THE PEELITES

1846–1857

THE PEELITES
1846-1857

by

Wilbur Devereux Jones

Arvel B. Erickson

OHIO STATE UNIVERSITY PRESS

Copyright © 1972 by the Ohio State University Press
All Rights Reserved

Library of Congress Catalog Card Number 79-157717
International Standard Book Number 0-8142-0162-8
Manufactured in the United States of America

to

DONALD GROVE BARNES

Table of Contents

Preface

This book is a short study of the nineteenth-century British statesmen known as the Peelites. Often resembling a mutual admiration society and professing loyalty to the leadership and principles of Sir Robert Peel, they were men of liberal-conservative views, who, though never a political party as such, nevertheless possessed more talent and often more power than any other political section during the years from 1846 to 1857.

Much has been written about the life and work of the leading Peelites—Aberdeen, Graham, Gladstone, and Peel—not only in biographical and autobiographical works, but also in monographs and general histories of the nineteenth century. As yet, however, no specific study of any length has been made of the Peelites as a group; in fact, no one has yet attempted to clearly identify them, to determine their actual numbers from time to time, or to assess their role in British public life. The very years of their activity are among the most neglected in British history. This study seeks to fill this void.

Lists of members of the Peelite section are herein provided for the years during which this group had some sort of corporate existence. While considerable study has gone into the preparation of these lists, and statistical nets were devised to catch as many Peelites as possible, certain difficulties were encountered in creating them that could not be wholly overcome. These difficulties are discussed frankly in the text and in appendix 2. The writers are confident only that their lists provide general guides to the Peelite rank and file during the years under discussion.

For this work the authors have relied heavily upon primary

sources at various repositories in Great Britain. As all students of nineteenth-century British history are acquainted with the major secondary works dealing with this period, we have included in the bibliography only those to which reference has been made in the footnotes.

Professor Erickson wishes to acknowledge with grateful thanks sabbatical leaves granted by Case Western Reserve University, research grants from the Social Science Research Council and the American Philosophical Society, and the kind and efficient service of the staffs of the British Museum and the Public Record Office. He also wishes to acknowledge the kind permission of Sir Fergus Graham to quote from the manuscripts at Netherby.

Professor Jones wishes to acknowledge the many kindnesses extended to him by Lady Pentland and the late Charles A. Gladstone, and to extend thanks to them and to the duke of Wellington for permission to quote from the papers of their illustrious ancestors. He desires also to make note of the efficient assistance of the staffs at the University of London, Hughenden Manor, Nottingham University, and the Surrey Public Record Office.

Arvel B. Erickson
Wilbur Devereux Jones

January 23, 1970

List of Abbreviations

A number of abbreviations are used in the footnotes to refer to the documentary sources and to oft-quoted secondary works. The former are followed, whenever possible, with their file numbers; the secondary works, by their volume and page numbers.

ARCHIVAL SOURCES

AP	Aberdeen Papers, British Museum
ADP	Admiralty Papers, Public Record Office
BP	Brougham Papers, University of London
CP	Cardwell Papers, Public Record Office
CLP	Colchester Papers, Public Record Office
CO	Colonial Office Papers, Public Record Office
DP	Disraeli Papers, Hughenden Manor
EP	Ellenborough Papers, Public Record Office
GP	Gladstone Papers, British Museum
GOP	Goulburn Papers, Surrey Public Record Office
GRP	Graham Papers, Netherby
GNP	Granville Papers, Public Record Office
IP	Iddesleigh Papers, British Museum
MP	Martin Papers, Public Record Office
NP	Newcastle Papers, Nottingham University
NPP	Napier Papers, British Museum
PP	Peel Papers, British Museum
PRP	Portland Papers, Nottingham University

RIPP	Ripon Papers, British Museum
RP	Russell Papers, Public Record Office
WP	Wellington Papers, Apsley House

PUBLISHED WORKS

GMEM	Charles Greville, *The Greville Memoirs*. Edited by Lytton Strachey and Roger Fulford. 7 vols. London: Macmillan and Co., 1938.
M&BDIS	W. R. Monypenny and G. E. Buckle, *The Life of Benjamin Disraeli*. 2 vols. New York: The Macmillan Co., 1916.
MGLD	John Morley, *The Life of William Ewart Gladstone*. 3 vols. New York: The Macmillan Co., 1903.
PGRA	Charles S. Parker. *The Life and Letters of Sir James Graham 1792–1861*. 2 vols. London: John Murray, 1907.
PPE	Charles S. Parker. *Sir Robert Peel*. 3 vols. London: John Murray, 1899.
B&EVIC	Queen Victoria. *The Letters of Queen Victoria*. Edited by A. C. Benson and Viscount Esher. 3 vols. New York: Longmans, Green and Co., 1907.
SHER	Lord Stanmore, *Sidney Herbert, Lord Herbert of Lea*. 2 vols. London: John Murray, 1906.

PART 1

*Origins of
the Peelite Section
1845-1847*

CHAPTER 1

THE PEELITES IN BRITISH HISTORY

Every work dealing with mid-nineteenth-century British political life must mention the Peelites at certain points in the narrative, especially in 1846, 1852, and 1855. On numerous occasions the Peelites played a vital role in the legislative process. Their support (or lack of active opposition) was of overriding importance to the first three Governments which succeeded that of Sir Robert Peel, and their influence extended for an indefinite period beyond the fall of Lord Aberdeen's government in 1855. Yet, despite their importance in contemporary political affairs, they float as fragments in historical space, lazily orbiting the political scene, their presence known to all students of the period, but their numbers and influence as yet only partly understood. Just who they were, and what was the exact nature of their political organization, are questions which have been only partly answered.

The truth of this statement becomes at once obvious if one checks the references to the Peelites in the books on his library shelves. One of the older works[1] refers to them as a "distinct parliamentary group," which numbered 105 after the 1847 election, from 40 to 50 following that of 1852, and which lost its identity after the Peelites seceded from Palmerston's government in 1855. E. L. Woodward estimates the Peelites to have numbered about 100 in 1847 and approximately 35 in 1852, and considers them to have been numerically unimportant after the election of 1857.[2] More recent works also tend to be vague or to differ among themselves, respecting the Peelites. They are regarded as an "independent force" in Parliament by Asa Briggs, who states further that many Peelites returned to the Conservative fold between 1846–52, that there were more defections during the 1852–57 period, and their final defeat came in the last of these years.[3] Philip Appleman regards the Peelites as a "party" which had about 40 members in 1853—a party

1. J. A. R. Marriott, *England since Waterloo*, pp. 190, 211, 239.
2. *The Age of Reform, 1815–1870*, pp. 162, 165, 168.
3. *The Age of Improvement*, pp. 419–21.

which dissolved after the break-up of the Aberdeen coalition.[4] G. M. Young describes them simply as the friends of Sir Robert Peel, who moved across the political stage, making Conservatism a little less Tory, and Liberalism a little less Whig.[5] Robert B. McDowell concludes that the moment of decision came in mid-1852, when the Peelite party concluded that their ideas could best be realized through a Liberal coalition.[6] On the other hand, J. B. Conacher in a recent work, which deals only with the period of Lord Aberdeen's government, hints that the Peelites had some sort of existence until 1859.[7]

If authors of works on the Victorian era encounter some difficulties in adequately describing the Peelites, how much more perplexing they are to textbook writers, who must discuss them in a sentence or two, unshielded by modifying paragraphs! To call them simply "Peelites," as many do, neatly avoids the issue, for this bald term does nothing to define the nature of their group, save to associate it with Peel. If the term "Peel's Friends" is used, most historians, knowing that the standoffish Peel had few friends, conclude that the Peelites were few in number—a parliamentary group composed of officers and only a few rifle-bearers. If they are referred to as the "Peelite Party," the reader immediately imagines a functioning parliamentary mechanism complete with treasury, platform, leaders, and whips. The difficulty in selecting a name to describe and define the Peelite group is compounded by the fact that political observers in their own time differed regarding just who they were and what their organization should be called.

In searching for an adequate label for the Peelites, the historian must ultimately attempt to cut his way through a dense thicket of available facts and in the end may discover that their historical reality is so complex that the Peelites defy any neat definition such as one expects to find in a survey text. Although we think of them primarily in political terms, the Peelites were men-in-society, playing their individual roles in the economy of the period, choosing friends and pastimes, encouraging certain types of associations and

4. Philip Appleman, ed., *1859: Entering an Age of Crisis*, pp. 168–70.
5. *Victorian England: Portrait of an Age*, p. 82.
6. *British Conservatism, 1832–1914*, p. 46.
7. *The Aberdeen Coalition, 1852–1855*, p. xi.

discouraging others, aiding or ignoring contemporary churches in their missions—in other words, helping as individuals to create not only the political but also the economic, social, and religious environments of Victorian Britain. A comprehensive study of the Peelites would have to include detailed investigations of the ideas and attitudes of a large number of men beyond the Peelite leaders so that some conclusions might be reached as to the homogeneity or heterogeneity of the Peelites as men-in-society.

Unless he severely limits the membership of the Peelite group by adopting some narrow definition of it, the historian finds such a comprehensive analysis far beyond his reach. It is true that biographies of Peelite leaders are available, and one might study and compare them and call his conclusions a synthesis of the Peelites as men-in-society. But such a work would exclude those among "Peel's Friends" who have not been the subjects of biographies, not to mention a much larger number of statesmen who were friends of his friends, and more or less looked to them for political leadership. Then, if one decides that the traditional "112" should form the basis for his investigation of the group in depth, he rapidly discovers that few have had biographers and even their obituary notices provide little information about them.

Yet, if the Peelites present an insuperable challenge to historical writing, the same situation obtains with respect to the Chartists, the Anti-Corn Law League, and to all of the political parties. In their studies of these groups, historians are likely to read the private papers and speeches of their leaders, and to describe the group as a whole on the basis of the facts found in a limited number of sources. The assumption and justification for so doing is that the rank and file would not have accepted their leadership had they not agreed with their leaders. If the political group being studied is wholly monolithic and totalitarian, this reasoning is probably sound; but the further it moves toward a democratic structure, the more ineffective this method becomes.

In the case of the Peelites, this technique of studying the few and applying one's conclusions to the many breaks down almost completely, for no political group within the broad confines of the Anglo-American political tradition ever put so much stress upon the right of its members to hold individual opinions and was so unwilling to form a conventional political structure and chain of command.

Faced with this situation, the historian must simply admit that his methodology is inadequate and simply do the best he can by first making a serious attempt to identify the Peelites and then going on to study their voting records on political, economic, social, and religious issues. If one follows this method, the Peelites should emerge, if not as men-in-society, at least as men in political life; and some generalizations might be induced to provide a firmer basis for an appraisal of their ideas and influence than exists at the present time.

CHAPTER 2

THE CABINET CRISIS OF 1845

If the term *Peelite* is made synonymous with *Free Trade Conservative*, we face the difficulty of defining the position of William Sebright Lascelles, the Conservative member from Wakefield. The Free Traders had been active in the West Riding area after the 1841 election,[1] and Lascelles was apparently one of their converts. Be this as it may, Lascelles, brother of Lord Harewood and brother-in-law of Lord Morpeth, voted for a committee on the Corn Laws in 1843 and supported their outright repeal in 1845. Thus, as a Free Trade Conservative, he was a "Peelite" before Peel's public adherence to free trade formed the section.

To avoid this difficulty, we must further qualify our definition of *Peelite* by adding to "Free Trade Conservative" the requirements that he was a member of Parliament who voted with Peel during the 1846 divisions or who joined the group later. This last phrase is important. Without it, William E. Gladstone, who—though a member of Peel's government—occupied no seat in the 1846 Parliament and could not be counted among the Peelites.

The vote of Lascelles is but one bit of evidence that the free trade propagandists had done their work well and had called into existence an indefinite number of Free Trade Conservatives well before the Corn Law Crisis of 1845–46. The Free Traders stressed that the increasing population, development of railway communications between town and countryside, and improved agricultural techniques combined to make abundant production, rather than high prices, the key to future British agricultural prosperity. These arguments had caused some Conservative newspapers to modify their views as to the necessity of the Corn Laws and had even made Free Traders out of some landlords.[2] But one must not overstress

1. See F. M. L. Thompson, "Whigs and Liberals in the West Riding, 1830–1860," *English Historical Review* 74 (April, 1959).

2. Mary Lawson-Tancred, "The Anti-League and the Corn Law Crisis of 1846," *The Historical Journal* 3, no. 2 (1960). The motives of the most outspoken of these Free Trade converts, Earl Fitzwilliam, are examined in David

the success of the Free Traders among the land-based Conservatives. Before 1846 there were few Free Trade Conservatives among the country bankers, rural solicitors, land agents, millers, and corn dealers; and the agricultural constituencies maintained strong pressure upon their representatives to preserve the Corn Laws.

Under these circumstances, the Conservative converts to free trade held their views in secret and refrained from joining Lascelles on the Corn Law divisions, which makes the problem of dating their conversions a complex one. According to G. M. Young, the most eminent of these secret converts Sir Robert Peel moved slowly toward free trade not because of political considerations but because he believed cheap food would mean low wages and the loss of rents to the landowners would not be compensated for by advantages to the working classes.[3] Asa Briggs has described Peel as a pragmatist rather than an ideologist, who, once convinced that the Corn Laws were not necessary for British agriculture, was ready to repeal them whenever it became clear that public suffering would result from their retention.[4] Both of these interpretations are probably sound, but they do not pinpoint the moment when the prime minister became a covert Free Trader and began his vigil, awaiting the appropriate time when his changed view could be made public. Sir James Graham's well-known letter of December, 1842, in which he suggested that the next changes would be to "open trade," was probably addressed to one he knew was in general agreement with him on the subject;[5] but the earliest direct evidence of Peel's abandonment of the Corn Laws appears in a Gladstone memorandum of November 22, 1843, which noted that Peel had expressed a strong opinion to the cabinet that the next change in the Corn Laws would be to total repeal.[6] This meager

---

Spring, "Earl Fitzwilliam and the Corn Laws," *American Historical Review* 59 (January, 1954).

3. Young, *Victorian England*, p. 43.

4. Briggs, *Age of Improvement*, p. 321.

5. *GRP.* Graham to Peel, December 30, 1842. Graham showed Free Trade inclinations in his *Coin and Currency* pamphlet of 1826. The story of Graham's conversion to the principle is found in Great Britain, Parliament, *Hansard's Parliamentary Debates*, 3d ser., 83 (1846): pp. 710–25.

6. *GP,* BM 44777. Gladstone Memorandum, Nov. 22, 1843.

evidence suggests that Peel and Graham were covert Free Traders in 1842 and made known their views to the cabinet the following year. Gladstone accepted their point of view as early as 1844,[7] and Sidney Herbert evidently had joined their group some time before the crisis of November, 1845.

The story of the cabinet crisis resulting from the potato famine has been told in many places, and it is unnecessary to trace it in any detail here; but, despite all that has been written, a few questions must be raised and, if possible, answered. Peel's legion of admirers, from his own day to the present,[8] have been concerned with establishing the "selflessness" of his motives and the detached statesmanship transcending partisan considerations that governed his conduct during these months. The impression is that "right" emerged victoriously without planning and behind-the-scenes maneuvering on the part of the prime minister, who was concerned only with the public good.

Granting without hesitation that Peel acted according to his concept of the public good, this does not mean that he ceased to function as a politician who was determined, first, to thwart the Protectionists and, second, to carry the repeal himself. This first objective had to be attained if repeal were to be carried at all, and, as for the second—why should Peel have wished to trust this all-important project to anyone else? If the events of November–December, 1845, are interpreted on the basis of these two assumptions, they enhance Peel's stature as a politician without doing any damage whatsoever to his character.

Late in December, Peel told the queen quite frankly that, if he had resigned in November, the Protectionists would have been able to take over the Government and a revolution would have resulted, but a month later it was too late.[9] It was, therefore, Peel's policy to

7. Anthony Wood, *Nineteenth Century Britain, 1815–1914*, p. 142.

8. Spencer Walpole, *A History of England from the Conclusion of the Great War in 1815*, 4:404. Walpole noted that four prominent men lived through this period, Grey, Peel, Cobden, and Russell, but the greatest name was that of Peel. Harvey Glickman contends that the Conservatives have no coherent, active tradition as a party, and that the highest places have gone to men like Peel, Disraeli, and Churchill, who transcended previous policy. See: Harvey Glickman, "The Toryness of English Conservatism," *The Journal of British Studies* no. 1 (November, 1961).

9. B&EVIC, 2:78. Memorandum by Albert, December 25, 1845.

advance so cautiously in November that neither Stanley nor Wellington, the two Protectionists who might possibly have formed a government, would have an excuse for resigning and breaking up the Government at that moment. On November 1, therefore, Peel proposed suspension of the Corn Laws; but when he refused to set a time limit to the suspension, Stanley became suspicious and concluded he really meant repeal.[10] The prime minister hastily wrote a conciliatory letter to his powerful subordinate denying that he wished to advise the queen that the Corn Laws should be removed,[11] and Peel's proposals to the cabinet on November 6 merely called for scaling down the duties. When even these were rejected, Peel refused to make an issue of it and thus avoided a crisis at that time.

Meanwhile, the Free Traders were busy strengthening Peel's position vis-à-vis the Protectionist majority in his cabinet by whipping up public sentiment for an abandonment of the Corn Laws and mobilizing public opinion against a possible Protectionist government. Then came Lord John Russell's open letter of November 22 in favor of open trade in corn, which—as Greville was quick to note—far from embarrassing Peel, actually was of service to him.[12] The growth of urban feeling against the Corn Laws and the commitment of the Whigs to their abolition so strengthened Peel's position that he could state flatly to the cabinet on November 25 that the existing Corn Law could not be maintained. The prime minister in his memorandum of November 29 called for a suspension and reconsideration of the Corn Laws, and gave his colleagues time to reconsider the whole question.

Then came the cabinet sessions of December 2, 4, and 5. As no minutes of these important meetings are available, we are left to reconstruct the situation and procedure from scraps of evidence gathered here and there. Those must have been trying sessions indeed! Graham gave powerful support to Peel, and Herbert did what he could, though youthful and unsure of himself and deeply concerned with party unity. Among the other members of the Commons, Lincoln dreaded the reaction of his Protectionist father; Lord Granville

10. See Wilbur Devereux Jones, *Lord Derby and Victorian Conservatism*, p. 111.

11. Ibid. The crossed-out portions of Peel's draft letter evidently were designed to strengthen the denial.

12. *GMEM*, 5:243–46.

Somerset feared his strong-willed brother; and Peel's oldest friend and his chancellor of the exchequer, Henry Goulburn, seems to have been violently opposed to repeal. The reactions of the cabinet ministers in the Lords were even more discouraging. Aberdeen supported Peel, but was uninformed in economic affairs; Stanley would not budge; Buccleuch talked of resignation; Ripon feared the destruction of the party; Wellington opposed repeal; and Lyndhurst argued against it with the skill of a lord chancellor. The ruin of British agriculture, the destruction of the Conservative party, loss of public character, the triumph of democracy, and a host of other ominous predictions were advanced by these men, who, save for Stanley, were shortly to become Free Trade Conservatives.

Peel's plan for a gradual, but complete abolition of the corn duties was so ill-received by the cabinet as a whole that the prime minister finally concluded it was impracticable to continue with it. Many of the members would have supported him unwillingly, not because they approved the proposals, but because they wished to maintain the Conservatives in power;[13] and in this state of mind they were hardly fit to wage an effective parliamentary battle, so Peel was ready to explore the alternatives. He had to know whether or not Stanley or Wellington might expect to replace him, so he put a question to the cabinet about as follows: Was it in the public interest that an attempt be made to form a government based on support of the Corn Laws, or the Protectionist principle?[14] Their responses indicated that no member of the cabinet was ready to form a Protectionist government.[15] Peel therefore asked whether he should resign immediately because the cabinet would not give unanimous support to his proposals, or stay on and introduce his plan in Parliament in anticipation of defeat and resignation. Peel himself favored resignation, and in this he had the almost unanimous support of the cabinet members.

At the time of his resignation on December 5, Peel told the queen that if he had continued, Stanley would have undermined his position in the Lords, and Buccleuch would have done the same in Scot-

---

13. Sir Robert Peel, *Memoirs by the Right Honourable Sir Robert Peel.* Lord Mahon and Edward Cardwell, Trustees. 2 vols (London: John Murray, 1856), 2:221.

14. *PP*, BM 40461. Peel to Wellington, December 14, 1845.

15. Ibid. Wellington to Peel, December 14, 1845.

land. He also feared that the Radicals, angered by his appropriation
of their favorite measure, might join the Protectionists against him.[16]
By early December, however, Peel had accomplished his purpose of
thwarting the Protectionists. The question that remained was who
would draw up the repeal measure and pass it through Parliament.

The conduct of Lord John Russell, who was summoned to form a
government, has attracted unfavorable comment from some authorities. Some years ago F. H. Baring traced Russell's reluctance to form
a government to his domestic situation, and the Protectionist views
of Lords Lansdowne and Clarendon.[17] Trevelyan concluded that the
Whigs feared the Protectionist peers, lost their nerve, and hoped
Peel would carry repeal with a minimum of public disturbance.[18] A
recent article stressed the "selflessness" of Peel's conduct during this
crisis and dubbed Russell's reservations about accepting Peel's as-
surance of support as "excessively cautious, if not churlish."[19] These
writers provide a fairly large number of motives for Russell's refusal
to which the 100-vote Conservative majority in the Commons must
certainly be added.

Peel was undoubtedly aware of Russell's difficulties, and any interpretation of his plans and motives revolves around the question,
Did he seek to encourage or discourage Russell? Peel assured Russell
through the queen on December 8 that he would support a repeal
measure which provided for the gradual extinction of the Corn Laws,
accompanied by relief of unduly onerous charges on agriculture; but
he also desired an increase in the naval and military estimates, which
had to be presented in a manner that would not disturb the Anglo-
French entente. What Peel promised, then, was to support Russell
if he adopted Peel's views on the corn question and Aberdeen's views
on foreign policy. Not satisfied with Peel's assurances, Russell wanted
further concessions regarding the nature of the repeal plan, and information as to whether or not Stanley or Wellington was ready to
form a Protectionist government. Peel secured the information Rus-

16. *B&EVIC*, 2:58. Memorandum by Albert, Dec. 7, 1845.

17. F. H. Baring, "Lord John Russell's Attempt to Form a Government in
1845," *English Historical Review* 23 (April, 1908).

18. George M. Trevelyan, *British History in the Nineteenth Century,
1782–1919*, p. 273.

19. F. A. Dreyer, "The Whigs and the Political Crisis of 1845," *English
Historical Review* 80 (July, 1965).

sell desired regarding Stanley and Wellington and pledged support to a repeal measure such as Russell envisaged in his famous letter of November 22.

Up to this point Peel's promises and activities were encouraging, if somewhat cautious; but when Russell requested further assurances on December 15, his attitude became much less cooperative. After conferring with Graham, Lincoln, and Herbert, Peel flatly refused to give pledge in advance for the measure Russell might draw up, and he warned that his previous promises had bound only his friends and himself, not the Conservative party. So Russell, on December 16, told the queen he must decline office if Peel did not support an immediate repeal of the Corn Laws; and, on receiving this news, Peel again consulted his friends, this time including Aberdeen and Goulburn. He replied that he still supported the views Russell had expressed in his letter of November 22, but he would not pledge himself on details or be "fettered" by a "previous engagement." Lord Grey's attempt to secure a verbal clarification of the Peelite position from Herbert met with a rebuff.[20]

One can hardly escape the conclusion that Peel's offers of cooperation were highly qualified and that Russell had some reason to be dubious about them. Coming as it did atop all his other difficulties, this Peelite attitude may have tipped the scales against Russell's accepting office and caused him on December 19 to abandon his attempts. If, as Disraeli believed, Russell hoped to destroy the Conservative party by handing back the "poisoned chalice" to Peel, he was merely postponing rather than abandoning office and at the same time securing an important political objective. One can never be sure just what Russell or Peel expected to happen or how far either of them could look into the months of 1846, and this renders any certain interpretation of their motives impossible.

20. *SHER*, 1:58. Herbert Memorandum, undated.

CHAPTER 3

THE NEW PEELITE GOVERNMENT

Peel's attitude, which Trevelyan described as "gleeful," and the fact that he was well prepared to resume direction of British affairs strengthen the suspicion that he hoped, and perhaps expected, that Russell would fail. At a cabinet meeting on the evening of December 20, Peel demanded carte blanche in drawing up the repeal measure; and all of his colleagues, except Lord Stanley, rallied to his support. He then went on to rearrange his cabinet.

The changes made by Peel in December were obviously designed to strengthen his position in the Lords, that powerful citadel of Protectionism. The earl of Dalhousie, a very efficient supporter, received cabinet rank as president of the Board of Trade. To secure the powerful debating services of Lord Ellenborough, Peel placed him at Haddington's office, the Admiralty. Haddington received the Privy Seal, which was vacated by the duke of Buccleuch, and Buccleuch became lord president of the Council, which had been made vacant by the death of Lord Wharncliffe. Stanley's position at the Colonial Office was given to Gladstone.

One might state that all of the officers in Peel's powerful Government were ipso facto Peelites and let it go at that, but a brief examination of their individual positions provides some insight into the complex nature of Peelism. A Peelite of purest hue would be one who was a friend of the prime minister, who followed him, and who believed in free trade. Among the cabinet officers in the Commons only Graham, Gladstone, Herbert, and Lincoln were Peelites by these three tests. Lord Granville Somerset, brother of the Protectionist seventh duke of Beaufort, was a less enthusiastic Free Trader and was probably closer to Wellington than to Peel.[1] Henry Goulburn had been Peel's intimate friend since Alfred Club days during the war, and he followed him in this crisis; but he was no Free Trader and supported Peel as a bulwark against unrestrained democracy.[2]

Proceeding alphabetically through the members in the Lords,

1. *WP.* Somerset to Wellington, December 1845.
2. Peel, *Memoirs*, 2:201–07. Goulburn to Peel, November 30, 1845.

14

Aberdeen's motive for supporting Peel was unique—Peel provided him with an opportunity to carry out his foreign policy. Some years later Aberdeen told the queen that "he did not pretend to understand the question of Free Trade,"[3] but in 1845 he wished to shut Palmerston out of office so he could remove the last (he believed) cause for serious quarrel with the United States. He had created an entente with France and seemed to have separated that country from the United States; now all that was needed to complete his grand design for lasting peace was to settle the Oregon question. A repeal of the Corn Laws would be highly popular in the United States, and Aberdeen planned to take advantage of this situation to embark on a new, hard-line policy, which would break the stalemate over the Oregon issue and force a compromise.[4] Lord Aberdeen was a friend of Peel and followed him, but he was a Free Trader only by chance.

The duke of Buccleuch in early December believed the potato famine was being used as a pretext for repeal of the Corn Laws and had seriously considered resigning. He therefore accepted his new cabinet post on December 22 with considerable reluctance and approved repeal because it seemed now to be a matter of necessity rather than expediency to settle the troublesome issue.[5] Buccleuch may also have been influenced by his fellow Scotsman Aberdeen but he does not seem to have been particularly close to Peel. He was therefore a Peelite only in the sense that he followed Peel in 1845–46.

Although Peel had been very kind to Lord Dalhousie when he went out of office early in December, granting him the position of clerk register of Scotland at £1200 a year, Dalhousie's letter to Wellington on December 12, which ended "I even hope that I may again serve under you in some future Government,"[6] suggests that he looked to Wellington rather than Peel for leadership. Yet he was not unfriendly to Peel, and not only followed him in this crisis, but believed in free trade, so he must be considered a Peelite in every sense.

3. *B&EVIC*, 2:356. Memorandum by Albert, February 23, 1851.

4. This hard-line policy was accomplished by his letter to Edward Everett of January 3, 1846, and his "thirty sail of the line" threat to Louis McLane. See Wilbur D. Jones and J. Chal Vinson, "British Preparedness and the Oregon Settlement," *Pacific Historical Review* 22 (November, 1953).

5. Peel, *Memoirs*, 2:255. Buccleuch to Peel, December 22, 1845; AP, BM 43201. Buccleuch to Aberdeen, December 29, 1845.

6. WP. Dalhousie to Wellington, December 12, 1845.

Lord Ellenborough, the former governor general of India who had been recalled by the East India Company in 1844 for his expansionist activities, gross insubordination, and other sins, believed that the Government had not defended him properly at the time; and for this disservice he blamed Lord Ripon, and probably Peel as well.[7] But he followed Peel and seems to have been a moderate Free Trader; it was only in the friendship area that he fell down. On accepting office in the "now only possible government," Ellenborough wrote a friend that he was siding with Wellington, who had decided to remain in the cabinet.[8] As for Peel—there is no reason to believe that Ellenborough even liked him, and certainly he did not regard the prime minister as a friend.

Very little information is available regarding Lord Haddington's attitudes. There is no evidence that he supported free trade in the cabinet discussions of November and December, and we must assume that he went along with repeal only to keep Peel in office. That he was friendly to Peel is evident from the letter he wrote to the prime minister when he accepted the Privy Seal.[9] Lord Aberdeen classed Lord Lyndhurst with Stanley and Goulburn as almost "violent" in his opposition to repeal during the cabinet sessions,[10] and his biographer states that the lord chancellor stayed on because he was unwilling to desert the Government.[11] One of his few available letters for this period indicates that Lyndhurst believed the Government could not carry the repeal.[12] Lyndhurst's attachment to the Conservative government was strong; to Peel, fairly firm; and to free trade—practically nil in 1845.

Lord Ripon had fought the battle for freer trade for more than thirty years and had been theoretically an advocate of free trade since early in the century; but he was by nature unusually cautious and by intellectual bent so appreciative of opposing points of view that he was often immobilized. Still, as an original Free Trader, a follower of Peel, and one of the prime minister's best friends, Ripon

7.   Wilbur Devereux Jones, *"Prosperity" Robinson*, pp. 252–58.
8.   *EP*. PRO 30/12–21. Ellenborough to Redesdale, December 26, 1845.
9.   *EP*. PRO 30/12–21. Haddington to Peel, December 25, 1845.
10. *MGLD*, 1:283.
11. Sir Theodore Martin, *A Life of Lord Lyndhurst*, p. 410.
12. *BP*. Lyndhurst to Brougham, December 24 (?), 1845.

qualified as a Peelite on all three counts. St. Germans had always been a Protectionist, but in December he was ready to accept repeal "if accompanied by some compensation to the farmers for the loss of protection."[13] Once he had made this decision, St. Germans became one of the most reliable of the Peelites and met all three of the proposed tests.

The attitudes and motives of the duke of Wellington, the most powerful figure in the Lords, have been discussed in many places. There is almost complete unanimity of opinion that he was never a Free Trader, and many scholars conclude that his relations with Peel were never intimate, and sometimes uneasy. Being the son of a self-made man, Peel was probably never wholly relaxed when with the great, landed aristocrat;[14] and the lack of intimacy in their relations was probably as much Peel's fault as Wellington's. The duke remained at his post in 1845 because he did not want to desert the queen and because he still cherished faint hopes that the Conservative party might be saved.

Aside from certain members of his cabinet, Peel received support, encouragement, and friendship from Lord Heytesbury, who, as lord lieutenant of Ireland, sent Peel information which helped create the crisis of 1845. Heytesbury welcomed Peel's return to office not because of his attachment to free trade, but because he felt all minor considerations should be abandoned in order to preserve the empire from revolution.[15] Later, the apparent success of free trade was to make genuine Free Trade Conservatives out of many statesmen who, in 1845, followed Peel from entirely different motives.

13. *PP.* BM 40480. St. Germans to Peel, December 22, 1845.
14. Wood, *Nineteenth Century*, p. 138.
15. *PP.* BM 40479. Heytesbury to Peel, December 25, 1845.

CHAPTER 4

THE BY-ELECTIONS AND THE UNSEATED PEELITES

Because Sir Robert Peel's mood seemed so cheerful when he reconstructed his Government, some authorities have interpreted this to mean that he anticipated little opposition to repeal from members of the Conservative party.[1] This interpretation is too thin. A letter written by St. Germans which recalled a conversation he had with Peel circa December 23, 1845, seems to provide vital evidence regarding Peel's state of mind. "I remember asking you," St. Germans wrote, "when you offered me a seat in the Cabinet whether after what had occurred you expected to be able to carry on the Govt., you told me that you did not. It was therefore under no impression that I was joining a durable administration that I accepted your offer."[2] This indicates that Peel expected to be repudiated by his party. Whether he anticipated the ruinous schism that developed is another matter.

That the rank and file of the Conservative party would not forsake Protection without a fight was evident from the by-elections. Gladstone was to experience acute political embarrassment because of their opposition. He had been warned before accepting office by an election agent from Newark borough named Robert Caparn that his constituents expected him to be sound on the Corn Laws, and in his reply (which was never sent) Gladstone wrote that he was "indisposed to disturb great questions" save for weighty reasons.[3] When he accepted the Colonial Office, Gladstone was quite aware that he would face the opposition of the duke of Newcastle at Newark; and he decided to search for a more friendly constituency. Lincoln suggested that he stand for Nottinghamshire North, vacant by the death of Henry Gally Knight, but Gladstone replied that his political convictions would not permit him—"without an extreme necessity"—to become a democratic candidate against the "local proprietary."[4] For a time Gladstone considered Wigan, only to be chased off by the Pro-

1. Lawson-Tancred, *The Anti-League*, p. 164. See also Trevelyan, *The Nineteenth Century*, p. 273.

2. *PP*. BM 40480. St. Germans to Peel, June 24, 1846.

3. *GP*. BM 44363. Caparn to Gladstone, December 14(?), 1845; Gladstone to Caparn, December 15, 1845.

4. *MGLD*, 1:287. Gladstone to Lincoln, date not shown.

tectionist opposition,[5] and he remained a minister with portfolio and no parliamentary seat until the fall of Peel's government, a striking symbol of Protectionist wrath and power.[6]

Lord Lincoln also realized that his accepting office in the reconstructed Government would cost him the support of his father, the duke of Newcastle, and his seat at Nottinghamshire South. A contest there would inevitably have become a trial of strength between Peelites and Protectionists;[7] and Lincoln, short of funds if not electioneering ability,[8] applied unsuccessfully to the discredited party agent, Francis R. Bonham, for a seat elsewhere.[9] So he tried for Nottinghamshire South, facing the opposition of Thomas B. T. Hildyard, who was supplied with funds by the Protectionist committee and by his own father, who called him the "deluded victim of bad counsel." Lincoln was easily defeated. After another unsuccessful appeal to Bonham,[10] he turned to his father-in-law, the duke of Hamilton. The Peelite incumbent for Falkirk District, William Baird, obligingly vacated his seat; and with the help of the duke, Lincoln won a narrow victory there.

A lesser member of the Government, Captain Henry John Rous, brother of the earl of Stradbroke, on taking a seat at the Admiralty chose voluntarily to permit his Westminster constituents to pass on his conduct. It was a tactical mistake. His opposition did not come directly from the Protectionists, but from a Whig named General Sir George de Lacey Evans. Lord Ernest Bruce, Lord Francis Egerton, and Lt. Col. Thomas Wood, prominent Peelites, rallied to the aid of Rous; but the Protectionists marched to the polls en bloc and gave Evans the votes he needed for victory.[11] Rous's position in the Government did not require him to have a seat, and he did not find one.

5. *Illustrated London News*, April 11, 1846.

6. It is interesting to note that Peel defended the right of a cabinet officer to continue in office without a seat in Parliament. See *PP*. BM 40479. Peel to Heytesbury, February 21, 1846; *MGLD*, 1:288.

7. See John Golby, "A Great Electioneer and His Motives: The Fourth Duke of Newcastle," *The Historical Journal* 8, no. 2 (1965).

8. Sidney Herbert offered to loan money to Lincoln so that he could avoid the "ruinous interest" charged by the banks. Whether Lincoln accepted the offer is unknown. *NP*. 11930. Herbert to Lincoln, February 15, 1846.

9. *NP*. 11866. Lincoln to Bonham, January 10, 1846.

10. Ibid. 11868. Lincoln to Bonham, February 28, 1846.

11. *GMEM*, 5:297–301. See also *EP*. PRO 30/12–3. Ellenborough to Hardinge, June 4, 1846.

Not all of the Peelites who accepted positions in the Government and submitted themselves to their constituents for reelection were as unsuccessful as Rous and Lincoln. Ralph Neville, a lord of the Treasury, won an uncontested election at Windsor; Swynfen T. Carnegie, who held a like position in the Government, managed to defeat a Protectionist opponent at Stafford Borough; and the Peelites could also celebrate the victory of George Percy Smy.he, who had succeeded Viscount Canning as undersecretary for Foreign Affairs, at the borough of Canterbury.

One of the more interesting constitutional questions which arose during this period involved whether or not a Conservative, elected as a Protectionist and turned Free Trader, was obligated to let his constituents pass on his change of viewpoint. Peel steadily maintained that Parliament had a right to determine this change of policy without seeking renewed authority at an election.[12] But many British voters did not share his view and called upon their representatives to resign forthwith once their apostasy had become known; and some of the Conservative members did not agree with the prime minister regarding the resignation obligation. Lord Ashley[13] embarrassed the Government by first submitting his controversial Ten Hours Bill to Parliament[14] and then resigning his seat, along with his Dorsetshire colleague Henry Charles Sturt. The Protectionists quickly found such strong opponents for them that Ashley and Sturt decided not to contest for the seats.

Sir Thomas Fremantle was another who refused to adopt the prime minister's no-election attitude. He held his seat at Buckingham under the patronage of the Protectionist duke of Buckingham; and, upon hearing of his changed opinions, a group of Fremantle's constituents called upon him to resign. The Conservative party whip apparently recognized the justice of their demand by taking the Chiltern Hundreds.[15]

12. See Betty Kemp, "Reflections on the Repeal of the Corn Laws," *Victorian Studies* 5 (March, 1962).

13. "The practical reality of Tory paternalism during Peel's ministry rests, upon closer examination, almost solely on the greatness of Lord Ashley." (David Roberts, "Tory Paternalism and Social Reform in Earl Victorian England," *American Historical Review* 63 [January, 1958]).

14. See Norman Gash, "Ashley and the Conservative Party in 1842," *English Historical Review* 53 (October, 1938).

15. Benjamin Disraeli, *Lord George Bentinck*, pp. 189–90.

A number of other Peelites, either voluntarily or under pressure from their constituents, took the Chiltern Hundreds or a Stewardship of Her Majesty's Manor at Hempholme, including Francis Charteris (Gloucestershire East), George Darby (Sussex East), William Henry Dawnay (Rutlandshire), Lord Henniker (Suffolk East), Sir Horace B. Seymour (Sussex East), and Thomas B. C. Smith (Ripon). The seats of all these members went to Protectionists, most of whom appeared in Parliament in time for the crucial division of February 27, 1846. Baillie Cochrane, Peelite member for Bridport, won his election by a single vote; but the contest was investigated by a parliamentary committee, and his seat was awarded to a Liberal candidate. At Selkirkshire, Alexander Pringle was replaced by Allan Eliott Lockhart, another Peelite, so the Government did not lose by this exchange.

Still another category of by-elections resulted from deaths, and the succession of certain members to their titles. At Buckingham Borough, Sir John Chetwode (deceased) was succeeded by the Protectionist Colonel Hall, and a Protectionist also secured the seat of Lord Grimston at Hertfordshire when the latter went to the Upper House as the earl of Verulam. The seat at Lichfield, vacated by Lord Leveson when he succeeded to the title of Earl Granville, brought in Edward L. Mostyn, who declared that Peel's new policy merited consideration. He thereafter became a fairly dependable Peelite.

The election in this category which captured the most popular attention involved the West Riding seat of John Stuart Wortley, where some 30,000 electors spoke for about a million people, which was vacated by Wortley's translation to the Upper House as Lord Wharncliffe. This large constituency was so prestigious that Lord George Bentinck believed its acquisition by a Protectionist might encourage the Lords to throw out any repeal measure passed by the Commons;[16] but after a lengthy and careful weighing of their prospects for success, the Protectionists did not contest the seat, and, as the Peelites put up no candidate, it went to the powerful Whig, Lord Morpeth. Due to the activities of the Free Traders, however, Yorkshire as a whole was a Peelite stronghold.[17]

16. *PRP.* PwH 193a. Bentinck to Portland, Jan. 2, 1846.
17. See J. T. Ward, "West Riding Landowners and the Corn Laws," *English Historical Review* 81 (April, 1966). Ward's list of Peelites with York-

The results of these by-elections of early 1846, when the repeal of the Corn Laws was the major issue, could hardly have been reassuring to the Peelites. Sixteen of the seats, contested or uncontested, were won by professed Protectionists, including Buckingham Borough (2), Chichester, Dorsetshire (2), Gloucestershire East, Hertfordshire, Midhurst, Newark, Northamptonshire South, Nottinghamshire South, Nottinghamshire North, Rutlandshire, Ripon, Suffolk East, and Sussex East; the Peelites were successful in only half as many elections, including Antrim, Bridport, Canterbury, Falkirk, Lichfield, Selkirkshire, Stafford, and Windsor. Among those Peelites who lost their seats during these by-elections, only Sir Horace B. Seymour managed to acquire one (Antrim) in time for the crucial divisions on the Corn Laws. Lord Lincoln did not return to Parliament until May, 1846; and Ashley, Charteris, and Gladstone were without seats until the 1847 election.

It might be said, then, that George Darby, William H. Dawnay, Sir Thomas Fremantle, Lord Henniker, Henry John Rous, and Thomas B. C. Smith formed a special class of Peelites. They were Peelites, along with Ashley, Charteris, and Gladstone, who never had a chance to vote against Protection in 1846; and for most of them, it was the end of the political road.

One might ask the question, What would have happened if Peel had shared Ashley's constitutional views and decided he must dissolve and go to the country on the repeal issue? The 2–1 victory of the Protectionists over the Peelites probably can not be advanced as proof of a similar victory if the election had been general, for the victories of the former came mainly in county constituencies rather than in constituencies which would represent, however roughly, a cross section of the nation. Lord George Bentinck, it is interesting to note, complained that Protectionist candidates were difficult to find even for county contests,[18] which suggests that Protectionism, with its overtones of selfish interest, had been successfully undermined and

---

shire connections includes William S. Lascelles, Sir George Cockburn, Richard M. Milnes, Thomas G. B. Estcourt, Captain Henry Meynell, and Lord Ernest Bruce.

18. "In all the Counties where there have been vacancies in the course of the last few months the difficulty has invariably been to find a Candidate & the Constituents have had in almost every case to pay the expenses of their Representative" (*PRP*. PwH 207a. Bentinck to Portland, Feb. 14, 1846).

discredited by the Free Traders, even though the dwindling number of individuals who clung to Protection probably did so the more tenaciously because of the mounting weight of the attack upon it.

To counterattack the Peelites successfully at a general election, the Protectionists would have had to find a large number of candidates to meet their opponents in the main area of their strength—the English boroughs; and, based on Bentinck's statement, one must conclude they could not have found men for such contests. Reasoning from this assumption, one might conclude that, insofar as the relative strength between Peelites and Protectionists is concerned, the results of an election in 1846 would not have differed substantially from that actually held in 1847. Whether or not Peel was constitutionally and morally right in refusing to dissolve in early 1846 might be argued one way or the other, but one can hardly doubt that he was pragmatically right in postponing the contest until the initial tidal wave of bitterness had somewhat subsided.

CHAPTER 5

PREPARATIONS FOR THE BATTLE

In his memoirs Sir Robert Peel neglected to state exactly how the controversial repeal measure was drawn up, and some vagueness therefore surrounds its origins. His letter to Lord Ellenborough of December 25 shows that he had given up the idea of suspension, partly because of uncertainty as to the success of an indemnity, and was then considering the provisions of his bill.[1] No cabinet meetings were held until January 12, and most of the members of his Government seem to have been kept in the dark about the proposed measure until that time. A note in Greville indicates that Graham had a hand in constructing the bill,[2] and there is an important retrospective reference by Dalhousie in 1847 which recalled that he, Sir George Clerk, and Henry Goulburn had prepared "the alterations intended to be made in the tariff" without the aid or knowledge of any of the secretaries of the Board of Trade.[3] If this letter refers to the repeal measure, then five individuals—Peel, Graham, Dalhousie, Clerk, and Goulburn—brought it into being.

The halfhearted support, fear, and even hostility of many cabinet members probably convinced Peel of the wisdom of postponing cabinet discussions of the measure until the imminence of the parliamentary session would discourage time-consuming controversies. Had the whole cabinet been taken into his confidence at this stage, it seems likely that Ripon, St. Germans, and probably some others would have insisted upon more tangible compensation to the agricultural interest for the loss of Protection than was included in the bill; and this concession might not only have swung additional votes in its favor but also have reconciled a larger number of Conservatives to Peelite leadership. But Peel changed his mind about making concessions to the agricultural interest, and the full cabinet of January 12 seems to have approved his plan without much discussion.[4] After the meeting

1. *EP.* PRO 30/12–21. Peel to Ellenborough, December 25, 1846.
2. *GMEM,* 5:281–82.
3. *NP.* 12228. Dalhousie to Lincoln, November 18, 1847.
4. On December 12, Peel was in favor of a "very liberal dealing as to

was over, the duke of Wellington sent Peel a letter he had received from the duke of Rutland warning that their success in repealing the Corn Laws might encourage the Anti-Corn Law League to go on to something else[5]—which might be interpreted as an implied remonstrance by Wellington himself.

The prime minister, in choosing the mover and seconder of the address, apparently desired to give an impression of Conservative party unity. Lord Francis Egerton (Lancashire South), a sturdy advocate of Protection, was asked to move the address, and Edmund B. Denison (West Riding, Yorkshire), to second it. Although Greville makes some reference to Egerton's conversion to free trade, the latter accepted Peel's proposal with the reservation that his acceptance would not bind him to an unqualified support of the Government.[6] Denison, a member of the Central Protection Society, later told the Commons that Peel had not revealed his plans at the time this request for his services had been made. When the House divided on Peel's measure, Denison joined the Protectionists in opposition, but Egerton supported the Government and at the end of the session was rewarded with a peerage.

Finding a mover and seconder in the Lords proved a more laborious task than in the Commons, for the resignation of Lord Stanley, who had acted as leader under Wellington,[7] had caused rumors and deep suspicions regarding the Government's intentions. The chief whip, Lord Redesdale, after writing a number of letters to Wellington, resigned his position.[8] Wellington invited Lord Winchester to move the address, but received a friendly refusal,[9] and the duke turned next to Lord Home, who accepted.[10] Lord Farnham agreed to second the motion, provided that it did not commit him to an un-

---

pecuniary burdens," but on December 25, when his position was much stronger, he said he would give "compensation" only when it would promote "social development," and on the latter, not the former, ground. See Peel, *Memoirs*, 2:228. Graham to Russell, December 12, 1845, and *B&EVIC*, 2:78. Memorandum by Albert, December 25, 1845.

5. *WP*. Rutland to Wellington, January 12, 1846.
6. *PP*. BM 40461. Peel to Wellington, January 17, 1846.
7. *EP*. PRO 30/12–21. Colchester to Ellenborough, December 28, 1845.
8. *WP*. Redesdale to Wellington, December 25, 28, 1845, January 1, 1846.
9. Ibid. Winchester to Wellington, January 13, 1846.
10. Ibid. Home to Wellington, January 14, 1846.

qualified support of the Government,[11] and Wellington thought his search had ended. But Farnham had second thoughts on the subject and, two days before the meeting of Parliament, sent his regrets.[12] Embarrassed and annoyed, Wellington was ready to do the seconding himself when Baron de Ros, a Protectionist who later voted against repeal, came to his rescue and accepted the dubious honor.[13]

Support for the repeal measure might have been obtained, or opposition to some extent neutralized, by an astute distribution of offices and honors, and Peel at this moment seems to have been more willing to use these political devices than he was to be at the end of his term of office. The marquess of Camden and the marquess of Hertford each received the Garter, and Lord Liverpool, a Civil Knight Grand Cross of the Bath. All of these peers were to vote for a repeal of the Corn Laws. Lord Essex, patron of Sir George Clerk's seat at Stamford, was offered a lord lieutenancy, which he declined for reasons of health; but he also became a Peelite lord. On the other hand, the gift of the lord lieutenancy of the West Riding in Yorkshire to the earl of Harewood failed to win him over, and Wellington's offer of a favor to Lord Stanley was politely refused.[14]

The support of the press would no doubt have been of great value to the Government—a fact which seems to have been understood by Aberdeen and Lincoln, if not by Peel. John Thadeus Delane of the *Times* sometimes lent a helping hand to Lord Aberdeen in his conduct of foreign affairs; and either as repayment, or from a desire to help Peel, the foreign secretary early in December told Delane that Wellington would support Peel in revising the Corn Laws. This gave the editor a "scoop" and caused some embarrassment to Sidney Herbert,[15] but it failed to enlist the *Times* behind the Peelites. Lord Lincoln, working through his friend John Douglas Cook, a former *Times* employee, also attempted to secure that newspaper's support; but he met with only modest success. John Walter, the chief propri-

---

11.   Ibid. Farnham to Wellington, January 14, 1846.

12.   *PP*. BM 40461. Farnham to Wellington, January 20, 1846.

13.   Ibid. Wellington to Peel, January 20, 1846.

14.   *WP*. Stanley to Wellington, January 18, 1846.

15.   The rumor went around that a Mrs. Caroline Norton, for whom Herbert had a romantic attachment, had sold this story to the *Times*. See Office of the Times, *The History of the Times*, 2:4–13; and *SHER*, 1:63.

etor of the newspaper, nursed a grudge against Peel and Graham, who had opposed his political ambitions.[16] Their change of views on the Corn Laws also cost the Peelites the support of the *Morning Post*, which had hitherto been favorable to the Government; and in the columns of that newspaper, Peel changed from a statesman of "eminent qualifications" to the leader of a "motley band of placemen, trimmers, Traitors, Whigs, Radicals, Leaguers, and democrats of all shades."[17] During the vital first six months of 1846, the Whigs and their allies had considerable support from the press, and the Protectionists likewise received encouragement from this source; but the Peelites had little for which to thank the gentlemen of the Fourth Estate.[18]

Although the Peelite leaders took few effective steps to build support for their plans in or outside the Commons or Lords, Peel's policy of secrecy prevented the growth of a strong antirepeal bloc during the weeks between the cabinet crisis and the opening of Parliament. This is clear from the activities and letters of some of the potential Protectionist leaders. Late in December, Lord Colchester suggested to a friend that Lord Stanley be called upon to lead the Protectionists in the new Parliament;[19] but the former colonial secretary, torn between his allegiance to Protection and a lingering loyalty to his former colleagues, did nothing to elevate himself to such a position. Lord George Bentinck believed that strong pressure from the Protectionists would force Peel to return to his former views on the Corn Laws, and he mentioned this possibility to Stanley, who did not think Peel would submit to this type of coercion.[20] As late as January 17, neither Bentinck nor Stanley was completely convinced that Peel planned total abolition;[21] and until his apostasy had become patent, they were in no position to rally an effective opposition to his plans.

The Whig leaders were in a somewhat similar position—unable to

---

16. Walter believed that Peel and Graham had encouraged a parliamentary committee to unseat him in 1841, and later had opposed his standing for Windsor Borough.

17. Wilfred Hindle, *The Morning Post, 1772–1937*, p. 156.

18. *GMEM*, 5:297–300.

19. *CLP*. PRO 30/9–2 (2). Mayo to Colchester, January 2, 1846.

20. *PRP*. PwH 200a. Bentinck to Portland, January 20, 1846.

21. Ibid. PwH 198a. Bentinck to Portland, January 17, 1846.

act until they were sure what Peel planned to propose;[22] and, because of Russell's declaration of November on the Corn Laws and refusal of office the following month, their ability to maneuver was severely restricted. They could hardly join the Protectionists in opposition; and, if they attempted to liberalize Peel's measure, they would risk uniting their opponents. Before the meeting of Parliament, Peel contacted Lord John Russell through John Young to explain how he planned to treat the events of December in his explanation to Parliament,[23] but this gesture to the Whigs was probably as much a convenience to himself as to them. Convinced that Russell would have to support their repeal measure, Peel and Graham seem to have been completely certain as to the outcome of the debates on it.[24]

Graham did not think it worthwhile to attempt to make a head count of the repeal supporters in the Commons, so confident was he of success; and the estimates made by two other observers of the scene indicate the reason for his certainty. While Greville thought the Conservatives would divide into 200 Protectionists and 180 Peelites, Lord George Bentinck, who was very active at the time in Protectionist affairs, predicted that only 180 Conservatives would desert the prime minister on a repeal division.[25] Both of these calculations gave the Peelites too much strength, but they suggest why Graham did not bother to count noses before the meeting of Parliament.

Whether, as Trevelyan suggested, Peel could have carried more of his party with him had he taken them into his confidence during these weeks, rather than treating them with contempt,[26] is an interesting question; but the evidence suggests that Peel's overriding desire was to repeal the Corn Laws, and considerations for the future of the Conservative party that he had previously built seems to have played a negligible role in his plans and procedures.

22. *RP.* PRO 30/22–5A. Le Marchant to Russell, January 5, 1846.
23. Ibid. Young to Russell, January 20, 1846.
24. *GMEM*, 5:282.
25. *PwH.* 196a. Bentinck to Portland, January 14, 1846.
26. Trevelyan, *The Nineteenth Century*, p. 269.

CHAPTER 6

THE CORN LAW DEBATES IN THE COMMONS

The passage of the repeal of the Corn Laws through the Commons took almost four months, the delay being caused partly by the interferences of other pieces of legislation at times but mostly by the determination of the Protectionists to stage such an impressive resistance that the Lords would be encouraged to defeat or at least mutilate the measure. Peel first laid his proposals before the Commons on January 27, debate began on February 8, and the first of three major divisions took place on February 27, 1846. This was the division that created the traditional "112 Peelites."

They were: Acland, Thomas Dyke, Jr. (Somerset West); A'Court, Edward Henry (Tamworth); Attwood, John (Harwich); Baillie, Henry James (Inverness-shire); Baillie, Hugh Duncan (Honiton); Baird, William (Falkirk Dist.); Baldwin, Charles Barry (Totness); Baring, Henry Bingham (Marlborough); Baring, William Bingham (Thetford); Barkly, Henry (Leominster); Beckett, William (Leeds); Benbow, John (Dudley); Bodkin, William Henry (Rochester); Botfield, Beriah (Ludlow); Bowles, Adm. William (Launceston); Boyd, John (Coleraine); Bruce, Ernest A. C. B. (Marlborough); Buckley, Edmund (Newcastle-under-Lyme); Cardwell, Edward (Clitheroe); Carnegie, Swynfen T. (Stafford Bor.); Clerk, Sir George (Stamford); Clive, Robert Henry (Shropshire South); Cockburn, Sir George C. (Ripon); Copeland, William Taylor (Stoke-upon-Trent); Corry, Henry T. L. (Tyrone); Cripps, William (Cirencester); Damer, George L. D. (Portarlington); Dickinson, Francis Henry (Somerset West); Douglas, Sir Charles E. (Warwick Bor.); Douro, Marquess of (Norwich); Drummond, Henry Home (Perthshire); Dugdale, William Stratford (Warwick North); Eastnor, Viscount (Reigate); Egerton, Lord Francis (Lancashire South); Egerton, William Tatton (Cheshire North); Escott, Bickham (Winchester); Estcourt, Thomas G. B. (Oxford University); Fitz-Roy, Henry (Lewes); Flower, Sir James (Thetford); Glynne, Sir Stephen R. (Flintshire); Godson, Richard (Kidderminster); Gore, Montagu (Barnstaple); Goulburn, Henry (Cambridge University); Graham, Sir James Robert (Dorchester); Greene, Thomas (Lancaster); Gregory, William Henry (Dublin City); Grimsditch, Thomas (Macclesfield); Hamilton, Lord Claud (Tyrone); Hamilton, William John (Newport, I. W.); Hanmer, Sir John (Kingston-upon-Hull); Herbert, Sidney (Wiltshire South); Hervey, Lord Alfred (Brighton); Hogg, James Weir (Beverley); Hope, George William (Southampton); Hornby, John (Blackburn); Hughes, William Bulkeley (Carnarvon Dist.); James, Sir Walter Charles (Kingston-upon-Hull); Jermyn, Earl (Bury St. Edmunds); Jocelyn, Robert Viscount (Kings Lynn); Johnstone, John J. Hope (Dumfriesshire); Johnstone, Sir John V. B. (Scarborough); Kelly, Sir Fitzroy (Cambridge Bor.); Kirk, Peter (Carrickfergus); Lascelles, William Sebright (Wakefield); Legh, George Cornwall (Cheshire North); Lockhart, Allan Eliott (Selkirkshire); Lyall, George (London); Macgeachy, Forster Alleyne (Honiton); Mackinnon, William Alexander (Christchurch); McNeill, Duncan (Argyllshire); Mahon, Viscount (Hertford Bor.); Mainwaring, Townshend (Denbigh Dist.); Martin, Charles Wykeham (Newport, I. W.); Masterman, John (London); Meynell, Capt. Henry (Lisburn); Milnes, Richard Monckton (Pontefract); Mostyn, Edward M. L. (Lichfield); Neville, Ralph (Windsor); Northland, Viscount (Dungannon); Oswald, Alexander Haldane (Ayrshire); Owen, Sir John (Pembroke Dist.); Patten, John Wilson (Lancashire North); Peel, Jonathan (Huntingdon Bor.); Peel, Sir Robert (Tamworth); Pennant, Edward G. D. (Carnarvonshire); Polhill, Captain Frederick (Bedford Bor.); Praed, W. Tyringham (St. Ives); Reid, Col. George A. (Windsor); Reid, Sir John Rae (Dover); Russell, Jesse D. W. (Staffordshire North); Sandon, Viscount (Liverpool); Seymour, Sir Horace B. (Antrim); Smollett, Alexander Jr. (Dumbartonshire); Smythe, George Percy (Canterbury); Somerton, Lord (Wilton); Stewart, John (Lymington); Stuart, Henry (Bedford Bor.); Sutton, John Manners (Cambridge Bor.); Thesiger, Sir Frederic (Abingdon); Tollemache, Frederick J. (Grantham); Tomline, George (Shrewsbury); Trench, Sir Frederick W. (Scarborough); Vernon, Granville Harcourt (Retford East); Villiers, Viscount G. A. F. (Cirencester); Wall, Charles Baring (Guildford); Wellesley, Lord Charles (Hampshire South); Whitmore, Thomas Charlton (Bridgenorth); Wood, Col. Thomas (Brecknockshire); Wood, Thomas Jr. (Middlesex); Wortley, James A. Stuart (Buteshire); Wynn, Charles W. W. (Montgomeryshire); Young, John (Cavan).

Although the division list in *Hansard* for February 27 seems accurate, similarities and even duplications of names, one apparent misspelling, and occasional ambiguous descriptions of party affiliations in the 1846 edition of *Dod* give rise to some uncertainties as to the positive identity of the famous "112." The Peelite list included herein provides the names of 112 probable Conservatives who voted for repeal on February 27;[1] but if the name of Viscount Newry and Morne, who paired in favor of repeal, is added, then the total Conservative vote rises to 113.

Using this Peelite list as a basis, we might go on and compare it with the results of the next great division, held on March 27, to determine just how stable was this new section at a later stage of the battle. On March 27, only 98 of the original 112 (or 113) seem to have been present and voting, but four others paired for repeal for a total of 102 votes. The votes of the absentees were made up for partly by those of Viscount Newry, who paired for a second time, and of Thomas Bunbury, Christopher Turnor, and possibly Colonel William Verner.[2] If these votes are counted, then the Peelite strength on March 27 was 106 votes.

1. Most of the 112 in this list were selected because *Dod* identified them as Conservatives, Liberal Conservatives, or Moderate Conservatives or, failing any of these descriptions, as members of the Carlton Club. This system permitted the identification of 108 Peelites. Two of the names on the list, Allan Eliott Lockhart and Edward M. L. Mostyn do not appear in *Dod*, and George Cornwall Legh's name seems to have been misspelled "Leigh" on the division list, but all three appear to be readily identifiable Conservatives, and this raises the total to 111. One is then left to choose between William Feilden and William B. Hughes to secure the extra vote. The former is identified in *Dod* as one who "sometimes" voted Conservative, but he was not unfavorable to the ballot, hardly the mark of a Conservative. Hughes is included in this list on the strength of a statement made by Sir John Young much later, which read: "No reliance can be placed even for a day on either B. Denison, or W. B. Hughes. The former has little courage . . . the latter was promised something by Sir Robert Peel . . . and the hope of attaining this object is what has really kept him with us" (*GP.* BM 44327. Young to Gladstone, August 10, 1852). This indicates that Hughes was a member, though not a very reliable one, of the Peelite Section down to 1852. It should be noted that in another place *Hansard* lists only 109 Conservatives on this division (*Hansard*, 3d ser., 85:271). See appendix 2 for an attempt to reconcile the Peelite list in this work with the analyses in *Hansard*.

2. Colonel William Verner, a soldier, Orangeman, and close friend of Peel, was an "unattached Conservative" from Armagh. If *Hansard's* listings are accurate, Verner voted against repeal on February 27, paired in favor of it on March 27, and voted against it on May 15. And he is not the only one who presents a peculiar problem for any historian of the Peelites. If the listings

The third of the great divisions on the measure came on May 15. This time 101 of the original 112 Peelites were present and voting, Viscount Newry voted in person, and six more paired for a total of 108 votes. Thomas Bunbury and Christopher Turnor again voted for repeal to raise the total to 110. The new recruits were Lord Lincoln, Captain James Lindsay (whose election was cleared on March 31), and Lord Granville Somerset, for a grand total of 113 votes. If we add to this total the five of the original 112 who were absent, and the potential votes of Gladstone and Lord Ashley, who had not yet found seats, then Gladstone's estimate of Peelite strength as "approaching 120" seems very accurate.[3]

Although the Peelite section was not nearly so loquacious during the debates as one might have expected considering the surfeit of talent in their ranks, some twenty-two of them braved the hostility on their own side of the House to clarify their positions before the vote of February 27, and four more spoke during the later stages of the battle. This means that we have on hand explanations—some informative, others brief—for about one-quarter of the Peelite section. These speeches, however, probably provide most of the motives which caused these Conservatives to break with party dogma, and they also reveal the unusual ideological composition of the Peelite section.

For purposes of discussion, the speakers might be divided into four general categories, though most of them expressed a number of reasons for following Peel. The first group would include the convinced and enthusiastic Free Traders, such as Peel and Graham. Edward Cardwell, William H. Gregory,[4] Sidney Herbert, Colonel

---

of pairs on the March 27 division are accurate, then Aaron Chapman voted for repeal on that occasion, and William H. Gregory, Alexander H. Oswald, and Thomas C. Whitmore voted against it. Yet on May 15 Chapman voted against repeal, Gregory voted for it, Oswald paired for it, and Whitmore, one of the original Peelites, was listed as an "Absent—No." The division of May 15 offers insoluble problems in the "Absent—No" column. One finds there the names of J. Attwood, H. J. Baillie, C. B. Baldwin, Lord F. Egerton, J. Hornby, A. Oswald, W. T. Praed, T. C. Whitmore, and Hon. J. S. Wortley. But Baillie, Egerton, Oswald, Praed, and Wortley seem to have paired in favor of repeal.

3. *MGLD.* 1:351.

4. Gregory maintained that agriculture in the past had flourished in spite of Protection, not because of it (*Hansard*, 3d ser., 83:682).

Thomas Wood Jr.,[5] Sir George Clerk (vice-president of the Board of Trade, who had the task of answering Disraeli), William S. Lascelles,[6] Charles W. W. Wynn,[7] Forster A. Macgeachy,[8] Bickham Escott, and Sir John Rae Reid[9] should probably be included in the category of convinced Free Traders.

A second category of speakers, while they might make references more or less friendly to the theory of free trade, stressed the necessity of ending a controversy that had become dangerous. Colonel Thomas Wood was anxious to remove an issue which had been dividing the manufacturing and agricultural interests of the nation.[10] Henry J. Baillie, who did not anticipate that universal prosperity would result from repeal, dreaded the effects of a prolonged struggle between the landed gentry and the "mass of people."[11] Henry Barkly feared that the middle classes might rouse the masses against the gentry.[12] Similar anxieties seem to have loomed large in the attitudes of William B. Baring and Viscount Villiers.[13]

A third category of Peelite voters appear to have been motivated primarily by their confidence in the prime minister. Lord Northland "still thought that the measures proposed by the right hon. Baronet were unnecessary," but he preferred that Peel, rather than Russell, should perform the operation of cutting out Protection.[14] Granville Harcourt Vernon wished that Peel had proposed a fixed duty of 5s., but he had accepted his leadership since 1836 and would continue to be a member of his group.[15] In this category no individual was

5. Ibid., pp. 909–11.

6. Lascelles denied that restriction was an article of Tory faith and made friendly references to Russell which foreshadowed his switch to the Liberals in 1847 (ibid., pp. 563–65).

7. Wynn declared that he had been opposed to restrictions since 1815 (ibid., p. 775).

8. Macgeachy regarded repeal of the Corn Laws as the first of many important measures for the welfare of the people (ibid., 8:1449–56).

9. Reid declared his belief in every part of Peel's measure (ibid., pp. 802–3).

10. *Hansard*, 3d ser., 84:325.

11. Ibid., pp. 661–67.

12. Ibid., p. 1308.

13. Ibid., pp. 1247–48; ibid., pp. 855–56.

14. Ibid., pp. 908–9.

15. Ibid., 84:1465–66.

more prominent than Lord Sandon, whom Peel had encouraged to speak early in the debate for the purpose of stressing loyalty to his leadership.[16] Sandon "disapproved the measure proposed, and yet he intended to support it with his vote" because he desired to follow the enlightened opinion of the nation as represented by Peel.[17]

A fourth category of speakers advanced a variety of motives for their positions on this issue, which can only be described as miscellaneous. Some of them were mildly or strongly critical of the prime minister. Francis H. Dickinson, Bickham Escott, Sir John Hanmer, and even Colonel Thomas Wood believed that immediate repeal was preferable to the gradualism of Peel's plan.[18] Montagu Gore would have preferred the repeal measure to have been brought forward "by the noble Lord opposite."[19] But all of these critics were in a position similar to that of the disappointed office seeker,[20] Richard M. Milnes, who explained that Russell's refusal of office had left him no alternative but to support Peel even though he lacked confidence in him.[21]

The chancellor of the Exchequer, Henry Goulburn, confessed that he had opposed repeal back in November and traced his changed viewpoint to the reports of an impending and terrible calamity in Ireland.[22] Charles W. Martin admitted that repeal had come sooner than he had expected but urged that Britain, as the world's leading commercial nation, should point the way to others.[23] Granville H. Vernon, mentioned above in the third category, also stressed improvement of Anglo-American relations as an additional reason for his support of repeal.[24]

No historian dealing with politicians could be so naïve as to omit

16. *BP.* Peel to Brougham, February 8, 1846.

17. *Hansard,* 3d ser., 83:601.

18. Ibid., pp. 983–84; ibid., 84:422; ibid., p. 533; ibid., p. 720.

19. Ibid., 83:1405.

20. Milnes had sought the position of under secretary for Foreign Affairs, basing his claim on nine years of party service. See *GP.* BM 44215. Milnes to Gladstone, January 14 and 19, 1846; and T. Wemyss Reid, *The Life, Letters, and Friendships of Richard Monckton Milnes First Lord Houghton,* pp. 370–71.

21. *Hansard,* 3d ser., 83:1456–57.

22. Ibid., 84:51.

23. Ibid., 83:793.

24. *Hansard,* 3d ser., 84:1465–66.

from consideration the most powerful of all motivations in analyzing the positions of the various Peelites at this time—the motive of political expediency. That many of the Peelites made the politically correct choice at this time is evidenced by the simple fact that they were reelected in 1847. But there was more than one of those rare birds in politics—the politician who places his personal convictions above his political needs—among the Peelites; and, as we have seen, some of them paid the ultimate political price for their apostasy before the repeal measure ever came to a vote. Certain others, especially Colonel Thomas Wood (whose Brecknockshire constituents were circulating a petition to force his resignation), Thomas Dyke Acland Jr., and Bickham Escott, appear to have gone against the wishes of their constituents. None of them was to be elected in 1847.

There is still another motive evident in many of the speeches, which, though vague, suggests that some of these former Conservatives—as often happens to politicians of that political hue when they come into prolonged contact with exponents of a contemporary movement—had caught the progressive fever and were dissatisfied with their previous political postures. "Let us look at the movements which have taken place within the last sixteen years," Baillie Cochrane urged the House, "the development of industries, the progress of invention, the extended intercourse. America within the last six years brought within twelve days, China within two months, goods conveyed forty miles an hour, letters sent from Penzance to Caithness for one penny."[25] Many Conservatives must have asked themselves the questions, Am I passé? Are my ideas really fitted to the emerging society? That most important of contemporary Conservative leaders had written in December: "The political current seems steadily setting in a direction which leaves me high & dry on the beach."[26] While many of the Conservatives joined Lord Stanley on that beach, the Peelites were determined to go with the current—at least for a time.

25. *Hansard*, 3d ser., 83:570–71.
26. *EP*. PRO 30/12–21. Stanley to Ellenborough, December 29, 1845.

CHAPTER 7

THE LORDS AND THE CORN LAWS

When the Peel government was restored to power in late December, Wellington wrote Lord Aberdeen that he intended to do everything in his power to keep the queen's government together, and to reconcile the Lords to the course it would probably follow;[1] and, despite the flood of protests he received from various members of the aristocracy, the duke adhered faithfully to his intentions.

Redesdale had warned Wellington as early as December 9 that he would not give up the Corn Laws;[2] Lord Mahon had taken the same position on December 20,[3] and the crescendo of protests and desertions reached such an intensity after Peel's return that Wellington wrote Lord Ellenborough a long and gloomy letter on January 8, which observed that the scenes of 1830 were being reenacted, and the party was disintegrating.[4] There is nothing in Wellington's correspondence to indicate a belief that Peel's government could endure; on the contrary, the duke urged Lord Stanley to prepare himself to lead the forces of conservatism.[5]

The power and influence of Wellington in the Lords is so widely recognized there is no need to dwell on the subject, save to note that without the duke's guiding hand, the Upper House might well have come into conflict with the Commons over the repeal issue. Less widely recognized is the fact that there were some members of the Lords who looked to Peel rather than to Wellington for leadership. The eccentric Lord Brougham offered his powerful debating services to Peel, not to the duke;[6] and the proxies of the marquess of Ailsa and the duke of Leeds were sent to the prime minister, not to Wellington.[7] The latter had once been a Melbourne supporter.

1. *AP.* BM 43060. Wellington to Aberdeen, December 23, 1845.
2. *WP.* Redesdale to Wellington, December 9, 1845.
3. Ibid. Mahon to Wellington, December 20, 1845.
4. *EP.* PRO 30/12–6. Wellington to Ellenborough, January 8, 1846.
5. Jones, *Lord Derby,* pp. 116–17.
6. *BP.* Peel to Brougham, January 23, 1846.
7. *PP.* BM 40661. Peel to Wellington, February 21, 1846.

It is, indeed, difficult to understand the exact relationship between Peel and Wellington. For example, there was the Irish Representative Peerage question, which arose in February when the first baron Dunsandle sought Wellington's aid in securing a representative peerage. The duke replied he no longer had influence over the selection of the Irish representative peers, and that Dunsandle must contact Peel.[8] On being contacted Peel refused to promise aid to Dunsandle on the ground that the general rule was for the Government not to commit itself beyond the first vacancy, and that Lord Desart had already been selected by the Irish peers for the position.[9] Peel evidently believed that the Irish peers elected representatives from among candidates approved by the Government through its Irish secretary. Why, then, did Dunsandle apply first to Wellington, and not to Peel or the Irish secretary? "Although the Duke may apparently settle who shall be elected as Irish Representative Peers," Ellenborough wrote in March, "you may be assured that he endeavours so far as he can to ascertain the wishes of the Irish Peers."[10] So we are left to wonder just who really determined the selection of the Irish peers, but the chances are Ellenborough's account was actually more accurate than that of Peel, for it is fairly well established that Lord Stanley succeeded to Wellington's influence over the selection of both Irish and Scottish peers.[11] All of which indicates that the relations between Peel and Wellington were so distant that the former was unaware of the latter's influence in this important area, and this is further confirmed by the fact that Graham, rather than Peel, advised Wellington regarding party tactics in the Lords.[12]

The Lords spent many weeks waiting for the Corn Bill to come to them from the Commons, and the duke did what he could to prepare his fellow aristocrats for the surrender. Despite the fact that most observers regarded Peel's concessions to agriculture as distinctly minor in nature, Wellington put a good face on it and assured his friends that the plan would confer "great advantages" upon the land.[13]

8. *WP.* Wellington to Dunsandle, March 3, 1846.
9. *PP.* BM 40461. Peel to Wellington, May 2, 1846.
10. *EP.* PRO 30/12–34. Ellenborough to Lady Kilmaine, March 17, 1846.
11. See Jones, *Lord Derby*, p. 207.
12. *WP.* Graham to Wellington, February 7, 15, 16, 1846.
13. Disraeli, *Bentinck*, p. 37.

More than one was frankly skeptical, and a motion was made in the
Lords for a committee to study the tax burdens on land. Graham advised Wellington to accept such a committee provided that its work
did not interfere with the passage of the repeal measure, and the
duke did so.[14] Encouraged to do so either by the duke or by his
example, Lords Talbot, Essex, and the duke of Northumberland made
public announcements in support of repeal;[15] but Howe, Sandys and
some others made such assurances privately.[16] Strangely, Wellington's correspondence contains only a few letters from peers transmit-
ting their proxies to the duke, but the large number of such instru-
ments he had on hand for the division suggests that Wellington made
a major effort to secure the proxy votes of peers who preferred not
to be present on the division.

While Wellington was thus exerting his influence in support of the
queen's Government, the Protectionists did what they could to evolve
a counter strategy. During February they seemed to be gloomy regarding their prospects, even despairing. The duke of Richmond
acted as their informal leader, and their tactic was to move an amendment to the repeal measure asking that the issue be decided at a general election.[17] But the majority in the Commons on February 27,
smaller than had been expected, encouraged the Protectionists to
plan a more vigorous course. Lord Stanley became their leader in
March with Lords Malmesbury and Eglinton as whips, and plans
were laid for a stout attack on the second reading.

It was clear, however, that the measures of the Protectionists did
not match those of the Government. Lord George Bentinck counted
about 150 lay peers on the Protectionist side in early March, and they
were unable to increase their numbers appreciably.[18] Their strength,
such as it was, lay in two sources—the debating powers of men such
as Lord Stanley and Lord Ashburton (a Free Trader of the 1820s
era), and the secret sympathy for their cause cherished by a large
number of the Lords who did not join them. Had they been able to

14. *WP.* Graham to Wellington, Feb. 15, 1846.

15. *Illustrated London News*, Feb. 7 and 14, April 18, 1846.

16. *WP.* Howe to Wellington, Feb. 5, 1846; Sandys to Wellington,
February 10, 1846.

17. *PRP.* PwH 206a. Bentinck to Portland, Feb. 14, 1846.

18. *PRP.* PwH 213a. Bentinck to Portland, March 10, 1846.

find some high ground upon which to make their fight, the Protectionists might well have carried the day; but their cause was tarnished with selfish economic interest.

Lords Buccleuch and St. Germans seem to have acted as the Peelite whips in the Lords; and they collaborated with the Whig leaders, Lords Normanby and Bessborough, in working out a schedule for the passage of the bill. Their original schedule, which turned out to be too rapid, called for a first reading on May 18, the second sometime after May 25, and the committee stage to begin on June 4. The reason for this haste seems clear enough. Although the Disraeli-Bentinck plan to oust the Government on the Irish Coercion Bill had not been worked out when the schedule was originally drawn up, the difficulties encountered by the Government in passing its Irish measure apparently forewarned Peel that haste was in order.

Wellington's difficulties in planning the order of speakers for the debate were somewhat lesser than he had encountered on the address, but Lord Ripon complicated matters for a time. Wellington wished him to move the second reading, so that he could keep Dalhousie (in whom he seems to have had great confidence) in reserve to answer Stanley and Richmond, but the aging Ripon, after first accepting the duty had second thoughts about it, fearful, no doubt, that his many speeches on the Corn Laws since 1815 would be quoted against him, and asked that Dalhousie be given charge of the measure.[19] It took a letter from Peel to make Ripon reconsider and to place himself at the point of the offensive platoon.[20]

A spirited debate on the second reading of the bill began on schedule on May 25, and the great division which created the Peelite lords was taken three days later. Tracing down the Peelite lords among the 211 members on the winning side is no easy task, and the list included herein may or may not be one hundred percent accurate. Some lords occupied rather ambiguous political positions. For instance, the duke of Leeds, once a Tory, was classified as a Liberal after 1838, and Lord Brougham had had a long record of Whig Radicalism; yet both of these members committed themselves to Peel at this time and might be considered Peelites. Peel kept in close contact

19. Jones, *Robinson*, p. 268.
20. *PP*. BM 40461. Peel to Wellington, May 22, 1846.

with Brougham.[21] Another complicating factor in listing the Peelite lords is posed by the Lords Ecclesiastical, who naturally avoided a close identification with either of the parties.

The vote of the churchmen on the May 28 division is particularly interesting. Eighteen of them, of whom seven might be classified as Peelites, voted in favor of repeal, as against twelve who voted with the Protectionists. As fourteen of the great churchmen were dependent upon land rather than the Ecclesiastical Commission for their

TABLE 1

PEELITE LORDS OF THE MAY 28, 1846, DIVISION

LAY LORDS PRESENT

Dukes
5th duke of Buccleuch
1st duke of Wellington

Marquesses
2d marquess of Abercorn
2d marquess of Camden
2d marquess Cholmondeley
9th marquess of Huntly
3d marquess of Londonderry
2d marquess of Ormonde
14th marquess of Winchester

Earls
4th earl of Aberdeen
2d earl of Bandon (I)*
4th earl of Bathurst
5th earl of Buckinghamshire
3d earl of Chichester
3d earl of Clanwilliam
2d earl of Clare
5th earl Cornwallis
4th earl of Courtown
10th earl of Dalhousie
7th earl of Denbigh
3d earl of Devon
1st earl of Ellenborough
6th earl of Essex
9th earl of Galloway
5th earl of Glasgow
9th earl of Haddington
11th earl of Home (S)*
1st earl Howe
5th earl Jersey
3d earl of Liverpool
4th earl of Mornington

2d earl of Mt. Edgcumbe
1st earl of Ripon
3d earl of Romney
3d earl of Rosslyn
6th earl Shaftesbury
3d earl of St. Germans
2d earl Talbot
2d earl of Verulam
11th earl of Westmorland

Viscounts
1st viscount Canning
3d viscount Hawarden (I)*
6th viscount Strathallan (S)*
3d viscount Sydney

Barons
12th baron Blayney (I)*
3d baron Calthorpe
3d baron Carteret
2d baron Churchill
1st baron Delamere
2d baron de Tabley
2d baron Forester
2d baron Glenlyon
1st baron Heytesbury
1st baron Lyndhurst
2d baron Manners
1st baron Prudhoe
4th baron Rivers
8th baron Rollo (S)*
1st baron Sandys
3d baron Thurlow
2d baron Wharncliffe
2d baron Wodehouse

21. *BP.* Peel to Brougham, May 26 and June 13, 1846.

ECCLESIASTICAL LORDS PRESENT

Bishop of Chester
Bishop of Lichfield
Bishop of Lincoln
Bishop of Oxford

PROXY VOTES

7th duke of Argyll
7th duke of Leeds
3d duke of Northumberland
1st marquess of Ailsa
1st marquess of Bristol
2d marquess of Bute
4th marquess of Hertford
8th marquess of Tweeddale (S)*
1st earl Amherst
3d earl Caledon (I)*
1st earl DeGrey
2d earl Dunraven (I)*

4th earl of Kingston
10th earl of Lindsey
12th earl of Pembroke
2d viscount Melville
1st baron Bexley
3d baron Castlemaine (I)*
2d baron Downes (I)*
1st baron Seaton
11th baron Ward
Archbishop of Canterbury
Bishop of Carlisle
Bishop of London

* (I) = Ireland; (S) = Scotland; (P) = Proxy.

income, it is clear that some of them voted against what the Protectionists believed was to their economic interest.[22] There was certainly no church "policy" on this issue, and the churchmen seem to have been entirely free to follow their own convictions.[23]

In addition to the 18 votes cast by the churchmen, 193 votes in behalf of repeal were cast by the lay lords, of which 83 might be classified as Peelite votes. Thus the Peelite lords, lay and ecclesiastical together, cast 90 votes of the 211 total, or slightly more than 42% of it; whereas, in the division in the Commons on February 28, Peelite votes made up only 33% of the total for repeal. Aberdeen's and Buccleuch's appeals to the Scottish peers did not prevent about two-thirds of them from voting with the Protectionists, and Wellington was also unsuccessful in winning over the Irish peers. The disinclination of many of the lords to take a personal part in the struggle is indicated by the large number of proxy votes cast—73 for and 38 against—on this division.[24] On the basis of these few statistics one might conclude

22. *Hansard*, 3d ser., 87:448–49.

23. Ibid., pp. 304–6.

24. Before the debates in the Lords, a Whig leader warned St. Germans that he would not use his proxies to reverse a vote of the Lords present at a division, which was a clear warning to the Peelites to have their followers present and voting (See *PP*. BM 40480. St. Germans to Peel, May 17, 1846). This warning was evidently taken quite seriously, for the Peelites had 73% of their

that the Free Trade majority in the Lords was an English majority, well-supported by the church vote, and that the Peelite strength in the Lords, at that moment, was greater than that in the Commons.

After the victory of May 28 there was a short delay before the House went into committee on June 15, where the Protectionists were expected to attempt to substitute a higher fixed duty on grain than the 1s. levy Peel provided for in his measure. The duke of Buckingham proposed that the 1s. be raised to 10s., only to be defeated, then came a motion to raise the 1s. to 5s., which most of the lords probably favored secretly; but it was beaten also. These and other defeats raised the temper of the Protectionists as the sessions went by. "I have never known it so bad as last night," Wellington wrote Peel on June 23.[25]

Though strong in numbers, the Peelites in the Lords made a wretched showing during the debates, the burden of which was carried by Lord Brougham and the Whigs. Ripon, though old and ill, spoke a number of times; Haddington, Dalhousie, Londonderry, and Essex contributed speeches to the cause. But the usually eloquent Ellenborough was unimpressive; and Aberdeen, Heytesbury, and Lyndhurst might just as well have absented themselves until the time came to vote. In certain cases, especially that of Lyndhurst, their silence was undoubtedly due to lack of conviction as to the wisdom of the measure; but part of it may have stemmed also from a reluctance to cross swords with their Protectionist friends and associates led by Stanley, not from fear but from the hope and expectation that they could unite with them again politically once this crisis had passed.

Under these circumstances it is more difficult to identify the real Free Traders in the Lords than in the Commons. Certainly there were some of these. Ripon told the House that he had always been a theoretical Free Trader, and this was quite true.[26] Lord Haddington noted that he had long ago told his friends that the Corn Laws were not necessary for the well-being of British agriculture; Dalhousie condemned the Corn Laws as both "oppressive and unjust";

---

voters present on the division, while the Opposition members who voted with them mustered only 57% of their voting strength in person.

25. *PP.* BM 40461. Wellington to Peel, June 23, 1846.

26. See Jones, *Robinson,* pp. 54–58.

Essex stated that if only 20 peers voted for repeal, he would be among them; and the marquess of Bute denied that Protection was beneficial to agriculture. In their explanations to the House, these lords stood stanchly for repeal and therefore merit being classified as Peelites in a theoretical sense. One might add to these Lord Dunraven, whose letter to St. Germans stated a belief in the "present expediency & permanent wisdom" of repeal,[27] and Lord Howe, who seems to have been won over to the cause.[28] Certain others, such as Lord Ellenborough,[29] the duke of Leeds,[30] and the marquess of Tweeddale, who was in faraway Bengal and had his proxy cast by Buccleuch,[31] are known to have really favored a moderate fixed duty, and they probably represent the secret opinion of most of the Peelite lords.

Late in the debate the Protectionist, Lord Gage, observed that Wellington's prestige had passed the measure, and there is abundant evidence to support this view. In his speech Lord Londonderry stated frankly that his support for the measure was based on confidence in Wellington, and this motive is strong in the letters of Lord Clare, Lord Bute, Lord Home, Lord Sandys, the duke of Argyll, and Lord Mt. Edgcumbe.[32] Among these lords, Sandys was also a strong supporter of Peel.[33] To keep Peel, or Wellington and Peel, in power certainly was a powerful motive among many of the Peelite lords.

Still another motive—one difficult to document and impossible to

27. *PP.* BM 40480. Dunraven to St. Germans, April 6, 1846.
28. *WP.* Howe to Wellington, February 5, 1846.
29. Ibid. Ellenborough to Wellington, June 15, 1846.
30. Ibid. Leeds to Peel, February 19, 1846.
31. *Hansard,* 3d ser., 87:952.
32. See *EP.* PRO 30/12–21. Clare to Ellenborough, January 29, 1846. *WP.* Bute to Wellington, January 14, 1846; Home to Wellington, January 15, 1846; Argyll to Wellington, March 31, 1846; and Mt. Edgcumbe to Wellington, May 12, 1846.
33. *WP.* Sandys to Wellington, February 10, 1846. "It is my intention to support the measure proposed by Sir Robt. Peel," he wrote, "thinking it most important that he shall remain at the Head of the Government." Certain of the lords are very difficult to classify. *Dod* lists the marquess of Winchester as a Melbourne supporter, but Wellington asked him to move the address in January. In his refusal Winchester expressed "every good wish & for the success & prosperity of the Measure of Her Majesty's Present Ministers" (*WP.* Winchester to Wellington, January 13, 1846). For this reason he has been included on the list of Peelites.

measure—probably also influenced the attitudes of the Peelite lords. The British aristocracy had shown superlative survival instincts in the past by giving a little to retain the remainder, and they were to continue to display this quality in the future. Their instincts urged that it was unwise to demand the retention of a system which was widely presented as outside, and even hostile to, the general interests of the nation as interpreted by the Commons. Thus, there was in 1846 no repetition of the scenes of 1831–32, and the Lords rode the current of the times.

CHAPTER 8

PEEL AS THE PARTY LEADER

The available evidence seems to indicate that Peel's decision to abandon party leadership had been made as far back as December, when he informed St. Germans that his new Government was not likely to last. Graham had reached a similar conclusion by April, if not before.[1] Neither of them seems to have discussed the subject with Wellington, who himself had had grave doubts as to the Government's future, but had rallied his forces in the Lords to support and preserve the queen's government . Because of having done so, Wellington was not ready to give up without a fight.

The passive attitude of Peel and the pugnacious policy of Wellington clashed that June when the life of the Government was threatened by the Irish Coercion measure. Wellington urged Peel to "strike first" and use a threat of resignation to disarm the coalition forming against him,[2] but Peel replied in a pedagogic tone, insisting that threats of resignation should be reserved "for rare and very important occasions."[3] This was a strange observation indeed! The implication was that preserving the Government was unimportant. When Brougham urged the prime minister to save his Government by abandoning the Coercion Bill, Peel explained that his convictions and concern for the character of his Government would not permit him to abandon a measure necessary for the public good.[4] During the debate on the coercion measure, far from appearing crestfallen, Peel appeared confident and happy that the moment of his retirement would not be long postponed.[5]

The Protectionists, like Wellington, misinterpreted the plans of the close-lipped Peel. Bentinck feared that an election held with Peel still in power would create a "terrible division" within Conservative ranks, and this led him to help hatch the plot to oust him.[6] Yet dis-

---

1. *GRP.* Graham to Hardinge, April 6, 1846.
2. *PP.* BM 40461. Wellington to Peel, June 8, 1846.
3. Ibid. Peel to Wellington, June 9, 1846.
4. *BP.* Peel to Brougham, June 9, 1846.
5. Disraeli, *Bentinck,* p. 171.
6. *PRP.* PwH 220. Bentinck to Portland, June 9, 1846.

solving and holding an election was the last thing that Peel and Graham wished to do. They agreed that an election would drive them into the company of the Anti-Corn Law League, with whom they agreed only on commercial policy and whose other activities they considered dangerous.[7] There was actually, then, a basic objective shared by Peel and Bentinck at this time—that there should be no general election.

Wellington could neither understand nor appreciate Peel's desire to retire. Just before the crucial defeat in the Commons that led to Peel's resignation, the duke wrote Peel a very long letter, noting that the queen wished him to continue in office—always a very powerful motive for Wellington—and suggesting some rather desperate expedients to avert defeat; but Peel refused to remain responsible for Ireland without the Coercion Bill and expressed doubt that even a new Parliament would pass it.[8]

On June 26, the day after his defeat in the Commons, Peel held what Gladstone called the "shortest cabinet I ever knew" to inform his colleagues that a Conservative party could not be formed so long as he remained in office, and so he proposed to resign and recommended that they follow his example; then he left town without even informing Wellington of his plans for the following Monday. The duke subsequently made inquiry and was informed of Peel's plans through the duke of Buccleuch.[9] Peel's eulogy of Cobden in his speech of June 29 was interpreted by Aberdeen as the formal severing of his connection with the Conservative party.[10]

Peel's followers had almost all laid themselves open to charges of inconsistency or worse; some had placed their political careers in jeopardy by supporting him; and, according to the customary rules of the political game, they were justified in expecting that their loyalty might be acknowledged by some tangible reward by the prime minister. Faithful Heytesbury asked for a step-up in the peerage;[11] the

7. *PGRA.* 2:41. Graham to Heytesbury, June 20, 1846; *PP.* BM 40461. Peel to Wellington, June 21, 1846.

8. *PP.* BM 40461. Wellington to Peel, June 21, 1846; Peel to Wellington, June 23, 1846.

9. *WP.* Buccleuch to Wellington, June 29, 1846.

10. *GP.* BM 44777. Memorandum No. 61.

11. *PP.* BM 40479. Heytesbury to Peel, June 22, 1846.

duke of Buccleuch sought a British peerage for his friend Lord El-gin.[12] Peel refused both requests on the ground that the peerage "is already too numerous."[13] The peerage for Lord Francis Egerton, son of the duke of Sutherland, was considered by Peel to rest on "special grounds," and it was granted. Peel also offered to revive the barony of Windsor for the wife of Robert Henry Clive, son of the earl of Powis, but Clive refused the favor because the public might conclude his actions had been motivated by expectations of "family advantage."[14]

In his distribution of baronetcies, Peel seems to have been quite uninfluenced by political considerations. The request of William A. Mackinnon—according to his own description, "the only person connected with the land who voted with you on the first reading of the corn bill"[15]—was ignored, but this honor went to Thomas Franklin Lewis (a Liberal), William Feilden (unclassifiable), John Somerset Pakington (a Protectionist and later a member of Lord Derby's Governments), John Gladstone (another Protectionist), William Verner (another Protectionist), and Moses Montefiore (the Jewish leader) in recognition of his high character and eminent position in the ranks of a loyal and estimable class of Her Majesty's subjects.[16] Henry Bruen, a loyal Protectionist, was also offered a baronetcy, but he apparently turned it down,[17] as did the Peelite lawyer and member for Oxford, Thomas G. B. Estcourt, who did not want to compromise the complete independence of his position in the Commons, whatever a former Conservative turned Peelite may have meant by that.[18]

Peel's followers did not even share much in the crumbs of patronage that fell from the prime minister's table. Peel turned down the Protectionist, the fifth earl De La Warr, who sought an army commission, and also the Peelite Sir Horace B. Seymour, who sought an Admiralty promotion, on the ground that he should not advise Wellington and Ellenborough in matters that fell wholly within the juris-

12. Ibid. Peel to Buccleuch, July 1, 1846.
13. Ibid.
14. Ibid. Clive to Peel, June 24, 1846.
15. *PP.* BM 40479. Mackinnon to Peel, June 24, 1846.
16. Ibid. Peel to Montefiore, June 28, 1846.
17. Ibid. Peel to Bruen, June 24, 1846.
18. Ibid. Estcourt to Peel, June 26, 1846.

diction of their respective departments.[19] When a church living at
Great Munden fell vacant, Peel hastened to give it to a Mrs. Mary
Dawson, who had an "urgent private claim on me,"[20] so he did not
have to choose among the applications for it received from such supporters as Baron Glenlyon, the marquess of Londonderry, Lord Lincoln, Sir George Clerk, Sir George Cockburn, and Charles Barry Baldwin. John Masterman, Peelite member for London, failed to secure
a minor job for a friend, but one was given in fulfillment of a promise
Peel had once made to the now-deceased Lord Wellesley.[21] One of
Brougham's scientist friends received a small grant from the Royal
Bounty;[22] a Quaker-poet named Bernard Barton received a small
pension, as did John Ramsay McCulloch for his "many useful publi-
cations on political economy."[23] Peel also complied with Lord Mahon's request for small pensions for three ladies, two of whom were
described as "aged and distressed."[24]

No contemporary politician could accuse Peel of wielding his patronage power to help his friends and punish his enemies. As one
examines the motives he advanced for bestowing favors, beyond set-
tling his personal obligations—reward for distinguished public service, excellence of character, contributions to the arts and sciences,
severe hardship—one must be impressed by the idealism of the prime
minister. Not all contemporary leaders shared his lofty views as to the
proper uses of patronage. When a peer commended to Lord John
Russell Peel's system of rewarding merit rather than political sub-
servience, Russell replied curtly that Peel's policy would turn the
peerage into a "Great Council of Venice" and secure its extinction
within fifty years.[25]

---

19. Ibid. Peel to Seymour, June 30, 1846. Peel told Seymour that he had
adhered to this rule even in the case of his own son. He seems, however, to have
hedged a bit in the case of another of his connections, who wished to be placed
on the list of candidates for the purchase of commissions (*PP*. BM 40594. Peel
to Somerset, June 27, 1846).

20. *PP*. BM 40479. Peel to Mrs. Dawson, June 22, 1846.

21. *BP*. Peel to Brougham, June 30, 1846.

22. Ibid. Peel to Brougham, March 28, 1846.

23. *PP*. BM 40479. Peel to McCulloch, June 28, 1846.

24. Ibid. BM 40494. Peel to Mahon, June 27, 1846.

25. *RP*. PRO 30/22–6F. Westminster to Russell, September 7, 1847; Russell to Westminster, September 9, 1847.

Peel's activities upon his return to office in December were a negation of party politics. He refused any compensation to his former followers save on the basis of social improvement, made a moral issue out of the repeal of the Corn Laws, willingly resigned the highest office, ignored the claims of his supporters for patronage, bestowed favors on Protectionists, and suddenly and bluntly severed all party ties. He slighted the peers, ignored the press, and kept almost everyone, except Graham, in doubt as to his intentions. These extraordinary attitudes for a premier seem to have been based on the assumptions that virtue should be its own reward, even in politics, that the Peelites had supported his measures, not himself, and that politics needed to be lifted to a higher plane above political expediency. Disraeli traced Peel's strange political posture to a deficient knowledge of human nature;[26] Wellington, to Peel's failure to understand the importance of party politics.[27]

These attitudes were probably an expression of Peel's unusual character rather than a conscious pose, but at this juncture in his career, when the most serious charges of betraying his party's trust were being lodged against him, Peel was probably more than ever anxious to divorce his conduct from any shadow of personal gain, and he probably deeply appreciated the motives of Clive and Estcourt when they refused his offers.

Either Peel and his followers acted from personal motives, in which case they had betrayed their party; or they had sacrificed themselves for a principle, which gave the highest moral tone to their conduct. Most of their contemporaries reached the latter conclusion regarding Peel and the Peelites; and the movement thus began on a new, high plane of politics and emerged as the foremost political expression of the moral idealism of the Victorian age.

26. Disraeli, *Bentinck*, p. 230.
27. *EP.* PRO 30/12–6. Wellington to Ellenborough, January 8, 1846.

PART 2

While Peel Still Lived 1846-1850

CHAPTER 9

THE END OF THE 1846 SESSION

When the newly formed Russell government faced the Commons in July, the seating arrangements in the House were more than a little misleading. Bentinck and the Protectionists remained on the Government side, having pledged qualified support to Russell,[1] while the Peelites, who had lately received Russell's support in the Corn Law struggle, sat opposite. Meanwhile, in the Upper House the Peelites crowded around Lord Stanley and the Protectionists, who occupied the Opposition benches. On the surface it appeared that the Peelites were consistent in their seating arrangements, while the Protectionists were not, but the attitudes of the two toward each other, and toward the Government, were much more complex than mere seating arrangements implied.

The position of Peel was, of course, of first-rate importance. Just what was Peel's position? According to one authority, he was resentful toward the Protectionists who had deserted him rather than toward the Whigs who had replaced him.[2] Although this statement contains a modicum of truth, it is quite misleading. In certain individual cases Peel harbored some resentment,[3] but this certainly did not express itself in his distribution of patronage; and after his retirement from office he kept almost as aloof from his former followers as from the Protectionists. If one can reduce his attitude to a single factor, that factor was a strong desire to pursue a perfectly independent course in Parliament and to consider measures, not men.

Thus, when Russell, seeking to strengthen his Government, asked Peel's permission to recruit among his followers, Peel replied they

---

1. Bentinck pledged his support if Russell did not attack the Irish Church or give Cobden a prominent place in his Government. *RP*. PRO 30/22–5B. Beauvale to Russell, July 7, 1846.

2. J. B. Conacher, "Peel and the Peelites, 1846–1850," *English Historical Review*, July, 1958.

3. Peel's letters for the period are remarkably free of traces of resentment, save in the case of Charles Newdigate, whom he classed with Bentinck and Disraeli. *PP*. BM 40594. Peel to Edmund Peel, June 22, 1846. Graham seems to have reacted more emotionally and vowed he would never unite with the 73 factious Conservatives who had helped overthrow Peel. *MGLD*, 1:296.

were quite free to make their own decisions but would probably reject his offers.[4] Later when Lord Lyndhurst sought Peel's aid in reconstructing the Conservative party, he refused, but again indicated that the Peelites were free to make whatever political connections they wished.[5] So far as their nominal leader was concerned, the Peelites could join the Whigs or Protectionists, or remain as independent members of the House.

Peel's detached attitude offended more than one of his former followers, who still looked to him for leadership. One day in August, while riding to the Horse Guards, Wellington encountered Peel, who sought to pass by without more than a formal salutation, but the duke detained him and expounded his views on the political situation. Peel listened politely, then replied: "Good-bye. I am glad to see you so well!" "And this is the man," the duke exclaimed, "for whom I have been sacrificing myself during the last six months."[6]

Even if Wellington had been able to overcome his discouragement with the course of events as well as the limiting factor of his advancing age, his new position prevented his assuming leadership in reconstructing the Conservative party. At the queen's request, and with Peel's blessing, he had retained his position as commander of the Forces; and, although this did not actually make him a member of the Government—he had occupied a similar position in the Goderich Government in 1827—the disheartened duke used his office as a means of retiring from the tangled political scene. And when Lyndhurst sought his services in reconstructing the party, the duke replied that his position would not permit him to act in concert with any party not connected with the administration.[7]

As of July, 1846, then, the Peelites were a political party without leaders. Or were they a party at all? Their contemporaries were not sure. Greville and other observers during the January-June, 1846, period had called them simply the "Government" or, rarely, the "Peelites." After they left office a Whig party worker referred to them as the "remnant of Peel's party," and the "112."[8] Stanley at times used the term "112."[9] Late in 1846 Goulburn called the group "our friends,"

4. *PP.* BM 40480. Peel to St. Germans, October 3, 1846.
5. Martin, *Lyndhurst*, p. 418.
6. *EP.* PRO 30/12–21. Ellenborough to Clare, August 29, 1846.
7. Martin, *Lyndhurst*, pp. 418–20. Wellington to Lyndhurst, July 23, 1846.
8. *RP.* PRO 30/22–5B. Bannerman to Russell, July 25, 1846.
9. *BP.* Stanley to Brougham, July 25, 1846.

and "our party."[10] The variety of these terms used by a Whig, a Protectionist, and a Peelite suggests that in later 1846 the utmost confusion existed regarding their status and that their identity as a stable section of the Commons had yet to be achieved. Some observers rather expected them shortly to find their way back into one of the organized parties or sections.

Lord John Russell, hoping to remove the "exclusiveness" label from his Government,[11] to strengthen it, and to speed the process of dissolution among the Peelites made offers in July to three of the foremost younger members of the Peelite group—Lincoln, Dalhousie, and Herbert. Their replies were quite uniform: they could not, without loss of public character, join an administration which had displaced the Government to which they had belonged.[12] Undaunted, Russell turned next to Graham and offered him a position on the permanent council of the duchy of Lancaster. Graham at first refused, but later accepted when he learned the queen had expressly desired his services.[13] Thus, although he had failed to enlist the younger men, Russell had been able to establish some tenuous ties with two very prominent Peelites, Wellington and Graham; and this encouraged the hope for more Peelite aid in the future.

After the repeal of the Corn Laws, the balance of the session might have been uneventful had Russell decided simply to renew the Sugar Duties, which expired that July; and, as a minority prime minister, this might even have been a logical course. But he seems to have seen in this issue a chance to please his Liberal and Radical followers, deepen the gulf between the Protectionists and Peelites, and, at the same time, by attacking the so-called "Sugar Monopoly," to reestablish his leadership of the free trade movement, a position he had abandoned to Peel when he had refused earlier to take office in December.[14]

The bill that Russell introduced that July called for a diminution of the tariff on sugar until it reached a low, fixed point in 1851, which

10. *AP.* BM 43196. Goulburn to Aberdeen, December 12, 1846.

11. See: Donald Southgate, *The Passing of the Whigs, 1832–1886*, p. 211.

12. *RP.* PRO 30/22–5B. Dalhousie to Russell, July 2, 1846; Herbert to Russell, July 2, 1846. *NP.* 12699a. Lincoln to Russell, July 2, 1846.

13. *RP.* PRO 30/22–5B. Graham to Russell, August 30 and September 2, 1846.

14. See F. A. Dreyer, "The Whigs and the Political Crisis of 1845," *English Historical Review* 80 (July, 1965).

would eliminate the preferential treatment previously extended to sugar grown in the British West Indies. This would place free-grown sugar into competition with slave-grown sugar, and thus the issue went beyond mere free trade policy and had strong moral overtones. Lord George Bentinck was quick to spot this weakness in the Government's case, and decided to offer the same amendment that Lord Sandon, now a Peelite, had moved against Russell's Government in 1841 —that the proposed reduction was unjust and impolitic, and would stimulate slavery at the expense of free labor. No one was sure how the "112" would vote in this situation. One Whig observer thought 40 would back Bentinck, while half as many would follow Peel in support of the Government;[15] Stanley anticipated that Peel would support the measure, but thought it impossible to predict the voting pattern of his followers.[16] The situation posed a highly interesting question—the Peelites had placed free trade ahead of party connection earlier in the year; would they now give it precedence over the antislavery crusade?

When the results of the division of July 28, 1846, were recorded, the Government had won by a 265–135 margin of which the original "112" provided 51 votes, three of which were pairs. These Peelites, who had very strong attachments to free trade, were:

A'Court, Edward H.	Hamilton, William J.
Attwood, John	Hanmer, Sir John (pr.)
Baring, William B.	Herbert, Sidney
Barkly, Henry	Hervey, Lord Alfred
Benbow, John	Hogg, James W.
Botfield, Beriah	Hornby, John
Carnegie, Swynfen T.	James, Sir Walter C.
Clerk, Sir George	Jermyn, Earl
Dickinson, Francis H.	Jocelyn, Viscount
Douglas, Sir Charles	Johnstone, Sir John
Eastnor, Viscount	Lascelles, William S.
Escott, Bickham	Lyall, George (pr.)
Flower, Sir James	Mackinnon, William A.
Goulburn, Henry	Martin, Charles W. (pr.)
Graham, Sir James	Milnes, Richard M.
Greene, Thomas	Mostyn, Edward L.

15. *RP*. PRO 30/22–5B. Bannerman to Russell, July 25, 1846.
16. *BP*. Stanley to Brougham, July 25, 1846.

Neville, Ralph	Stuart, Henry
Oswald, Alexander	Sutton, John M.
Owen, Sir John	Thesiger, Sir Frederic
Peel, Jonathan	Tomline, George
Peel, Sir Robert	Trench, Sir Frederick
Polhill, Capt. Frederick	Wall, Charles B.
Russell, Jesse D. W.	Wood, Col. Thomas
Sandon, Viscount	Wortley, James S.
Seymour, Sir Horace B.	Young, John
Smythe, George P.	

In seeking to cull the followers of Peel, one must consider the question of whether these 51 members were supporting Peel or Russell, because they were on the same side. Glancing ahead to the election, it would appear that this division for two of them, Henry Barkly and William S. Lascelles, marked their transition into the Liberal party, as Barkly in 1847 ran as a Liberal Free Trader, and Lascelles, as a Liberal. Milnes called himself a "Moderate Conservative" who supported Russell, which would probably place him in the same class as the others and reduce the Peelite total to 48.

Fifty of the original "112" Peelites chose to stay away from this division, and eleven either voted or paired with the Opposition. These seceders included Henry J. and Hugh D. Baillie (both of whom had West Indian connections), Charles B. Baldwin, William H. Bodkin, William T. Copeland, Henry H. Drummond, Montagu Gore, Lord Claud Hamilton, George W. Hope, John Masterman, and George A. Reid. There would seem to be no common factor, economic, occupational or otherwise, to link the members of this group together or to explain why they voted as they did on this occasion, save for the cases of the two Baillies.

The results of this important division might be interpreted in two quite different ways. From the standpoint of getting out the vote, the showing of the Peelites was not very impressive, as even less than fifty percent of their potential voters were present. On the other hand, if one considers that the moral issue of slavery was involved, the mustering of 48 votes in support of free trade indicates a very firm adherence to the latter cause. Some of the Peelites evidently voted against their political or economic interests.[17]

17. Henry Goulburn had strong West Indian connections and probably voted in opposition to his economic interest on this occasion. "There is [in

Turning to the Upper House during these months, it is impossible to determine the strength of the Peelites there because division lists are lacking. There were some defections over the sugar issue. The strong Abolitionist, Lord Brougham, who had served the Peelites so well earlier in the year, reasserted his independent position not only by opposing the reduction of the preferential duties, but by attempting—unsuccessfully, as it turned out—to induce Lord Stanley to make a major issue of the measure.[18]

There appears to have been a much stronger impulse among both Protectionists and Peelites in the Upper House to close ranks than was true in the Commons. Lord Stanley could not fail to be encouraged by the number of Peelites who now sat on his side of the House and by the efforts of Londonderry, Ellenborough, and Lyndhurst to reunite the party. Lyndhurst especially was active, and contacted Peel, Wellington, and Stanley on the subject of reunion, but only the last of these gave him real encouragement.[19] Lord Aberdeen seemed to occupy a neutral position; Dalhousie was "decidedly adverse" to Stanley.[20] The *coup de grace* was given to Lyndhurst's well-meaning efforts by Lord George Bentinck, who in August renewed his feud against the Peelites by bringing unsubstantiated jobbing charges against Lyndhurst and Ripon.[21] By the end of the session only Lyndhurst, Brougham, and Ellenborough were cooperating with Stanley, while Haddington, Ripon, and Buccleuch looked to Peel for leadership (which was not forthcoming) and Dalhousie avoided acknowledging either Peel or Stanley as his leader.[22]

By the end of the session the Peelites had achieved a species of identity as a parliamentary section, having withstood both Russell's attempts to win over some of their important members and Lyndhurst's attempt to reunite the Conservative party in the Lords; and,

---

Liverpool] . . . indignation at . . . Lord Sandon, whose constant friends & supporters he has so traitorously deserted. I always said he would bolt . . . as a politician he is done at Liverpool" (*PRP*. PwH 68. Chapman to Bentinck, July 29, 1846). Sandon did not stand for Liverpool in 1847.

18. *EP*. PRO 30/12–21. Ellenborough to Stanley, July 25, 1846; Stanley to Ellenborough, July 25, 1846; *BP*. Stanley to Brougham, July 25, 1846.

19. Martin, *Lyndhurst*, p. 420. Lyndhurst to Stanley, July 8, 1846.

20. *WP*. Londonderry to Wellington, July 8, 1846.

21. Jones, *Robinson*, pp. 270–71.

22. *EP*. PRO 30/12–21. Ellenborough to Clare, August 29, 1846.

had Peel chosen to give strength and form to that section, he might have enlisted a hundred or so members in the Commons and perhaps eighty-five in the Lords. The Peelite section would have provided a haven for statesmen interested in moderate reform (save, perhaps, for the Church), but who were repelled by the democratic and even republican tendencies of the Radicals and Leaguers. Peel undoubtedly had greater political stature than Russell and might have taken from him enough Whigs and Liberals to organize a Liberal party strong enough to form an administration. An alternative course would have been for Peel to retire from the political scene completely, so that his followers would have given up all hope of his return to power and have found places in other sections of the Parliament.[23] The fact that Peel followed neither of these courses meant that the Peelites had to search for an identity and meanwhile lived in a limbo whose exact political nature confounded both their contemporaries and later historians.

In this search for a political identity, the autumn of 1846 was a climactic period, for the Peelites found themselves confronted with certain highly practical questions. What would be their posture when Parliament assembled? Would they try to function as a section or let nature take its course without plan or policy? These questions became the more pressing when the Conservatives made an effort to lure back some of the former members of their party. Lord Lincoln feared that Stratford Canning would succumb to the temptation to restore old ties.[24] Viscount Jocelyn accepted an invitation to visit Stanley at Knowsley.[25] Major Beresford, the Protectionist whip, entered into intimate political discussions with Edward Cardwell and Francis Bonham.[26] By December, Goulburn was convinced that "if we take

23. Gladstone's criticism of Peel's "false position" is discussed in J. B. Conacher, "Peel and the Peelites, 1846–1850," *English Historical Review* 73 (July, 1958.)

24. *PP*. BM 40481. Lincoln to Peel, August 27, 1846.

25. Ibid. BM 40597. Young to Peel, October 23, 1846.

26. Francis Robert Bonham had filled the position of Storekeeper to the Ordnance during 1841–45, but he tendered his resignation after an investigation into his connection with a British railway. Bonham was one of Peel's most attached friends and continued to be active in Peelite affairs down to 1852, when Aberdeen gave him a minor post. See N. Gash, "F. R. Bonham: Conservative 'Political Secretary,' 1832–1847," *English Historical Review* 63 (October, 1948).

no measures for collecting our friends I think that left altogether without a leader . . . the greater group will probably attach themselves
to Stanley, who was always popular with them."[27] Bentinck's presence in the Protectionist hierarchy helped prevent such defections,
and Stanley himself would not forgive Graham;[28] still there seems to
have been a strong tendency among the Peelites to continue to regard
themselves as Conservatives not only at this moment, but during the
balance of the decade.

What could be done? The aging Goulburn, who had sacrificed his
economic interest as well as his private opinions to the cause of free
trade, met with Cardwell, Bonham, Young, and Lincoln on December 11 to consider the situation. This group arbitrarily decided to
authorize Young to send circulars to "our friends," on the authority
of the members of the late Government who happened to be in London.[29] Herbert agreed to this procedure.[30] Graham did not, noting
that such organized activity would give the impression that Peel
wished to return to power, which was quite untrue. The most Graham
would do was to write Buccleuch, Aberdeen, and perhaps some others
that Peel would be on the Opposition bench when Parliament
opened, but would not send notes to his former followers.[31] Goulburn
was dissatisfied with this arrangement, but Peel merely restated his
policy of not trying to control the activities of other members of the
House.[32]

British politics would have been considerably less complex if the
other Peelite leaders had faced realities at this time and not continued
to harbor hopes for a third Peel administration; but they did not, and
even went ahead and sent the circulars. They were based on the
authority of the "Duke of Buccleuch, Lords Dalhousie, St. Germans
and Canning in one house; You [Lincoln], Mr. Goulburn, S. Herbert

27. *PP*. BM 40597. Bonham to Peel, November 12, 1846.

28. "I fear that I shall never act with him [Stanley] again in public life,"
Graham wrote. *AP*. BM 43190. Graham to Aberdeen, January 3, 1847. See
also Jones, *Lord Derby*, p. 115.

29. *AP*. BM 43196. Goulburn to Aberdeen, December 12, 1846.

30. *GOP*. II–23. Herbert to Goulburn, December 13, 1846.

31. *PGRA*. 2:53. Graham to Buccleuch, n.d. *AP*. BM 43190. Graham to
Aberdeen, December 26, 1846.

32. *PGRA*. 2:53. Peel to Graham, January 9, 1846.

in the other . . . ,"[33] and went out to 240 members, rather than the 112 first proposed. Some 90 replies were received, which suggests both the solidarity of the "112," and the hostility of some 150 former Conservative friends.

These circulars attracted some public attention. The *Manchester Guardian* stated that Young, Cardwell, and Bonham had sent notices to members of the "Peel faction,"[34] and that it was quite clear that Peel himself was not behind this apparent move to organize a party. The circulars therefore merely informed the political world that certain members of the Peelite group were determined to act together with or without the approval of the former prime minister. Peel does not seem to have been either particularly complimented or annoyed at this expression of loyalty; but an individual of his high intelligence must have realized, as Lord Stanley did, that so long as he sat in Parliament, Peel was bound to be a leader, whether he acknowledged his followers or not.[35]

33. *NP.* 12225. Young to Lincoln, December 17, 1846.
34. *Manchester Guardian*, January 13 and 16, 1847.
35. *BP.* Stanley to Brougham, January 7, 1847.

CHAPTER 10

THE IRISH RELIEF QUESTION

A rather strange coincidence of events took place just before Parliament opened in 1847. Lincoln, who had been working hard to strengthen the separate identity of the Peelite group, found himself contacted by letter by Lord Ellenborough, who, curiously enough, was seeking his aid in abolishing that identity by reconstructing the Conservative party. Ellenborough's communication was more than flattering. He noted that Lincoln's lofty social position, and his willingness the preceding year to submit to an election while Peel, Graham, and others refused to face their constitutents on the Corn Law issue, made him the natural leader of a reconstructed Conservative party in the Commons.[1] Lincoln replied that his youth and deficiencies disqualified him from such leadership even if the Protectionists would accept him, which seemed highly unlikely.[2]

This offer seems to have made a very deep impression on Lincoln, who took very great pride in his social position and thought it might, indeed, entitle him to a high position of leadership. He was by no means without ambition; and, although he never appears to have seriously contemplated a return to the Conservative party, an unexpressed conviction seems to have grown up within him that his country might look further and find a much less capable prime minister than he himself.

Parliament had hardly met before John Young, who had assumed the position of informal "whip" of the Peelite section, found that the fears of the autumn had been groundless. Young could report to Peel that Charles Bowyer Adderley (Staffordshire North) and Viscount Chelsea (Reading) had declared themselves to be followers of Peel; and a third, Colonel William Mure (Renfrewshire), had come out in support of free trade.[3] Was this to be a trend? Were the Protection-

---

1. *EP.* PRO 30/12–21. Ellenborough to Lincoln, January 3, 1847.

2. *EP.* PRO 30/12–21. Lincoln to Ellenborough, January 5, 1847.

3. Adderley seems to have had second thoughts regarding Peelism for he was to stand as a Protectionist in 1847; Chelsea did not return to Parliament in that year and hence was a very short-term Peelite. Mure, however, ran in 1847 as a Free Trade Conservative.

ists coming over to Peel, rather than the Peelites going over to Stanley? No one could be sure until a major division forced the individual members to commit themselves one way or the other.

No clear-cut free trade issue was in prospect at the moment, and the steady advance of corn prices from 49s. to 70s. during the past six months, despite the recent tariff adjustments, had removed the agricultural question from the realm of political controversy for the time being. In its place arose an issue in which the proper role of the national government was very much involved—the famine in Ireland. Russell proposed that both the Corn Laws and the Navigation Acts be suspended until September 1 as a means of encouraging the importation of food into Ireland, and Peel and Bentinck quickly went along with the plan; but beyond this initial step, unanimity of purpose quickly disappeared.

Lord George Bentinck quite rightly concluded that the government's relief program was woefully inadequate, and on February 4 he submitted his Irish Railways Bill, which was to be the *cheval de bataille* for the session. Correctly pointing out (even as Lord Stanley had done in the cabinet before he left it) that importing food into Ireland did not solve the problem because the Irish poor lacked means of purchasing it, Bentinck suggested a public works plan which has a rather modern ring to it. He suggested that the government advance funds at low rates of interest to the Irish railways for expansion purposes, provided the railways themselves would match the funds borrowed from the government, and that a large-scale program to employ 110,000 workers should be undertaken. He believed that this railway building would provide a powerful stimulant to the whole Irish economy.[4]

This bold scheme did not sit well with the economy-minded, laissez-faire Peelites. Graham, for one, was willing enough for the government to advance funds to landlords to drain their estates, but

4. Bentinck believed that his "political Fame" depended upon the success of this particular measure, and he warned his father that no person in their family should under any circumstances acquire a financial interest in the Irish railways. Bentinck's motives were lofty and pure; his economic vision, more acute than that of some of the contemporaries who derided him (*PRP*, PwH 225. Bentinck to Portland, February 19, 1847). John Young's condemnation of the measure as a selfish scheme to aid the stockholders in the Irish railways was not only ungracious, but—at least insofar as Bentinck was involved—also untrue. See *GP*. BM 44237. Young to Gladstone, February 17, 1847.

balked at its becoming involved in the railway industry.[5] Nor did
the scheme appeal to the prime minister, who threatened to resign
if it were passed over his opposition; and this threat was another good
reason for the Peelites to oppose Bentinck, the unpopular statesman
who announced he was quite prepared to replace Russell. Although
Peel would not promise Russell in so many words to oppose the
measure,[6] his attitude toward it was well known; and it may have
encouraged the Peelites to turn out in force.

The following members from the original "112" voted with Peel
against Bentinck's measure on February 16, 1847:

Acland, Thomas D. Jr.	Egerton, William T.	Martin, Charles W.*
Attwood, John*	Escott, Bickham*	Mostyn, Edward M.*
Baillie, Henry J.	Fitz-Roy, Henry	Neville, Ralph*
Baillie, Hugh D.	Flower, Sir James*	Owen, Sir John*
Baring, Henry B.	Godson, Richard	Peel, Sir Robert*
Baring, William B.*	Goulburn, Henry*	Pennant, Edward D.
Barkly, Henry*	Graham, Sir James*	Polhill, Frederick*
Beckett, William	Greene, Thomas*	Reid, George A.
Benbow, John*	Grimsditch, Thomas	Reid, Sir John R.
Bodkin, William H.	Hamilton, William J.*	Russell, Jesse W.*
Bowles, Adm. William	Herbert, Sidney*	Sandon, Viscount*
Bruce, Lord Ernest	Hervey, Lord Alfred*	Seymour, Sir Horace*
Buckley, Edmund	Hogg, James W.*	Stewart, John
Cardwell, Edward	James, Sir Walter C.*	Sutton, John M.*
Clerk, Sir George*	Jermyn, Earl*	Thesiger, Sir Frederic*
Copeland, William T.	Johnstone, Sir John*	Tollemache, Frederick
Corry, Henry	Kelly, Sir Fitzroy	Tomline, George*
Cripps, William	Lascelles, William S.*	Vernon, Granville H.
Dickinson, Francis H.*	Lockhart, Allan E.	Villiers, Viscount
Douglas, Sir Charles*	Lyall, George*	Wellesley, Lord Charles
Douro, Marquess of	Mackinnon, William A.*	Wall, Charles B.*
Dugdale, William S.	Mahon, Viscount	Wood, Col. Thomas*
Eastnor, Viscount*	Mainwaring, Townshend	Wortley, James S.*

These 69 Peelites were joined by Lord Lincoln, Captain James Lindsay,[7] Lord Granville Somerset, and William Mure Peelites of a

5. See: Arvel B. Erickson, *The Public Career of Sir James Graham*, pp.
296–98.

6. *PP.* BM 40598. Young to Peel, February 9, 1847.

7. A Peelite identification letter was written at this time by John Young
to Gladstone, who had asked him to investigate the political situation at Wigan.

slightly later vintage for a total of 73. Almost all of the Peelite members from Irish constituencies, however, were absent from the division or voted with Bentinck.

Another highly significant division took place on February 17, 1847, when the Commons considered the Factories Bill, which, during Lord Ashley's absence from Parliament, was introduced by another member. Involved was a maximum ten hour day for women and young persons in the factories. Certain of the "112" came to its support. These included:

> Baillie, Henry J.
> Beckett, William
> Benbow, John
> Bodkin, William Henry
> Dickinson, Francis H.
> Godson, Richard
> Grimsditch, Thomas
> Hervey, Lord Alfred
> Hornby, John
> Johnstone, Sir John
> Milnes, Richard M.
> Mostyn, Edward L.
> Owen, Sir John
> Polhill, Frederick
> Sandon, Viscount

But the following Peelites, larger in numbers, voted against it:

> Barkly, Henry
> Cardwell, Edward
> Clerk, Sir George
> Cripps, William
> Douglas, Sir Charles
> Egerton, William T.
> Escott, Bickham
> Flower, Sir James
> Goulburn, Henry
> Graham, Sir James R.

Young found it unfavorable and added: "If, however, you hear a different account from Bonham, Wilson Patten, or Capt. Lindsay, trust their account rather than mine." He added that Ireland was "quite mad" in favor of Bentinck's scheme, and Irish members who opposed it were regarded as enemies to their country (*GP.* BM 44237. Young to Gladstone, Feb. 17, 1847).

Gregory, William H.
Hamilton, Lord Claud
Herbert, Sidney
Lascelles, William S.
Lockhart, Allan E.
Neville, Ralph
Northland, Viscount
Oswald, Alexander
Patten, John W.
Peel, Sir Robert
Thesiger, Sir Frederic
Villiers, Viscount
Wall, Charles Baring

One cannot overlook the fact that many of the "official" Peelites, such as Sir Robert Peel, Sir James Graham, Edward Cardwell, and Henry Goulburn opposed this humanitarian measure, and this helps fix the boundaries of Peelite "liberalism."

Shortly before this division, indeed, a group of operatives of Lancashire and Yorkshire presented a petition to Peel in which they noted he had crushed their efforts to secure the ten-hour day in 1844, and had been a "forefront opponent" of it in 1846. Would he not support their measure this time, or suggest an alternative? To this request Peel replied somewhat stiffly that he would follow a course which he believed to be "just towards the working classes & conducive to their permanent welfare," but that he did not consider a restriction on factory working hours to be "good policy."[8] In adopting this attitude, Peel was at one with John Bright and John E. Roebuck, whose "radicalism" did not extend to giving this sort of protection to the working classes.

These were the more important divisions in Parliament before the election of 1847, and it might be in order at this point to discuss the state of the Peelite section at this time. A party to be a party must have a leader; and, though the Peelites recognized their leader, he did not recognize his followers. A party usually has a structure composed of officers with specific duties, and a treasury. Though John Young, acting with the advice of Lincoln, Gladstone, and some others, attempted to be a party whip, it cannot be said that the Peelites had either a structure or a treasury. The members of a party have the

8. *PP.* BM 40598. Peel to the Operatives of Lancashire and Yorkshire, February 13, 1847.

habit of voting together. This was hardly true of the Peelites. Those listed above on page 64 with asterisks by their names voted together on all three of the great divisions—February 27, 1846; July 28, 1846; and February 16, 1847. These 38 tried and true members, some of whom, like Corry and Seymour on the railways issue, and Goulburn and Sandon on the sugar bill, had voted against their immediate interests on occasion; but they form only one-third of the original "112," and less than that of the potential Peelite strength of 120 votes. Did they have a habit of voting together? Not a very entrenched one, it must be admitted; but this should have pleased their nominal leader, who was interested in measures, not party.

The Peelite situation was somewhat different in the nonelective Upper House, where the defense of aristocratic interests tended to make the major issue among the sections not so much an ideological one, but the posture from which those interests could be best defended. The Whigs offered a more flexible defense; the Conservatives a more fixed one; and the Peelites had to choose between them.

Lord Stanley was aware that the anomalous position of Peel, and the "escapades" of Bentinck made reconciliation in the Lower House impossible at the moment,[9] but he worked with some success among his peers. One of his major (if temporary) accomplishments during this session was the enlistment, on certain occasions at least, of Lord Dalhousie, who had been previously reluctant to acknowledge his leadership.

By March, Stanley was feverishly seeking some issue on which the Conservatives and Peelites might act together against the Government, and he thought he had found one in a minor measure involving the British distilleries. Having secured the support of Dalhousie, he next contacted Lord Ellenborough, who threw some cold water on the plan. It was certainly wise to demonstrate the "strength & coherence" of the Conservative party in the Lords at the earliest opportunity, but Ellenborough objected to Stanley's choice of issues. They needed something more important and dramatic, such as a defense of the established church or the Navigation Acts, if they were to rally the two sections of the party in opposition to the Government.[10]

As it turned out, no issue of a major nature arose during the ses-

9. *BP.* Stanley to Brougham, April 13, 1847.

10. *EP.* PRO 30/12–21. Stanley to Ellenborough, March 19, 1847; Ellenborough to Stanley, March 21, 1847.

sion, but Stanley persisted and decided to make a test case of the Army Service Bill on April 26. Learning that Wellington secretly opposed this measure,[11] Stanley attacked and called for a division upon it. The result was none too impressive. The marquesses of Ailsa and Londonderry (pr.), Earls Ellenborough and Romney, and Barons Heytesbury and Blayney joined Stanley on this occasion; so did the marquess of Winchester and Lord Brougham, but they were at best *soi-disant* Peelites at this time. St. Germans secured the votes of about twice as many Peelites, including that of Dalhousie, whose attachment to the duke evidently was much stronger than his newly formed bond with Stanley.

A second issue arose rather unexpectedly in June when Palmerston's policy of forcing the recall of the Portuguese Parliament—thus meddling in the domestic affairs of a foreign state—came under sharp criticism in the Commons. Although Stanley thought he had coordinated his plan of attack effectively and left the Lords for dinner the night of June 15 expecting that Brougham, Ellenborough, and some others would speak during the period he was at the table, Stanley returned to the House just in time for the adjournment. "I think . . . ," Stanley wrote Brougham the next day, "that personally I have some ground to complain, that on such a Question, brought forward in the name of the party, I should have been left wholly unsupported."[12] In a similar letter to Ellenborough, Stanley noted that "having been requested by the party generally" to bring the matter forward, he had a right to expect support.[13] The incident itself was rather trivial; its most interesting feature is the fact that Stanley addressed Ellenborough and Brougham as if they were members of his party, which, of course, they were not.

The only real gain made by Stanley in the Lords during early 1847 was establishing more cordial relations with the able and rising Lord Dalhousie, and Lord John Russell stepped in quickly to rob him of his prize. After being turned down by Sir James Graham when he offered him the governor generalship of India, Russell offered it to Dalhousie, who was urged to accept by Wellington. In doing so, Dalhousie made it clear to Russell that this did not "imply any separa-

11. *GMEM*, 5:440–43.
12. *BP*. Stanley to Brougham, June 16, 1847.
13. *EP*. PRO 30/12–21. Stanley to Ellenborough, June 16, 1847.

tion from the party with which I have acted, or any adherence, now or hereafter, to the Whigs."[14] Thus, Dalhousie went to India as a Peelite, succeeding two other Peelites, Ellenborough and Hardinge, and preceding another Peelite, Lord Charles John Canning, which meant that Britain's prized imperial possession experienced twenty years of Peelite administration. Ellenborough was noted there for his imperialism; Hardinge, for his moderation; Dalhousie, for his efficiency; Canning, for his clemency; but there seems to have been no "Peelite policy" toward India nor any administrative characteristic shared by these men save for a deep and serious interest in their task. Dalhousie's administration in India was the longest-lived, and by the time he returned to England in 1856 the Peelite section had almost faded from the political scene.

14. *PGRA.* 2:59. Dalhousie to Graham, August 10, 1847.

CHAPTER 11

THE ELECTION OF 1847

As the election campaign of the summer of 1847 was in sight, Lord Stanley for a time hoped that some arrangement might be made with the Peelites to prevent clashes between the two sections of the Conservative party, but because Peel refused to acknowledge his headship of a "section"—Stanley used the term to describe the Peelites—there was no one with whom he could make a deal.[1] So both sections went into the fray under the Conservative guidon and left it to the voters to determine which were true believers and which were heretics.

There were a few instances of cooperation between Peelites and Protectionists during the election. The prominent Peelite member for London, John Masterman, received the support of the Protectionist Thomas Baring, and acknowledged his ally's point of view by declaring he was "very jealous" about altering the Navigation Acts. He won his seat. The Peelite Lord Sandon seconded the nomination of the "high Conservative and Protectionist" Lord Mandeville for a seat at Westminster, but this mark of approval did not prevent his being snowed under. A curious instance of Peelite-Protectionist cooperation occurred in Glasgow, where the two sections evidently decided that half a loaf was better than none and backed the Liberal, John Macgregor, in order to defeat his more radical opponents.[2]

The Whigs, as keepers of the liberal tradition in British political affairs, might well have begun to regard the Peelites as interlopers, potential rivals for the leadership of the movement; at any rate, some signs of Whig hostility toward the Peelites had begun to appear. Le Marchant wrote Russell that he had asked Delane of the *Times* to cease writing articles about Peel and come out in support of the Whigs. Somewhat reluctantly, the editor agreed, and cancelled an article he was preparing about the former prime minister.[3] But this attitude of hostility was by no means characteristic of all of the Whigs.

1. *BP*. Stanley to Brougham, April 12, 1847.
2. *RP*. PRO 30/22–6D. Macgregor to Russell, July 17, 1847.
3. Ibid. Le Marchant to Russell, July (?), 1847.

A strange turn of events found Lord Henley, nephew of Peel and a Free Trader, receiving some support from the Whigs, while he was opposed by none other than Lord Ellesmere, who had been a member of the "112" and upon whom Peel had lavished his only valedictory peerage.[4]

The issues in the 1847 election varied from constituency to constituency, and the various candidates tailored their appeals to fit the views and prejudices of their particular electors. One contemporary newspaper observed in amusement: "The Conservatives have abjured Protection, and the Whigs are extending the power of the Church."[5] Among orthodox Conservatives the chief issues were probably Protection and Protestantism, neither of which had been exemplified by the Peelites, who had repealed the Corn Laws and had increased the grant to Maynooth, the Catholic college in Dublin. Had grain prices fallen in 1847, the Protection issue would probably have taken precedence; but in a period of agricultural prosperity, the second was the more important. "Maynooth has certainly destroyed several of our friends," Bonham observed after the election, "Free Trade hardly any."[6] But there were many local issues which influenced the voters here and there, not to mention the influence of powerful families, the personalities of candidates, and free spending, which probably were quite as important in determining the outcomes of local races as were the two main issues.

Peel's name had by this time acquired a powerful magnetism among many British voters. Individuals and committees from London, the West Riding, and North Lancashire—all "prestige" seats— tried to induce the former prime minister to abandon his small Tamworth constituency and to stand in their areas; but Peel refused these offers because the Tamworth voters had been loyal to him, sometimes under "trying circumstances."[7] He was evidently annoyed when a group from Hereford County sought to capitalize on his name by adopting one of his sons as a candidate, and there was a tone of asperity in his refusal.[8] The Peel name was also very much

4. Ibid. PRO 30/22–6E. Bedford to Russell, August 16, 1847.
5. *Illustrated London News.* July 31, 1847.
6. *PP.* BM 40599. Bonham to Peel, August 2, 1847.
7. *BP.* Peel to Brougham, April 18, 1847.
8. *PP.* BM 40598. Powell to Peel, April 6, 1847; Peel to Powell, April 8, 1847.

involved in the contest for the second seat at Peel's own Tamworth constituency, which had been held by Edward Henry A'Court, a member of the "112," and which was being sought by William Yates Peel, a brother of the former prime minister. A'Court's friends appealed to Sir Robert, who was the chief proprietor at Tamworth, hoping he would persuade his brother to withdraw from the contest; but Peel replied that it was his "fixed determination" not to influence directly or indirectly the contest for the second seat, and it was for the voters to decide whether or not A'Court "had done anything justly to forfeit their confidence."[9] Unable to bear the expenses of a contested election, A'Court withdrew from the field and left it clear for William Yates Peel, who was to become an inactive and obscure member of the Commons during the next few years. As an Uncommitted Conservative, William was not a regular member of the Peelite group, but a third brother, Jonathan Peel, reelected without opposition for Huntingdon Borough, was a member of the "112."

The second-in-command of the Peelite section, Sir James Graham, had forfeited the confidence of many of his Dorchester constituents and found it necessary to seek another seat. In February, Lord Londonderry had offered to help bring him in for Durham, but Graham turned down the offer because the constituency would not give him the "freedom of action" that he desired.[10] He also rejected advances from East Cumberland and Hull, but finally accepted an offer from Earl DeGrey, whose family had long had influence in Ripon, on condition that he be left free to follow "that course that my deliberate judgment may dictate."[11] Although DeGrey appears to have agreed to this condition, Graham must have known that Lord Ripon's brother—though a Peelite—was fairly "Orange" in his sympathies and much less liberal in religious matters.

Save for Sidney Herbert, whose Wiltshire South constituency returned him without a contest, the younger members of the Peelite inner circle were refugees from Protectionist wrath. Lincoln was not quite comfortable in his Falkirk District seat, where a considerable group of Ultra-Protestants were among the electors; and in January

9. Ibid. Peel to Grundy, June 3, 1847.

10. *Illustrated London News.* June 26, 1847. It also appears that the Londonderry influence in Durham was then on the wane.

11. *PGRA*, 2:57. Graham to DeGrey, date not shown.

he had taken soundings at Manchester.[12] They indicated a dangerous voyage, so he abandoned that radical constituency to John Bright and returned to the Falkirk contest. With the aid of his father-in-law, Lincoln was able to carry the election despite Ultra-Protestant opposition and "opium money."[13] But, like Graham, he had to consider thereafter the views of many of his constituents in religious matters, and Falkirk was hardly the liberal-type borough that Lincoln would have desired to represent.

Gladstone had been in a state of political suspended animation since he had left Newark a year and a half before and was naturally anxious to return to Parliament. Oxford University provided him his opportunity when Thomas G. B. Estcourt decided to retire from his seat there. Gladstone, with some belated support from Peel, waged a "fierce" and successful contest to win over the 3,300 masters of arts who held the right of election at the university, and emerged quite proud of his accomplishment. Peel at first preferred that Cardwell sit for Oxford;[14] it is tantalizing to speculate on how Cardwell's success at Oxford and Gladstone's finding a more liberal constituency would have influenced their later careers. As it was, Cardwell replaced Lord Sandon at Liverpool on a platform of "Commercial Freedom and Religious Toleration,"[15] and hence might expect his constituents to approve a liberal attitude in politics.

Save for Peel, Cardwell was the only member of the Peelite inner circle whose constituency gave him perfect freedom to act upon liberal principles. Graham had an Orange patron; Lincoln had many Ultra-Protestant constituents; Gladstone's constituents regarded the Conservative party as the bastion of the Established Church; Goulburn won at Cambridge University partly because of his recent vote for "more bishops";[16] and Herbert sat for an agricultural constituency that had been unexpectedly tolerant of his commercial views but might turn on him later. Lincoln's freedom of action was increased

12. *NP*. 11935. Herbert to Lincoln, December 12, 1846.

13. "I am sure of success in spite of opium money and R. Cathc. Endowment," Lincoln wrote (ibid. 11873. Lincoln to Bonham, July 30, 1847). He did not elaborate.

14. A. T. Bassett, *Gladstone to his Wife*, pp. 72–73.

15. *Liverpool Mercury*. July 23, 1847.

16. *PP*. BM 40452. Graham to Peel, July 22, 1847.

by the knowledge that he would be translated to the House of Lords ere long, but the others had to tread cautiously when they walked on liberal ground.

Peel's support of Gladstone at Oxford was apparently an exception to his general line of political conduct, which was to avoid any appearance of party leadership, and the lengths to which he carried this nonintervention is illustrated in the case of the seat at Scarborough. Sir Frederick W. Trench, who occupied the seat and had been one of the "112," informed Peel in April that he intended to retire from political life and suggested that his seat—a very safe one, according to Trench—be assigned to one of Peel's immediate "connexions," or to "our Friend," Sir George Clerk.[17] Clerk, another member of the "112," who had had a seat at Stamford under the influence of the Protectionist marquess of Exeter and had to give it up. In the 1847 election it went to a prominent Tory of the older generation, John Charles Herries. Clerk might have used the Scarborough seat and so, indeed, might have Graham, Gladstone, Cardwell, or Lincoln, but it does not appear that Peel offered it to any of them; at any rate, it fell to the earl of Mulgrave, a Liberal.[18]

The tabulation of the results of the 1847 election provided the names of the winning candidates, but it by no means clarified the positions of the various sections of the House of Commons. Charles Wood wrote gloatingly to Russell in August: "Peel's party as a party numerically speaking, is gone. . . . The protectionists are thoroughly beaten."[19] Among the many inaccurate and conflicting opinions regarding the election's results, Wood's observations stand out as the most inaccurate. Gladstone, who had estimated the 1846 strength of the Peelites as approaching 120, came closest among contemporary observers to agreeing with Wood when he calculated that their strength had been reduced by half.[20] Others were inclined to be much more generous to the Peelite cause and included in their ranks many whose hustings speeches showed a leaning in that direction. How untrustworthy these speeches were as a political guide was noted at the

17. *PP*. BM 40598. Trench to Peel, April 27, 1847.

18. Clerk was able to find a seat at Dover from which Sir John Rae Reid, another of the "112," had retired.

19. *RP*. PRO 30/22–6E. Wood to Russell, August 14, 1847.

20. *MGLD*, 1:351.

time by Lord Ellenborough, who wrote: "Its [the new Parliament's] complexion is to me revolting, for it is impossible not to see that many Conservatives & many Whigs & Radicals have got their elections under false pretences—the former truckling to Free Trade & the latter to Ultra-Protestantism."[21]

The contemporary confusion is strikingly illustrated by comparing the identifications made by two contemporary newspapers—the *Illustrated London News*, which provided an early analysis of the election results in the English and Welsh boroughs, dividing the members among the Whig, Protectionist, and Peelite sections,[22] and *The Times*, which offered a more comprehensive analysis of both borough and county members, whom they divided among the Liberals, Peelites, and Protectionists.[23]

The *Illustrated London News* located 73 Peelites in the English and Welsh boroughs, but one of them—Andrew Lawson—was subsequently defeated, so the total was 72; *The Times*, on the other hand, could find only 75 Peelites in all the boroughs in Great Britain. Comparing the two lists, we find the two newspapers agreed on the identities of only 57 Peelites in the English and Welsh boroughs, and that 41 of these were members of the "112." The other 16 included Lord Ashley, Henry Bayley Clive, Thomas S. Cocks, Octavius E. Coope, William Cubitt, John Duncuft, James W. D. Dundas, William E. Gladstone, Howel Gwyn, Lord Arthur Lennox, James Lindsay, John I. Nicholl, William Yates Peel, George R. Robinson, George J. Turner, and James Wyld. If both papers believed these men to be Peelites, there must have been some good reason for it; and that reason in most cases probably was their statements on the hustings, as reported in various newspapers. Yet, when we check their names in *Dod* for the new Parliament in 1847, we find that Henry B. Clive and Howel Gwyn were Protectionists, James W. D. Dundas was a Whig, John I. Nicholl and William Y. Peel were simply Conservatives, James Lindsay was an unpledged Conservative, and James Wyld denied being Whig, Tory, or Radical. Thus, the two newspapers, even when they agreed, did not locate 57 Peelites whose identifications were absolutely established.

21. *EP.* PRO 30/12–21. Ellenborough to Clare, August 23, 1847.
22. *Illustrated London News.* August 7, 1847.
23. *The Times* (London). August 13 and 17, 1847.

The additions (16) made by the *Illustrated London News* beyond the 57 noted above seem to have been selected without much rhyme or reason—at least so it appears when their names are checked with the identifications in *Dod*. Seven of them (Edward H. Baldock, Thomas Baring, Richard Blakemore, Sir James B. East, Sackville W. Lane Fox, George Hudson, and Edwin Lascelles) were listed as Protectionists; three (the earl of Euston, William S. Lascelles, and John Martin), as Liberals; one (Richard M. Milnes), as a Conservative supporter of Russell; and one (Andrew Lawson) was subsequently defeated, which leaves only four (Thomas Greene, Henry T. Hope, George Sandars, and Sir Henry P. Willoughby) Conservative Free Traders. The newspaper seems to have beat the bushes to flush out anyone who might resemble a Peelite for additions to its list.

As *The Times* included members from Scottish and Irish boroughs, as well as those in England and Wales, it was not so hard pressed to find Free Trade Conservatives who might be identified as Peelites. It added 18 to the 57 noted above, and ten of these (William Bolling, Samuel Christy, Alexander D. B. Cochrane, Henry Edwards, James Heald, William Keogh, Lord Lincoln, Viscount Newry, Viscount Northland, and Roundell Palmer) were Peelites in the sense that they were Conservative Free Traders; but an aura of uncertainty surrounded the other eight. Sir Robert Pigot, David Waddington, and Glynne Earle Welby appeared as Protectionists in the 1847 edition of *Dod*, William H. C. Plowden as a Conservative, Henry G. Sturt as a Moderate Conservative, Lord Patrick J. Stuart as a Moderate Reformer, John Peter Deering as a Conservative opposed to the Peel administration, and John Boyd as a repentant Conservative Free Trader who was now a High Conservative.

When it analyzed the county members, *The Times* was as kind to the Peelites as the *Illustrated London News* had been in its treatment of the English and Welsh borough representatives. It found 38 Peelites, who, added to the 75 in the boroughs, gave a total strength of 113—as many as they had for the division of February 27, 1846. There was ample justification for 15 of these, as they had been members of the original "112,"[24] and seven more showed strong leanings in the

24. These included Henry J. Baillie, Robert H. Clive, Henry T. L. Corry, Henry H. Drummond, William T. Egerton, Lord Claud Hamilton, Sidney Herbert, Duncan McNeill, Alexander H. Oswald, John W. Patten, Edward G. D.

direction of the Peelites, including Francis W. Charteris, George Dundas, William Mure, Viscount Seaham, and Lord Granville Somerset, who were Free Trade Conservatives; Viscount Drumlanrig, a Liberal Tory; and Hamilton K. G. Morgan, a Moderate Conservative; but the list included twelve Protectionists,[25] a Conservative (Sir William Verner), a Decided Conservative (William Lockhart), a Liberal (Chichester S. Fortescue), and a Whig (Richard G. Townley). One receives the impression that *The Times* also was interested in building up the membership of "Peel's Party."

It would certainly have been a boon to historians if Peel had scanned the lists and picked out his followers, but he did not; and the confusion evident in the newspapers is also to be found in the private correspondence of political leaders of the time. Lord Stanley, who had a strong interest in all things Conservative, wrote Brougham in August:

> The Elections are now over, but I have considerable difficulty in endeavouring to classify the Returns, so as to form any calculation at all to be relied on, of the relative strength of parties. I should be disposed to estimate all classes of 'Liberals' combined much as you do, at 325 or 330: the Peelite force is very doubtful. George Bentinck puts it as high as 120, Beresford as low as about 85. I take the fact to be that on all sides there will be a great number of loose fish, and of that class of independent Members which has been defined to be Members on whom nobody can depend.[26]

The Conservative leader added gloomily: "I am coming to Redesdale's opinion that if the Conservative Party is to be formed, it must be formed primarily in the Lords—but even there we are sadly disjointed."

Lord Brougham wrote a penetrating letter the following month:

Pennant, Alexander Smollett Jr., Lord Charles Wellesley, Charles W. W. Wynn, and John Young.

25. These included Sir Thomas D. Acland, Nathaniel Alexander, Thomas Bateson, Charles L. C. Bruce, Viscount Clive, Viscount Courtenay, Theobald Jones, Charles P. Leslie, William F. Mackenzie, Lord Norreys, George Rushout, and Richard Spooner. It should be observed that in *Dod* many Protectionists merely noted that they voted against repeal in 1846, but did not state specifically that they opposed free trade as such.

26. *BP.* Stanley to Brougham, August 20, 1847.

As to party my calculations agree to within 5 or 6 with Billy Holmes who . . . makes 85 Peelites—some 30 more than could have been expected. But then what right have we to call them Peelites—except some dozen or so? The others are so reckoned because they are not known to be Protectionists & are known not to be Whigs. For example, G. Damer (the Col.) & Douro have lately been staying with us & they may be much & naturally opposed to such leaders as G. Bentinck yet they have no kind of desire to follow Peel unless on the merit of any given question they happen to agree with him. Then Aberdeen justly observes that if by Peelites be meant men who respect Peel and would willingly join him were he again to come forward—but join him on specified grounds—there may be many more than 80 or 90. Yet as leadership & still more place is now out of the question with him, there can be no *party* of Peelites & in that sense of men to take office to carry out the Govt. Peel has nothing like a party—& yet in no other sense can any party be said to exist. . . . He will take his own line on each question . . . reckoning on the division between those called Peelites & the Protectionists to ensure him a considerable support indoors . . . a support for which he will have to pay no price by shaping his conduct to secure it.[27]

Whether or not his interpretation of Peel's tactic of securing support without paying for it was absolutely correct, the questions Brougham raised regarding the nature of the Peelite section were certainly acute. Materializing a Peelite section in rigid form out of the iridescent, amorphous mass of "loose fish" is certainly a difficult task, but scarcely more so than adequately describing the nature of the Government coalition,[28] or, for that matter, analyzing the position of Brougham himself. Yet we know that Brougham, the coalition, and the Peelites all existed during this era as political factors that challenge the historian's ingenuity to define and measure.

27. *EP.* PRO 30/12–21. Brougham to Ellenborough, September 23, 1847.

28. Supported as it was by 51 Whigs, 2 Whig Protectionists, 1 Whig Radical, 163 Liberals, 2 Liberal Protectionists, 1 Advanced Liberal, 1 Liberal Free Trader, 27 Radicals, 33 Reformers, 26 Repealers, 1 Liberal Repealer, 6 Free Traders, 2 Chartists, and 11 others who defy classification.

CHAPTER 12

THE PEELITE SECTION IN 1847

Before we try to answer the question, Was the election of 1847 a victory or a defeat for the Peelite section?, we must decide if the term *Peelite* adequately describes the political group and its conditions that we are attempting to define. The term *Peelites* is safe enough because it is so generic that the reader might imagine a dozen members or two hundred and not feel improperly restricted. If the term *Peel's Friends* is used, the meaning is more specific; but at the same time one might interpret it to mean Peel's social friends or Peel's political friends, and neither term is very meaningful. Among his social friends—not a very large group, it would seem—Peel included not only many nonpolitical figures, such as Russell Ellice of the East India Company, but politicians like Sir Robert Inglis, a strong Protectionist, and Lord John Chichester, a Liberal. If we use the term *Peel's political friends*, it might be taken to mean a small group of intimates such as Graham, Bonham, and Young or a very large body of members of Parliament who would accept his leadership. Used in the latter sense, Peel's political friends would include the whole body of Conservatives who were more or less pledged to free trade.

In this difficult situation, the safest course would seem to be to use the term *Peelites* in the sense that it was usually used at the time, which included both the actual Peelites (that is, those intimates who consulted among themselves and tried to collaborate with Peel) and the potential Peelites (those Conservatives who were reluctant to abandon their party label and generally supported free trade and a more liberalized approach toward political problem-solving). Thus, if we speak of the Peelite section, it can include a large potential force in Parliament.

One of the strongest arguments for using the term *Peelite section* lies in the fact that some statesmen of the time anticipated or feared that the loosely knit section might develop into a true political party and take over the political movement in Britain. "I do not think there is anything like an actual coalition [between the Peelites and the Government]," Stanley wrote, "but I have little doubt that there is a

79

very good understanding between the Government and many of Peel's followers; and that they, and he, will give a general support, till an opportunity occurs for damaging them."[1] Le Marchant reported a conversation with Delane of *The Times* to Russell: "Peel was he considered almost below zero in the estimation of the constituencies generally & his party wd. be insignificant as to numbers in the new Parliament. His hopes of course lay in breaking up the Liberal party."[2] That some of the leading Peelites hoped to lead the liberal movement in Britain seems fairly well substantiated by their activities from time to time, and that Russell realized and tried to avert this development is indicated by his frequent efforts to recruit among the Peelites, not only to strengthen his own position but also to weaken that of a competing section.

With these factors in mind, we might now try to answer the question, Was the election of 1847 a victory or a defeat for the Peelite section? The fact that only 69 of the original 112 Peelites returned to Parliament, roughly sixty percent of their original strength, suggests that the attrition was heavy and that the Protectionists took vengeance upon them at the polls; but a closer examination of the election results tends to modify these assumptions.

Only 37 of the original 112 Peelites were returned to their places without electoral contests. This lack of opposition might mean one of two things: that their constituents and patrons approved of their conduct or that the competing parties lacked funds or candidates to back opponents in these constituencies. Although this second consideration might have obtained in a few cases, the fact that the election of 1847 was a lively one and the search for seats both by the Government and the Protectionists was fairly intensive suggests that these 37 lacked opposition because potential challengers felt they could not be displaced. One might therefore assume that the voters and patrons of the 37 were by and large satisfied with their conduct in 1846.

Twenty-one other Peelites faced opposition at the polls but received a vote of confidence from their constituents, the dimensions of which varied markedly from place to place. Those heading their respective polls were John Attwood (Harwich) William Beckett

1. *BP.* Stanley to Brougham, August 20, 1847.
2. *RP.* PRO 30/22–6E. Le Marchant to Russell, (?), 1847.

(Leeds), John Boyd (Coleraine), William T. Copeland (Stoke-upon-Trent), Sir Charles E. Douglas (Warwick Bor.), Henry Fitz-Roy (Lewes), Lord Alfred Hervey (Brighton), John Hornby (Blackburn), Earl Jermyn (Bury St. Edmunds), Alexander Smollett (Dumbartonshire), and Thomas C. Whitmore (Bridgenorth). These eleven received a mark of approval only slightly less significant than the 37 in uncontested boroughs, but certain others had to fight for their political lives. John Masterman had a margin of only four votes at London; Frederic Thesiger (Abingdon) and Charles W. Martin (Newport, I.W.) won by only two votes, and Charles B. Baldwin (Totness) squeezed through by a single vote. Such narrow victories might be expected to cause the victors to tread circumspectly in the new Parliament.

TABLE 2

FATE OF THE "112" IN 1847 ELECTION

Won Uncontested

Henry J. Baillie	Allan E. Lockhart
Henry B. Baring	Duncan McNeill
William B. Baring	Viscount Mahon
Henry Barkly	Viscount Northland
John Benbow	Alexander Oswald
William Bowles	Sir John Owen
Lord Ernest Bruce	John W. Patten
Robert H. Clive	Jonathan Peel
Henry L. Corry	Sir Robert Peel
William Cripps	Edward Pennant
Henry H. Drummond	George A. Reid
William T. Egerton	Lord Somerton
Richard Godson	Frederick Tollemache
Thomas Greene	Viscount Villiers
Lord Claud Hamilton	Lord Charles Wellesley
Sidney Herbert	James S. Wortley
William B. Hughes	Charles W. Wynn
Viscount Jocelyn	John Young
Sir John Johnstone	

Won Contested

John Attwood	Earl Jermyn
Charles B. Baldwin	William A. Mackinnon
William Beckett	Charles W. Martin
John Boyd	John Masterman
William T. Copeland	Richard M. Milnes
Sir Charles E. Douglas	Alexander Smollett
Lord Douro	George P. Smythe
Henry Fitz-Roy	Henry Stuart
Henry Goulburn	Sir Frederic Thesiger
Lord Alfred Hervey	Thomas C. Whitmore
John Hornby	

TABLE 2 (*continued*)

Changed Seats

Edward Cardwell	William S. Lascelles
Sir George Clerk	Edward L. Mostyn
George L. Damer	Sir Horace B. Seymour
Sir James Graham	John M. Sutton
Sir John Hanmer	Charles B. Wall
James W. Hogg	

Retired

Thomas D. Acland, Jr.	John H. Johnstone
Edward H. A'Court	Sir Fitzroy Kelly
Hugh D. Baillie	Peter Kirk
William Baird	George C. Legh
Edmund Buckley	George Lyall
Sir George G. Cockburn	Forster A. Macgeachy
Francis H. Dickinson	Townshend Mainwaring
William S. Dugdale	Captain Henry Meynell
Viscount Eastnor	Ralph Neville
Lord Francis Egerton	W. Tyringham Praed
Thomas G. Estcourt	Sir John R. Reid
Sir James Flower	Jesse D. W. Russell
Sir Stephen R. Glynne	Viscount Sandon
Montagu Gore	Sir Frederick W. Trench
William J. Hamilton	Granville H. Vernon
George W. Hope	Colonel Thomas Wood
Sir Walter C. James	

Defeated

William H. Bodkin	Thomas Grimsditch
Beriah Botfield	Frederick Polhill
Swynfen T. Carnegie	John Stewart
Bickham Escott	George Tomline
William H. Gregory	Colonel Thomas Wood, Jr.

The other eleven members of the 112 abandoned their previous constituencies and acquired new seats. If they had abandoned single-member constituencies and had secured seats in such constituencies, it would be quite easy to determine who displaced whom and who the displaced, in turn, displaced; but this clear-cut situation did not obtain in most cases, and some doubt must exist. It would appear, however, that Protectionists or Uncommitted Conservatives acquired the seats of Clerk, Graham, and Wall; Liberals secured those previously occupied by Hanmer, Sutton,[3] and Mostyn; Free Trade Conservatives took over from Seymour and Lascelles; and Cardwell and Damer lost out to Whigs. Whom, then, did the Peelites displace?

---

3.   John M. Sutton was beaten in his try for reelection at Cambridge Borough, then won a telling victory at Newark, from whence the duke of Newcastle had driven Gladstone.

They replaced other Peelites in six cases, Conservatives in four others, and a Liberal in the last. Thus, the Peelites actually displaced more Conservatives (4) than were displaced by Conservatives (3).

Having accounted for the 69 of the 112 Peelites who returned to Parliament, the discussion now centers on those who did not. Thirty-three of their losses[4] came by retirement rather than defeat at the polls. In some cases the reasons for retirement are readily available: William Baird had given his seat to Lincoln in 1846; Lord Francis Egerton had gone to the House of Lords; Edward H. A'Court did not want to contest Tamworth with Peel's brother;[5] and Sir Frederick W. Trench retired for personal reasons.[6] Certain others, unlike that hardy perennial Charles W. Wynn, who was 72 years old, probably did not feel like going through contested elections at their ages; this group might include Hugh D. Baillie (age 70), Edmund Buckley (age 67), Sir George Cockburn (age 75), Thomas B. Estcourt (age 71), and Colonel Thomas Wood (age 70).[7] As eleven of the 33 seats involved returned Free Trade Conservatives, it is clear that many of those who abandoned their seats through retirement might have secured reelection. Of the remaining 22 seats, six went to Uncommitted Conservatives, five to Protectionists, nine to Liberals, one to a Whig, and another to a Reformer. Thus, 16 of the 33 seats were lost to the Peelite cause, but 17 went to Free Trade Conservatives or Uncommitted Conservatives who might cooperate with them. The retirement losses were heavy, but not disastrous.

The remaining ten of the original 112 Peelites were defeated at the polls. These included William H. Bodkin (Rochester), Beriah Botfield (Ludlow), Swynfen T. Carnegie (Stafford Borough), Bickham Escott (Winchester),[8] William H. Gregory (Dublin City), Thomas Grimsditch (Macclesfield), Frederick Polhill (Bedford Borough), John Stewart (Christchurch), George Tomline (Shrews-

4. Sir Fitzroy Kelly, included in the 33, retired from his seat at Cambridge Borough, then went down to defeat at Lyme Regis.

5. *PP*. BM 40598. A'Court to Charles A'Court, June 4, 1847.

6. Ibid. Sir Frederick Trench to Peel, April 27, 1847.

7. Wood wanted to take his ailing wife to Nice that winter but could not do so if a contested election (the outcome of which was in doubt) were in prospect (*PP*. BM 40596. Wood to Peel, July 25, 1846).

8. Escott was defeated in an attempt to hold his seat at Winchester, then lost again at Somersetshire West.

bury), and Col. Thomas Wood Jr. (Middlesex). Botfield and Carnegie were turned out by Conservatives; Bodkin lost to a Whig; Gregory, to a Repealer; Grimsditch, to a Chartist; and the others, to Liberals.

This brief survey seems to undermine the theory that the Protectionists took revenge on the Peelites at the polls in 1847; on the contrary, their chief opponents were sections of the Government coalition, who picked up eleven seats from the retiring Peelites, five of the eleven seats abandoned by the Peelites, and eight of the ten constituencies in which Peelites were defeated for a total of twenty-four seats. Protectionists and Uncommitted Conservatives together managed to secure only sixteen of these seats. The number of seats acquired by die-hard Protectionists (7) was quite small. The result, indeed, seems to show that the Peelites who lost out did so because they were too conservative, not because they had adopted a liberal position in 1846.

If we assume that the 69 Peelites from the original 112 who were reelected to the Parliament in 1847 formed the hard core of the section, they might be studied individually to determine whether or not some common "X" factor bound them together. One might first ask the question, Did the Peelite movement have a geographical orientation? A glance at the accompanying table, which names their constituencies, provides an answer to this. It is clear that Peelism was wholly absent in Ireland south of Cavan and west of Tyrone, and that it was stronger in western than in eastern Scotland as well as stronger in northern than in southern Wales. They held seats, either for borough or county constituencies, in more than half of the English counties, and were weakest in the Cumberland-Northumberland-Westmoreland-Durham area of the north. Peelites won in 20 percent of the Welsh constituencies, 13 percent of the Scottish, 10 percent of the English, and only 6 percent of the Irish. But, lest these statistics prove misleading, it should be added that 50 of their 69 seats were in England proper.

One might next ask, Were the Peelites successful in narrow or popular constituencies? About one-third of the Peelite constituencies had populations of 50,000 or more, and another third were in the 5,000–10,000 class. Populations of Peelite constituencies ranged from tiny ones such as Bridgenorth (pop. 1,931) and Honiton (pop. 3,773)

TABLE 3

THE SIXTY-NINE PEELITE CONSTITUENCIES

IN ENGLAND

Boroughs: Abingdon, Bedford, Blackburn, Brighton, Bridgenorth, Bury St. Edmunds, Canterbury, Cirencester (2), Dorchester, Dover, Dudley, Grantham, Harwich, Hertford, Honiton, Huntingdon, Kidderminster, Knaresborough, Lancaster, Launceston, Leeds, Leominster, Lewes, Liverpool, London, Lymington, Lynn Regis, Marlborough (2), Newark, Newport, I.W., Norwich, Pontefract, Ripon, Salisbury, Scarborough, Stoke-upon-Trent, Tamworth, Thetford, Totnes, Warwick, Wilton, Windsor. *Counties*: Cheshire-North, Hampshire-South, Lancashire-North, Shropshire-South, Wiltshire-South. *University*: Cambridge.

IN IRELAND

Boroughs: Coleraine, Dungannon, Lisburn. *Counties*: Cavan, Tyrone (2).

IN SCOTLAND

Boroughs: None. *Counties*: Argyllshire, Ayrshire, Buteshire, Dumbartonshire, Inverness-shire, Perthshire, Selkirkshire.

IN WALES

Boroughs: Carnarvon District, Flint District, Pembroke District. *Counties*: Carnarvonshire, Flintshire, Montgomeryshire.

to such giants as Cheshire North (pop. 217,650), and Tyrone County (pop. 312,956). Only in London (19,064) and Liverpool (14,970) were the Peelite members responsible to large masses of voters. About 55 percent of the Peelite constituencies had 1,000 or fewer voters, and Harwich had less than 200.

A number of the Peelite constituencies were considered to be under control of patrons. These included Bridgenorth (Whitmore family), Bury St. Edmunds (duke of Grafton and marquess of Bristol), Carnarvon Dist. (marquess of Anglesey), Cirencester (Bathurst family), Dorchester (earl of Shaftesbury), Dudley (Lord Ward), Hertford Bor. (marquess of Salisbury and Lord Cowper), Huntingdon Bor. (Lord Sandwich), Lymington (Sir H. Neale), Marlborough (marquess of Ailesbury), Newark (duke of Newcastle), Pembroke Dist. (Owen family), Ripon (Earl DeGrey), Tamworth (Sir Robert Peel), Thetford (duke of Grafton and Lord Ashburton), Warwick Bor. (earl of Warwick), Wilton (earl of Pembroke), and Windsor (Ramsbottom family). In certain cases, such as Sir John Owen at Pembroke, Sir Robert Peel at Tamworth,[9] and Thomas C. Whitmore

9. Peel probably would have been the first to deny that he held his seat at Tamworth through influence. "On purely public grounds, from confidence in the Rectitude of my intentions, they have repeatedly . . . reserved the Trust which they first committed to me soon after I had been rejected by the University of Oxford" Peel wrote (*BP.* Peel to Brougham, April 18, 1847).

at Bridgenorth, the influence seems obvious enough; but, as the duke of Grafton, the duke of Newcastle, the marquess of Salisbury, and Lords Ashburton, Sandwich, and Warwick were all Protectionists, it would appear that the Peelites in their constituencies won in spite of their influence rather than because of it. Possibly only a dozen Peelites were aided in their campaigns by the influence of patrons.

As the Corn Law struggle is often interpreted as a battle between town and countryside, one might expect that the Peelites would have come from the urban constituencies and ports which might thrive as a result of free trade. Some of the Peelites represented seaport constituencies, such as Carnarvon District, Dover, Harwich, Liverpool, London, Lyme Regis, and Scarborough, and others came from highly industrialized centers such as Blackburn, Lancaster Borough, and Leeds. But a sizable number of their constituencies were rural, or tied to the land. The two counties which furnished the most Peelite members (five each) were Yorkshire and Wiltshire—one well industrialized, the other quite agricultural. Many of their constituencies, such as Abingdon, Bedford Borough, Buteshire, Cavan, Marlborough, Thetford, and Warwick Borough had connections with the land, either as centers of agricultural production or distribution.

This brief survey of the 69 Peelite constituencies points up the difficulties involved in locating an "X" factor common to all of them which would provide a basis for the Peelite movement. Their constituencies were scattered and therefore nonsectional, and with the exception of the southern Irish, all of the British ethnic groups were represented among the Peelites, though the mix was more English than Celtic. Their members represented large populations and small ones, constituencies with many voters, and others with only a few. Some of the constituencies were urbanized; others were strongly agricultural. Nor can one find the "X" factor among the individuals who were members of the Peelite movement.[10]

It seems doubtful that the statistical approach, even if employed more minutely and skillfully than in this brief survey, would uncover the "X" factor, for that factor probably lies beyond the reach of even modern statistics. The Conservatives had been rooted in agriculture, and strongly attached to the Established Church. Peel had torn out

10. See appendix 1 for brief notes as to their positions in society and occupations.

the former and—to the more ardent Anglicans—had not seemed wholly sound in his attachment to the latter, which meant that large numbers of Conservatives, like the Peelites themselves, were not quite sure just what Conservatism involved. They knew that the type of Conservatism they desired was somewhat more mobile than it had been in the past, and one which might safely adapt British institutions to the changing needs of society. Any attempt to define the "X" factor more clearly than this is bound to run into many objections.

The confusion existing in Conservative ranks is vividly illustrated by the various descriptions the Conservatives gave to themselves in *Dod.* Aside from the 69 traditional Peelites and the Conservatives who identified themselves as having opposed repeal in 1846, there were Free Trade Conservatives, Liberal Conservatives, plain Conservatives, Moderate Conservatives, and two Tories, who together composed a band of 55 voters. Those called "Uncommitted Conservatives" on the accompanying chart are those who avoided stating or hinting their views on the free trade issue. This chart reveals why Stanley and others encountered so much difficulty in making a head count of the Conservatives.

TABLE 4

CONSERVATIVES OTHER THAN THE ORIGINAL PEELITES AND
PROTECTIONISTS IN 1847

FREE TRADE CONSERVATIVES

Lord Ashley	John Duncuft
(Bath)	(Oldham)
Marquess of Blandford	George Dundas
(Woodstock)	(Linlithgowshire)
William Bolling	Henry Edwards
(Bolton-le-Moors)	(Halifax)
Viscount Brackley	James Heald
(Staffordshire North)	(Stockport)
Francis Charteris	Henry A. Herbert
(Haddingtonshire)	(Kerry County)
Samuel Christy	Henry T. Hope
(Newcastle-under-Lyme)	(Gloucester City)
A.D.R.W. Baillie Cochrane	William Keogh
(Bridport)	(Athlone)
Thomas S. Cocks, Jr.	Lord Lincoln
(Reigate)	(Falkirk Dist.)
Octavius E. Coope	Sir Edmund C. Macnaghten
(Yarmouth)	(Antrim)
William Cubitt	William Mure
(Andover)	(Renfrewshire)

TABLE 4 (*continued*)

Viscount Newry and Morne
(Newry)
George R. Robinson
(Poole)
George Sandars
(Wakefield)
Viscount Seaham
(Durham North)
Thomas Sidney
(Stafford Bor.)

Lord Granville Somerset
(Monmouthshire)
Edmund Turner
(Truro)
George J. Turner
(Coventry)
John Walter
(Nottingham Bor.)
Sir Henry P. Willoughby
(Evesham)

UNCOMMITTED CONSERVATIVES

Viscount Francis Bernard
(Bandon)
Richard S. Bourke
(Kildare)
Wellington H. Cotton
(Carrickfergus)
Thomas J. Ireland
(Bewdley)
Sir Willoughby Jones
(Cheltenham)
Richard Kerr
(Downpatrick)
James Lindsay
(Wigan)
William B. M'Clintock
(Carlow County)

William Y. Peel
(Tamworth)
William H. Plowden
(New port, I.W.)
Ld. William J. Powlett
(St. Ives)
David Pugh
(Montgomery Dist.)
Christopher St. George
(Galway County)
Sir George H. Smyth
(Colchester)
David Urquhart
(Stafford Bor.)
Sir William Verner
(Armagh)

OTHER CONSERVATIVES

Liberal Conservatives
Henry Currie
(Guildford)
William E. Gladstone
(Oxford University)
Lord Arthur Lennox
(Yarmouth)
Roundell Palmer
(Plymouth)
Frederick R. West
(Denbigh Dist.)

Moderate Conservatives
Hamilton K. Morgan
(Wexford County)
Henry C. Sturt
(Dorchester)

Liberal Tory
Viscount Drumlanrig
(Dumfriesshire)

Tory
Francis R. Haggitt
(Herefordshire)

Those who contended that the Peelites lost the election might point out that some members from the 69, such as Damer, Douro, Milnes, William S. Lascelles, and probably many others, did not consider themselves to be members of a Peelite section and that only a few of the new men, such as Gladstone and Lincoln, could be positively identified as Peelites. Charles Wood may have reasoned in this manner when he wrote Russell: "Peel's party as a party numerically

speaking is gone."[11] On the other hand, Lord George Bentinck probably added most of the 55 Conservatives of various descriptions to
the 69 when he estimated Peelite strength at 120.[12] Two other observers, William Beresford, a Conservative,[13] and John T. Delane of
The Times,[14] estimated the Peelite section as 85 members.

Just how Beresford and Delane arrived at this figure of 85 is not
too clear. They might have used the 69 traditional Peelites as a base
and added Lord Lincoln, who had established his Peelite identity
later in the Corn Law debates along with James Lindsay and Lord
Granville Somerset, and Viscount Newry, who had been a proxy Peelite from the first. William Mure had announced his conversion to
Peelism early in 1847; Gladstone was widely known to be one of the
more influential Peelites; William Verner was an intimate friend of
Peel; William Y. Peel was a brother to the prime minister. These
members would bring the total to 77. Others who might be logically
added to the Peelite force were those who had resigned early in 1846
and had not been able to find new seats until 1847—a group which
included Lord Ashley, Francis Charteris, A. Baillie Cochrane, Lord
Arthur Lennox, and Henry C. Sturt. The other three might have been
added from any of the various groups of Conservatives.

It is probably impossible to state just how many Peelites there were
after the election of 1847. Indeed, if one had put the question—Are
you a Peelite?—to most of the various and sundry Conservatives on
the chart, they themselves probably could not have answered it. Most
of them had a Conservative bent, but Peel refused to lead them and
Bentinck had been fairly well discredited; so whom they would follow in the future would depend upon the issues and circumstances
that arose. Yet it is clear that the potential of the Peelite section was
great. If the Government pursued too radical a course, most of the
various Conservatives might have rallied around the 69, not to mention the more conservative Liberals; and the Peelites might have become the moderate, reforming party of the future.

11. *RP*. PRO 30/22–6E. Wood to Russell, August 14, 1847.
12. *BP*. Stanley to Brougham, August 20, 1847.
13. Ibid.
14. *RP*. PRO 30/22–6E. Le Marchant to Russell, undated, 1847.

CHAPTER 13

THE PEELITE SECTION IN THE 1848 SESSION

In late 1847 and during 1848 various forces were at work to reunite the Conservative party on the one hand and to prevent its reunification on the other. Reviving Chartism certainly favored the former movement; but the sharp financial panic of the autumn of 1847, which gave rise to discussions of financial and commercial policy, worked in the opposite direction. If the Peelite section was to remain distinct and form itself into a regular political party, it would be necessary for it to represent something more than a dissentient Conservative mood and to find defensible positions on outstanding issues.

The extent to which the Peelites did and did not develop positions on these questions is suggested by a study of the more important divisions that took place in the Commons during late 1847 and 1848. For purposes of analysis, it is convenient to call the sixty-nine original Peelites, Peelites, and the fifty-five Conservatives who were neither original Peelites nor members of the Bentinck-Disraeli group, Miscellaneous Conservatives. One found among the Miscellaneous Conservatives a subgroup who called themselves "Free Trade Conservatives," but their political behavior does not seem to have been sufficiently distinct to warrant their being separated from the Miscellaneous Conservatives as a whole.

If the Peelites and Miscellaneous Conservatives were brought together, they would have a force of 69 plus 55, or 124 votes, but the first of these numbers must be revised downward. William S. Lascelles ran in 1847 as a Liberal; and Richard M. Milnes ran as a Moderate Conservative who supported Russell—the first step that was to transform him into a Palmerstonian by 1857—so both should probably be subtracted from the Peelite total. William Cripps died in 1848, and the election of John Attwood was voided in March, 1848, which reduced the Peelite total by two more votes and brought it to 65. Thus, as their vote on important issues approached the full strength of 120, they were solidifying into a party.

Their most significant show of unity came early in the session when the Commons were debating a motion for a select committee on the commercial distress. On December 6 there was a division which might be interpreted as a test of strength with Bentinck and Disraeli voting in opposition to the Government, which was supported by Peel. The Miscellaneous Conservatives (30) gave Peel's position a stronger support than did the Peelite force (24), and there were only four defectors—Henry J. Baillie and John Masterman from among the Peelites, and James Heald and Sir Henry Willoughby from the Miscellaneous Conservatives. Although the two groups did not muster 50 percent of their total strength for the division, those present acted with praiseworthy unity.

Forming the committee on commercial distress gave rise to four separate divisions, two on December 13 and two on December 15, regarding which members should be included or excluded from it. These might, therefore, be considered political divisions and tests of Peelite political unity. On none of the divisions did they muster so large a force as on the December 6 division, but the number of Peelites and Miscellaneous Conservatives (*) who voted once or more with Peel and never voted against him was 61 and included the following:

Lord Ashley (1)*	H. Fitz-Roy (2)	R. Palmer (3)*
H. B. Baring (1)	W. Gladstone (4)*	J. Peel (3)
William Beckett (2)	R. Godson (2)	W. H. Plowden (1)*
John Benbow (1)	H. Goulburn (2)	G. A. Reid (1)
William Bolling (1)*	T. Greene (4)	Vis. Seaham (1)*
Richard Bourke (1)*	F. Haggitt (2)*	Sir H. Seymour (1)
John Boyd (2)	Sir J. Hanmer (1)	T. Sidney (2)*
Viscount Brackley (1)*	H. Herbert (2)*	Ld. G. Somerset (1)*
Lord E. Bruce (1)	Ld. A Hervey (2)	Ld. Somerton (1)
E. Cardwell (4)	J. Hogg (1)	H. C. Sturt (1)*
Sir G. Clerk (4)	J. Hornby (2)	J. M. Sutton (1)
A. B. Cochrane (1)*	T. Ireland (2)*	Sir F. Thesiger (1)
T. S. Cocks (4)*	Earl Jermyn (2)	F. Tollemache (1)
O. Coope (1)*	W. Keogh (2)*	E. Turner (1)*
H. Corry (3)	Ld. A Lennox (2)*	G. J. Turner (4)*
W. H. Cotton (1)*	Ld. Lincoln (4)*	J. Walter (1)*
W. Cubitt (1)*	J. Lindsay (4)*	F. R. West (4)*
Vis. Drumlanrig (1)*	W. Mackinnon (1)	J. S. Wortley (1)
H. H. Drummond (4)	Vis. Mahon (1)	John Young (4)
John Duncuft (3)*	H. K. Morgan (1)*	
George Dundas (2)*	E. Mostyn (2)	

It will be noted that there is one more Miscellaneous Conservative (31) than Peelites (30) in this list and that some of the former voted as regularly with Peel as did the Peelites.

There were only three defectors from both groups combined—William Mure and David Urquhart, who voted twice and both times opposite from Peel, and John Masterman, who voted against the Government on all occasions, including a motion to exclude Edward Cardwell from the committee on commercial distress. Three other Peelites and seven Miscellaneous Conservatives voted sometimes one way, sometimes the other.[1] Despite these desertions, the voting pattern of the two groups on political issues showed considerable unity, whether or not they voted primarily as followers of Peel, the Government, or their own inclinations. The least impressive aspect of the pattern was the high rate of absenteeism especially among the Peelites.

As Peel's fiscal policies had been the primary bond of unity among the Peelites, one would expect them to have been deeply interested in two divisions which came up during the course of the session—the first on February 17, when the Protectionist financial expert, John Charles Herries, moved to amend Peel's Bank Charter Act of 1844; and the second on June 9, when the same individual moved a resolution which stated that the Navigation Acts were essential to the national interest.

The panic of 1847, which had been brought on by a sudden contraction of credit, raised the question of responsibility: Had this been caused by "improvident" policies of the bank or by faults in the Bank Charter Act, which did not permit the bank sufficient control over the national currency? Herries proposed a modification of the act on the not illogical ground that the recent panic, which forced the government to suspend the restrictive parts of that act, had proved that a modification was sorely needed. Instead of rising to a man in defense of their nominal leader's financial wisdom, the Peelites turned out only fifteen of their number; and one of them, John Masterman, voted with Herries. Sixteen of the Miscellaneous Conservatives were

---

1. These included Robert H. Clive, Allan E. Lockhart, and Alexander Smollett Jr.; and Henry Edwards, James Heald, Sir Edmund Macnaghten, George R. Robinson, Christopher St. George, George Sandars, and Sir. Henry Willoughby.

present and voting, but seven of them agreed with Herries that Peel's act needed amendment.

Although the division on Herries's resolution regarding the Navigation Acts was merely a preliminary to the coming battle on the same issue the following year, the division of June 9, 1848, was important in revealing the shape of things to come. Although the Herries resolution did not force the members to take a stand on the issue (they could miss the division because repeal was not directly involved), it perhaps revealed who were the more ardent Free Traders among the Peelites and Miscellaneous Conservatives. Some 38 Peelites appeared for the division, 32 to vote against Herries, six to support him, while the Miscellaneous Conservatives furnished 20 votes against the resolution and twelve in support of it. A full 21 of both groups who had supported Peel on the political divisions did not appear for either of these.

The members who voted with Peel once or more on both the political and economic divisions were as follows:

H. B. Baring	H. Fitz-Roy	H. K. Morgan*
William Bolling*	W. Gladstone*	E. Mostyn
John Boyd	T. Greene	Sir H. Seymour
Lord E. Bruce	F. Haggitt*	J. M. Sutton
E. Cardwell	Sir J. Hanmer	Sir F. Thesiger
Sir G. Clerk	H. Herbert*	E. Turner*
A. B. Cochrane*	Lord A. Hervey	G. J. Turner*
T. S. Cocks*	J. W. Hogg	J. Walter*
H. T. L. Corry	W. Keogh*	F. R. West*
H. H. Drummond	Lord Lincoln	J. S. Wortley
John Duncuft*	J. Lindsay*	John Young

Of the 61 voters who had supported Peel on the political divisions, these 33 continued steady; 20 others were absent; and eight—including the Peelites John Benbow and George A. Reid, and the Miscellaneous Conservatives Richard S. Bourke, Viscount Brackley, William Cubitt, George Dundas, William H. Plowden, and Viscount Seaham—switched sides.

Four of the divisions might be used to secure information regarding the views of both Peelites and Miscellaneous Conservatives on religious issues, which had always been of the deepest concern to members of the Conservative party. Two of these involved archaic laws against Roman Catholicism; the other two related to the right of Jews to sit in Parliament. If one anticipated that the ex–Conservative party regulars would have been cautious on these issues, he would not be far wrong.

There remained on the statute books a number of anti-Catholic laws that had arisen during earlier periods of religious tensions, such as penalties for conducting worship services in a form other than that prescribed in the Book of Common Prayer and for acknowledging the spiritual or other authority of a foreign prince, certain restrictions on Roman Catholic property, and a prohibition against the publication and execution of bulls and other directives of the Pope—all of which were to be abolished by the Roman Catholic Relief Bill. Proponents argued that the laws were long outdated; Sir Robert Inglis contended that repeal of the laws would facilitate Roman Catholic recruiting in England and diminish the influence of the Established Church.

The Peelites disagreed with Inglis on the two divisions, but by a very narrow margin—17 to 16. The Miscellaneous Conservatives, on the other hand, gave him their support—19 to 16.

The Jewish Relief Bill created considerably more interest than the measure in behalf of British Catholics. The inspiration for this measure was the plight of Lionel Rothschild, elected to Parliament, but unable to take either the parliamentary oaths on the "true faith of a Christian," or his seat. Russell's own followers were divided on the issue;[2] but, according to Lincoln, Rothschild had enough influence in the City to force him to present the relief measure.[3] During the debate that followed, Russell contended that the British Constitution was inclusive, not exclusive, while Sir Robert Inglis insisted that it was designed for a Christian nation and that the forms and prayers of the House would be embarrassing to Rothschild if he were admitted. But, despite the opposition of most Conservatives, their leaders Lord George Bentinck and Benjamin Disraeli both voted to admit Rothschild; and hence the issue was by no means a clear-cut party clash.

2.   "I hear Lord Grey is against the Jew Bill," Lincoln wrote, "and the Duke of Bedford said . . . Ministers would do nothing on the subject *as a Government*" (*PP.* BM 40481. Lincoln to Peel, November 18, 1847).

3.   Lincoln wrote that Rothschild insisted upon no further delay, and "with the City Election hanging around his neck" Russell could not refuse (*NP.* 11943. Lincoln to Herbert, December 19, 1847).

This time Sir Robert Peel was present and voting on both occasions for the reform, but his example did not sway his nominal followers, who voted overwhelmingly—31 to 14—against Rothschild. This time it was the Miscellaneous Conservatives who were slightly more liberal. They voted against the bill by 30 to 14.

The results showed some interesting voting patterns. Henry L. Corry, Henry H. Drummond, Thomas Greene, and Charles W. Martin, among the Peelites, and A. Baillie Cochrane, Viscount Drumlanrig, William Mure, and Frederick R. West, among the Miscellaneous Conservatives, voted for the Catholics but against the Jews; while Henry Fitz-Roy and Frederick J. Tollemache, among the former, and Francis Charteris, William Cubitt, George Sandars, and David Urquhart, among the latter, took just the opposite position.

If we list the names of those who voted with Peel on the political, economic, and religious divisions (though Peel himself missed those involving the Catholics), the roll call is soon over—Edward Cardwell, Edward M. Mostyn, Sir Horace B. Seymour, and John M. Sutton, among the Peelites, and William E. Gladstone, Henry A. Herbert, William Keogh, Lord Lincoln, Edmund Turner, and Thomas Sidney among the Miscellaneous Conservatives.

The one debate that modern observers would probably select as being most involved with humanitarian reform during the session only involved two divisions in a small House. On March 16, 1848, Lord Ashley proposed that women who were entitled to parish assistance during their first pregnancy be permitted such assistance during later pregnancies if a medical man certified its desirability. Opponents stressed that the cost of medical relief had risen from £136,775 in 1838 to £175,190 in 1846 and carried the previous question, 50–37. Ashley withdrew his second motion, which involved medical certifications in cases where the baby might have to be destroyed to save the mother, but persisted in a third motion to appoint inspectors to check on medical facilities in work houses and among the poor of the unions, only to be defeated, 101–19.

The Peelites who voted for one or both of Ashley's propositions were Henry Fitz-Roy, Lord Claud Hamilton, Lord Wellesley, and James S. Wortley; whereas the Miscellaneous Conservatives provided eight votes—Lord Ashley, Viscount Drumlanrig, Francis R. Haggitt, Sir Willoughby Jones, Sir Edmund Macnaghten, William H. Plowden, George J. Turner, and Sir Henry P. Willoughby. Turner and Plowden, however, voted against the second of Ashley's motions. Whatever may be its significance, the fact is that the two men who styled themselves "Tories" supported Ashley.

There were, of course, a number of other divisions during this session of Parliament, but recording the vote on them would simply underline a fact which is made obvious enough by those already studied —that both the Peelites and the Miscellaneous Conservatives lacked ideological unity, and they exercised their independent judgments most of the time on the various issues of the day.

Certain tentative conclusions, however, might be drawn from studying the political, economic, religious, and humanitarian divisions recorded above. One certainly would be that both the Peelites and Miscellaneous Conservatives furnished fairly strong support for the Government on political issues, which suggests that they were anxious to maintain a political status separate from the Bentinck-Disraeli Conservatives; a second, that they would generally support issues involving the extension of free trade. On the other hand, they could not be rallied in support of the religious liberalism or the Ashley-type humanitarianism of the day. Under these circumstances, it seemed unlikely that they could become a "movement party" in serious competition with the Whig-Liberals.

Despite the rather narrow bases upon which they might found a new party, they might have carried considerable weight in the Commons if their votes were a decisive factor in a balance-of-power situation. This does not seem to have been the case. On all of the political issues, the Government could have won easily without the aid of the Peelites and Miscellaneous Conservatives; the same was true on the Bank Charter and Navigation Act divisions. The divisions on the religious issues were closer; and, if the Peelites and Miscellaneous Conservatives had voted as a unit against the Roman Catholic Relief Bill, it would have been defeated on the second reading. Their aid on the Jewish Relief measure was important, but not decisive.

There remains the problem of defining the Peelite section in the Commons during the session of 1848. Perhaps the best estimate of their numbers should be based on the list of those who voted together on both the political and economic divisions—33 voters, plus Sir Robert Peel; Sir James Graham, who missed the political divisions; and Sidney Herbert, who was out of the country, for a total of 36. This exclusive list included not only 21 original Peelites and nine Free Trade Conservatives, but two Liberal Conservatives, one Uncommitted Conservative, one Moderate Conservative, and one Tory. This seems to have been the nucleus of the Peelite section; the other original Peelites and Miscellaneous Conservatives might vote with them on certain issues, be absent (which was characteristic of the original Peelites), or vote with Bentinck-Disraeli. There is little to distinguish between the voting records of these "uncommitted" original Peelites and Miscellaneous Conservatives, save that the latter might have been even less liberal on religious issues.

The historian at the present time might make these identifications on the basis of the division analyses, but what guarantee is there that these "Peelites" were regarded as members of the Peelite section in their own day? A letter by Lord Lincoln following the division on the Jewish Relief Bill on December 17, 1847, stated: "The Majority was not so large as many expected, and in it were only 18 Peelites and 6 Protectionists."[4] A check of the division list shows that the original Peelites, Edward Cardwell, Sir George Clerk, Henry Fitz-Roy, James W. Hogg, Richard M. Milnes, Sir Robert Peel, George P. Smythe, Frederick J. Tollemache, Charles B. Wall, and James S. Wortley, and the Miscellaneous Conservatives, William Cubitt, William E. Gladstone, William Keogh, Lord Lincoln, Roundell Palmer, George R. Robinson, George Sandars, Thomas Sidney, and Edmund Turner, voted together on this division—19 in all; and, if we subtract Milnes (who was admittedly a regular supporter of the Government), the check is perfect, and these individuals must go down in history as bona fide Peelites, whatever may be the final decision regarding some of the others.

4. *NP*. 11943. Lincoln to Herbert, December 19, 1847.

CHAPTER 14

THE PEELITES IN THE 1849 SESSION

Both the political and economic backgrounds for the parliamentary session of 1849 were somber, even grim. The revolutionary wave had not yet receded in Europe; and although Chartism had achieved its last peak in 1848 and was on the wane, the conditions that had produced it were still present. Although the recession of 1846 had reached a turning point in the closing months of 1848,[1] the distress in the cities was mitigated by a decrease in food prices, which, in turn, brought depression in agricultural areas. The most tragic portion of the whole picture was the condition of Ireland, whose starvation and want proved the inadequacy of the relief program of the Russell Government.

Under these circumstances, and weakened by the deaths of two of his stronger supporters, Charles Buller and Lord Auckland, Lord John Russell went on another of his recruiting expeditions among the Peelites. There was a thought of securing St. Germans, who had refused a previous offer;[2] but Russell's primary interest was in the Commons and, specifically, in Graham, Herbert, and perhaps Lord Lincoln.[3] An offer was made to Graham in January, but he turned it down because he distrusted Palmerston's foreign policy and believed Russell's Irish and retrenchment policies were inadequate.[4] Graham had quit the Whigs once before and wished to avoid having to do so a second time.[5] The only recruit Russell had been able to win over was Henry Barkly, who accepted the post of governor of British Guiana in 1848, and hence was missing from the Peelite section in 1849.

Had Russell made an offer to Lincoln in January, 1849, we know

1. See A. D. Gayer et al., *The Growth and Fluctuation of the British Economy*, 1790-1850, 1:304-41.
2. *PP*. BM 40480. St. Germans to Peel, October 2, 1847; Peel to St. Germans, October 3, 1847.
3. *RP*. PRO 30/22–7E. Russell to Wood, January 6, 1849; Palmerston to Russell, January 9, 1849.
4. *PP*. BM 40452. Graham to Peel, January 12, 1849.
5. *GMEM*, 2:385.

that it would have been firmly declined.[6] Joining the Whigs in part-
nership was not distasteful to Lincoln; but at this time he believed
that the Peelites had only to wait and eventually they would play
the leading role in the coalition, an anticipation which proved quite
accurate. Palmerston sensed the danger, and later in 1849 warned
Russell that under certain circumstances many of their followers
might desert to Peel.[7] But the prime minister did not believe that
their friends would leave "our large party" to join Peel, whose "small
party" had refused to unite with the Whigs.[8]

Nebulous and ill organized as their "party" might be, the Peelites
were sought after by the Protectionists also. An obstacle to reunion
had been removed with the death of Lord George Bentinck in September, 1848, and Stanley probably kept open the Conservative leadership in the Commons as an invitation to the Peelites.[9] An informal
offer of the leadership, indeed, had been made to Goulburn in January, 1848, but his reaction had been much like Lincoln's was to be;
the Protectionists should join the Peelites, not vice versa. A year later,
when Disraeli learned that Graham had refused Russell's offer, he
seems to have encouraged a long-time Peelite proponent of reunion,
Lord Londonderry, to attempt to secure his services. Graham replied
that he could not join the party when its quasi leader, Lord Granby,
was attempting to revive Protection;[10] but his reaction was even more
negative than that. By this time Graham was convinced that the Whig-
sponsored Reform Act of 1832 had prevented the spread of revolutionary fever in Britain[11] and that a Protectionist government would
bring on class warfare,[12] so, after a short sojourn with the Conservatives, Graham was back in the "movement," and there he was to remain for the rest of his career.

Meanwhile, the "party" which was the object of both Whig and

6. *PP*. BM 40481. Lincoln to Peel, January 27, 1849.
7. *RP*. PRO 30/22–8F. Palmerston to Russell, April 14, 1849.
8. Ibid. Russell to Palmerston, April 16, 1849.
9. *PGRA*, 2:63. Peel to Graham, January 12, 1848. See also Jones, *Lord
Derby*, pp. 130–35. Bentinck had lost his leadership by voting in favor of Jewish
Relief in December, 1847, but he remained as a political factor until his death
less than a year later.
10. *PGRA*, 2:81–82. Graham to Londonderry, January 20, 1849.
11. *BP*. Graham to Brougham, October 20, 1848.
12. *GMEM*, 6:172.

Conservative concern had experienced some changes in its membership during 1848 and early 1849. Among the traditional Peelites, Henry Barkly had departed to Guiana, and William Bingham Baring had gone to the Upper House as the Second Lord Ashburton in August, 1848. However, as George C. Legh had reentered Parliament through a by-election of May, 1848, the estimated Peelite vote—65 in 1848—was only reduced to 64 in 1849.

There were many more changes among the Miscellaneous Conservatives. William Bolling and Edmund Turner, who had been fairly steady Peelites, both died in 1848; so did Lord Granville Somerset, who was too inactive to permit classification. William Y. Peel resigned his seat;[13] Octavius E. Coope, Thomas J. Ireland, Sir Willoughby Jones, and Lord Arthur Lennox were all unseated. On the basis of their voting records, none were true Peelites. Certain other Miscellaneous Conservatives of 1848,[14] and others in that classification in 1849,[15] voted with the Conservatives so consistently there is no need to continue to follow the records of the former or to add the latter to the list. All told, seventeen of the previous Miscellaneous Conservatives are dropped in 1849.

But the list must be supplemented by the addition of certain other members. The Free Trade Conservatives—Francis Baring, who replaced his brother William at Thetford; Lord John J. L. Chichester (Belfast), who poses a difficult problem for the historian;[16] Frederick Peel, the former prime minister's son and replacement of Henry Barkly at Leominister; and Joseph Sandars, who won a by-election at Yarmouth—and the Uncommitted Conservatives—Stephen Blair, who replaced William Bolling at Bolton-le-Moors, Edmund B. Deni-

13. As Peel did not resign his seat until after the beginning of the 1847–48 session, his name was retained on the list until 1849.

14. These include Viscount Bernard, the Marquess of Blandford, Richard S. Bourke, Wellington H. Cotton, Henry Edwards, William B. M'Clintock (Bunbury added in 1849), Christopher St. George, Henry C. Sturt, and Sir William Verner. The voting patterns of these members were studied in the 1849–50 sessions before dropping them.

15. These include Edward A. J. Harris, Joseph R. Mullings, and Joseph Napier.

16. Lord Chichester appears in *Dod* for 1849 as a Conservative who voted for repeal in 1846, and he might conceivably be numbered among the original Peelites save that his political position in 1846–47 appears to have been ambiguous.

son (West Riding, Yorkshire), James B. B. Estcourt (Devizes), and
Frederick W. C. Villiers (Weymouth)—are all added. Thus, the Miscellaneous Conservative list for 1849 is reduced by only nine votes
(55 to 46). Added to the 64 traditional Peelites, their total combined
strength for 1849 was 110.

The divisions which might be classified as political issues in 1849
were somewhat more interesting than those in 1848. There were
three, on February 2, on April 18, and on July 6; and what makes them
interesting is not only that they span the whole session, but that Peel
appeared in a somewhat different role on each occasion.

The division of February 2 resulted from Lord Granby's motion
to prolong the debate on the address. Peel was an absentee, and thus
could not influence the outcome one way or another. The Peelite turnout was very light—23 voted against Granby, and only three (Henry
J. Baillie, Richard Godson, and John Hornby) for him; and the Miscellaneous Conservatives practically ignored the division, splitting
8–2 against Granby.

The division of April 18 was one of those rare occasions when an
undoubted Peelite, who had the support of Peel, moved an amendment against the Government. Henry Goulburn moved the rejection
of the Government's Affirmation Bill on the third reading on the
ground that it extended the privilege of affirming, as opposed to oath-
taking, to people other than those Dissenters who had traditionally
refused to take oaths, and did not make sufficient provision for per-
jury in such cases. Four traditional Peelites (William Beckett, William T. Egerton, Henry Fitz-Roy, and John W. Patten) and six Miscellaneous Conservatives (Stephen Blair, Henry Edwards, James
Lindsay, Thomas Sidney, George J. Turner, and Sir Henry Willoughby) voted with Peel and Goulburn; none in either category opposed
them. This division found Peel voting with the more conservative portion of the combined section.

The division of July 6, 1849, came on Disraeli's motion that the
House go into committee on the state of the nation. For once Peel
rose and clarified his position. Since 1846 he had felt it his duty to give
a general support to the Government, he explained, because it faced
so many grave issues, and he wanted it understood that his vote
against Disraeli's motion did not constitute a blanket endorsement
of the Government's policies. The motion, he felt, involved free trade,

and he would not censure the Government for having followed that policy.[17] Was the vote a call to his followers? Was Peel once again assuming leadership?

If Peel desired to show his strength, the call was not wholly in vain. Forty of the traditional Peelites rallied to his support, and so did seventeen of the Miscellaneous Conservatives—a vast improvement over the showing they had made on February 2 when Peel was absent. Only four traditional Peelites (Henry J. Baillie, Richard Godson, John Hornby, and Lord Somerton) and three Miscellaneous Conservatives (Henry A. Herbert, Viscount Seaham, and Sir Henry P. Willoughby) did not heed the call. The showing of the Miscellaneous Conservatives seems especially significant, suggesting, as it does, an unwillingness to vote against Peel once he made a definite appeal.

In a strictly political sense, the Peelite section in 1849 might be said to contain the following members who voted with Peel on one or more occasions and did not oppose him on any:

Francis Baring*	Ld. Claud Hamilton	Sir Robert Peel
William Beckett	James Heald*	Edward D. Pennant
Stephen Blair*	Sidney Herbert	William H. Plowden*
William Bowles	Lord Alfred Hervey	Ld. William Powlett*
Ld. Ernest Bruce	James W. Hogg	David Pugh*
Edward Cardwell	William B. Hughes	George A. Reid
Francis Charteris*	Earl Jermyn	George Sandars*
Sir George Clerk	Sir John Johnstone	Joseph Sandars*
William T. Copeland	George C. Legh	Sir Horace Seymour
Henry L. Corry	Lord Lincoln*	Thomas Sidney*
Henry Currie*	James Lindsay*	George P. Smythe
Edmund B. Denison*	Viscount Mahon	Henry Stuart
Sir Charles Douglas	Charles W. Martin	John M. Sutton
Marquess of Douro	John Masterman	Sir Frederic Thesiger
John Duncuft*	Edward L. Mostyn	Frederick Tollemache
Henry Edwards*	Hamilton K. Morgan*	George J. Turner*
William T. Egerton	Viscount Newry*	Viscount Villiers
James B. Estcourt*	Alexander H. Oswald	Charles B. Wall
Henry Fitz-Roy	Sir John Owen	Lord Charles Wellesley
William E. Gladstone*	Roundell Palmer	James S. Wortley
Henry Goulburn	John W. Patten	John Young
Sir James Graham	Frederick Peel*	
Thomas Greene	Jonathan Peel	

17. *Hansard*, 3d. ser., 106:1429–30.

This combined group of 45 original Peelites and 22 Miscellaneous Conservatives(*) is fairly impressive in numbers, but even more so is the fact that only four of the former and five of the latter broke with the others on these divisions. Although they might not be consistent Peelites in a larger sense, both groups showed a definite dislike of dividing with Lord Granby or Benjamin Disraeli.

Before the session began, Sir James Graham wrote Lord Londonderry that he hoped the division on the Navigation Acts would help clarify the state of the parties in the Commons.[18] While there were other divisions involving economic or fiscal policy, the two divisions on this subject may be taken to determine the economic views of the Peelites who voted with their nebulous section on political divisions. The two divisions, on March 12 and April 23 were both brought on by motions of John C. Herries, the Protectionist financial expert. When the final results are studied, the Peelites who voted against the Navigation Acts, as well as with Peel on political divisions, were as follows:

Francis Baring*	Henry Goulburn	Hamilton K. Morgan*
Ld. Ernest Bruce	Sir James Graham	Frederick Peel
Edward Cardwell	Thomas Greene	Jonathan Peel
Francis Charteris*	James Heald*	Sir Robert Peel
Sir George Clerk	Sidney Herbert	George Sandars*
Henry L. Corry	Lord Alfred Hervey	John M. Sutton
Henry Currie*	James W. Hogg	Frederick Tollemache
Sir Charles Douglas	William B. Hughes	George J. Turner
John Duncuft*	Earl Jermyn	Viscount Villiers
James B. Estcourt*	Lord Lincoln*	Charles B. Wall
Henry Fitz-Roy	Charles W. Martin	John Young
William E. Gladstone*	Edward L. Mostyn	

This list probably does not reflect quite accurately the relative state of opinion on free trade between the original Peelite section as a whole and the Miscellaneous Conservatives. The former split 27-16 to repeal the Navigation Acts; the latter, 15-17. It would appear, then, that the fifteen Miscellaneous Conservatives who voted for repeal[19] were better "Peelites" than the sixteen original Peelites who voted to retain the Navigation Acts.[20]

18. *PGRA.* 2:81–82. Graham to Londonderry, January 20, 1849.

19. These included, in addition to those in the above list, Viscount Drumlanrig, Francis R. Haggitt, Henry T. Hope, John Walter, and Frederick R. West.

20. These included William Beckett, William Bowles, Robert H. Clive, Wil-

On many occasions the Peelites and the Miscellaneous Conservatives had remarkably similar voting habits, but on another issue in 1849 a notable difference appeared. Disraeli, on March 15, moved that there be a "more equitable apportionment of public burdens," which would give financial relief to the landowners. As the land was subject to the Poor Rate, the County Rate, the Highway Rate, the Church Rate, a land tax, and bore a third of the excise revenue from such items as malt and hops, while receiving only £62,206,319 out of a national income of £249,185,277, the case made by Disraeli seemed strong, and one might have expected the Original Peelites and Miscellaneous Conservatives to show some sympathy for the plight of the landowners. The latter did so, voting 17-10 in favor of the motion; the former did not, turning it down 23-0. Sympathy for the landowning class, then, seems to have been much more characteristic of the Miscellaneous Conservatives than of the Original Peelites.

There were no divisions involving Catholic relief during this session, so the two divisions on the Jewish Relief Bill, on May 7 and June 11, must serve as the 1849 test of the religious liberalism, or lack of it, existing among both parts of the section. A somewhat larger group, who voted also on the political and economic divisions, pledged themselves to Jewish relief. These included:

Francis Baring*	Lord Lincoln*
Edward Cardwell	Charles W. Martin
Francis Charteris*	Edward L. Mostyn
Sir George Clerk	Frederick Peel
Henry Fitz-Roy	Sir Robert Peel
William E. Gladstone*	George Sandars*
Sir James Graham	John M. Sutton
James W. Hogg	Frederick J. Tollemache
Earl Jermyn	Charles B. Wall

This list, however, would leave the erroneous impression that the Original Peelites were more liberal in their religious attitudes than were the Miscellaneous Conservatives. Actually, 30 percent of the total Original Peelite strength voted for Jewish Relief, as compared

---

liam T. Egerton, Richard Godson, Lord Claud Hamilton, John Hornby, George C. Legh, Viscount Jocelyn, Sir John Johnstone, John Masterman, Edward D. Pennant, George A. Reid, Alexander Smollett Jr., Henry Stuart, and Lord Charles Wellesley.

with 28 percent for the Miscellaneous Conservatives; and such Peelite names as Henry Goulburn and Jonathan Peel could be found among those opposing Jewish Relief. Although the percentage strength of the Original Peelites voting against relief was slightly smaller than that of the Miscellaneous Peelites (35% to 41%), the former actually cast more votes in opposition than did the latter (23–19). Religious liberalism was not characteristic of the majority of either part of the Peelite section; in fact, it was probably limited to about one-third, or even less, of the membership.

Electoral reform was another important area in which the two parts of the section displayed a unity of outlook. Joseph Hume, on June 5, brought in a Reform Bill to extend the franchise to all householders, reapportion the seats in Parliament, provide for the use of the ballot at elections, and limit the life of a parliament to three years. Only William Keogh, a Free Trade Conservative from Athlone, stretched his definition of true conservatism far enough to include such a measure; both the Original Peelites and the Miscellaneous Conservatives turned out in force to record their disapproval of it.

The Navigation Acts, for whose preservation Ellenborough hoped the two sections of the Conservative party in the Lords might act together, became an object of deep concern to Russell and Palmerston in April. The latter feared that a defeat on this issue in the Lords might cause the queen to send for Peel—with disastrous consequences. He continued:[21]

> But Peel can command a majority in the commons only with the support of the Whig party—and you might under the circumstances have to offer him support. Join him yourself as a Minister of his Govt. of course you could not; many of us your Colleagues would not do so either. There may be some who would; but you would be bound almost to hand your Party over to Peel, and to abdicate your own Position as Leader in his Favour—our Radicals would go to him whether you choose or not and a great many of our independent supporters might do the same.

Russell replied that the Radicals would "eagerly support" Peel, but he did not believe that any of their colleagues would do so.[22]

21. *RP.* PRO 30/22–6F. Palmerston to Russell, April 14, 1849.
22. *RP.* PRO 30/22–8F. Russell to Palmerston, April 16, 1849.

These letters are of importance in Peelite history because they reveal the great uncertainties regarding both Peel's position and the nature of his section. Palmerston in 1849 evidently believed that Peel under certain circumstances would accept the headship of a Government and that the Peelites would practically swallow the Whigs; Russell was not so sure Peel would accept the Government, even if it were offered to him, and evidently did not believe his acceptance would be followed by such widespread defections among his own followers as did Palmerston.

Far from attempting to use this delicate situation to return to power, Sir Robert Peel completely forsook his policy of aloofness and actively aided the Russell Government in its defense plans. He seems to have depended on Aberdeen, Lord Ashburton, Buccleuch, Hardinge, Ripon, St. Germans, and Wellington to uphold the Peelite free trade philosophy in the Lords.[23] But they must have known that Ellenborough, Brougham,[24] and an undetermined number of Peelite lords were acting with Lord Stanley.

Stanley made a major effort to bring in all Conservatives and Peelites for the battle, and, though some Protectionist lords were still resentful toward the shipping interest for having deserted them in 1846, he secured a large following, and the outcome of the contest seemed to be in doubt. Brougham launched the Protectionist debate on May 7, followed by Lord Stanley, who, according to Hobhouse, appealed "first to the Duke of Wellington, and then to God Almighty, asking the first to vote with him, and the latter to enlighten their Lordships' minds."[25] There was, so Greville observed, the greatest "whip-up" that "ever was known" for the division on May 8,[26] and for the Conservatives it proved to be a waste of time. Peelite votes gave victory to the Government, and the crisis that Palmerston had feared a month before never materialized.

The Peelite lords for and against the repeal of the Navigation Acts (with titles abbreviated) were as follows:

23. *PP*. BM 40601. Wood to Peel, Sunday, and May 18, 1849.

24. *BP*. Stanley to Brougham, Friday night, 1849.

25. Lord Broughton, *Lord Broughton, Recollections of a Long Life*, 4:237–38.

26. *GMEM*. 6:176.

For Repeal	Against Repeal
(D) Argyll	(D) Northumberland
(D) Wellington	(M) Ailsa
(M) Abercorn	(M) Hertford
(M) Bristol	(M) Huntly
(M) Ormonde	(M) Londonderry
(E) Aberdeen	(E) Bandon
(E) Chichester	(E) Bathurst
(E) Cornwallis	(E) Caledon
(E) DeGrey	(E) Ellenborough
(E) Denbigh	(E) Jersey
(E) Essex	(E) Romney
(E) Glasgow	(E) Rosslyn
(E) Howe	(E) Talbot
(E) Home	(E) Verulam
(E) Kingston	(B) Blayney
(E) Liverpool	(B) Castlemaine
(E) Pembroke	(B) Downes
(E) Ripon	(B) Forester
(E) St. Germans	(B) Lyndhurst
(V) Canning	(B) Rollo
(V) Hawarden	(B) Sandys
(B) Churchill	
(B) Rivers	
(B) Ward	
(B) Wharncliffe	
(B) Wodehouse	

Lord Brougham also voted with Stanley on this division, but he remains beyond classification.

In some respects the defeat on the Navigation Acts actually cleared the way for a reconciliation between the Protectionists and Peelites in the Lords because it was the last really important free trade issue of the period and was then decided once and for all in favor of the Peelites. It now became of the greatest importance to the reconciliators to find an issue which would bring the two wings of the party together. Religious questions found them in general agreement,[27] but

27.   The division on the second reading of the Jewish Relief Bill on May 25, 1848 may be taken as a fair sample of the thinking of the Lords in this area. Lord Stanley, of course, took a strong position in opposition to it, but it was Lord Ellenborough, a Peelite, who moved the rejection. Voting against Jewish Relief were the dukes of Buccleuch and Wellington, the marquess of Camden, the earls of Aberdeen, Bandon, Bathurst, Clanwilliam, Clare, Devon, Ellenborough, Galloway, Howe, Jersey, Romney, and Verulam, and Barons Blayney, Castlemaine, Churchill, Delamere, de Tabley, Forester, Rollo, and Sandys. On the other hand, 13 Peelites Lords voted for Jewish Relief, including such important members as the duke of Argyll, the marquess of Londonderry, the earl of St. Germans, and Baron Wharncliffe, and the attitude of the Peelite Lords

no religious issue on the horizon provided a vehicle for a major attack on the Government. What else might be used? Foreign affairs?

The latter seemed to offer interesting possibilities for party warfare and consolidation. Not only had Lord Palmerston undermined Lord Aberdeen's prized entente cordiale with France by blowing up the Spanish marriages issue, but he showed a strong inclination to meddle in the domestic affairs of the continental states and to lend some aid and comfort to revolutionaries. Lord Aberdeen had watched these developments with profound distaste. "Altogether," he wrote Brougham in 1849, "Europe is recovering from the Revolutionary mania in spite of us."[28] Although Aberdeen became increasingly "liberal" on domestic issues as the years went by, in foreign policy he remained conservative and monarchical.

Aberdeen was not the only Peelite to disapprove of Palmerston's vigorous conduct of foreign affairs. Sir Robert Peel, who had helped the Government to repeal the Navigation Acts and rose to its defense when Disraeli made a major attack on it in July, was careful to explain to the House that he did not approve all Government policies. Sir James Graham strongly distrusted Palmerston in 1849,[29] as did Henry Goulburn;[30] but Peel was opposed to bringing on a serious crisis which might be used by the Protectionists for their own political objects.

The situation, however, was quite different in the Lords. Aberdeen, even as a member of Peel's government, had insisted on formulating his own foreign policies, and in this area he was quite close to Lord Stanley, who was more interested in the price of corn and the Established Church than in international wrangles. For Aberdeen, voting to sustain the Navigation Acts would have violated Peelite policy; attacking Palmerston's intervention in the domestic affairs of other states would be sustaining it. Thus, after the division on the Navigation Acts, Stanley and Aberdeen opened a correspondence[31] and a tenuous connection which was to last into 1852.

---

was therefore quite similar to that of the Original Peelites and Miscellaneous Conservatives in the Commons.

28. *BP.* Aberdeen to Brougham, August 30, 1849.
29. *PP.* BM 40452. Graham to Peel, November 13, 1849.
30. *RIPP.* BM 40877. Goulburn to Ripon, September 12, 1849.
31. *AP.* BM 43072. Stanley to Aberdeen, June 18, 1849.

The first fruits of the Stanley-Aberdeen cooperation was an attack on the Government on July 20. They agreed that Lord Brougham should offer resolutions in the Lords to the effect that Palmerston's Italian policy constituted interference in the internal affairs of a sovereign state and displayed a want of "friendly feeling" toward an old ally. Aberdeen believed that Stanley had postponed the attack too long and had therefore made it ineffective. The resolutions were defeated, but on the division such Peelite regulars as Aberdeen, Buccleuch, Canning, Haddington, Heytesbury, and Lyndhurst voted with Brougham and Stanley.

In April, Palmerston had warned Russell that he was strong in the Commons but weak in the Lords; and the appearance of this Peelite-Protectionist coalition in July was a warning of the shape of things to come.

CHAPTER 15

1850: PEEL'S LAST SESSION

A mood of lassitude and dissatisfaction settled over the Peelite section as passing events made it clear that Peel would never again accept office.[1] Lord Lincoln, both for reasons of health and lack of interest, went abroad after the 1849 session and missed the important divisions of 1850; Graham was living a detached existence and—according to Young—"might be dead for all I have heard of him."[2] Aberdeen deplored Peel's lack of interest in foreign affairs;[3] Herbert was dissatisfied because Peel discouraged one of his immigration projects,[4] and Gladstone was so alienated that he contemplated the elevation of Lincoln or Herbert to the leadership of the Peelite section.[5]

One can understand the impatience of the younger set of Peelites. For them the past was merely prologue; for Peel the events of 1846 were the climax of his career, and he was observing the denouement, living an introspective life, and being wholly absorbed by the question, Had he or had he not been right? He so often defended his course in Parliament that Disraeli told Greville that Peel would do well to follow Cosimo Medici's example and "leave his character to posterity."[6] Free trade had become so much of an obsession with him that he did not even trust the Whigs to uphold it properly;[7] and when he went on trips, he studied the countryside for evidences of the truth or falsity of his free trade position.[8]

---

1. Jocelyn and Goulburn still cherished hopes in 1848 (and perhaps even later) that Peel would return to power. See *GMEM*, 6:83–84, and *CP*. PRO 30/48/8–50. Goulburn to Cardwell, October 1, 1848.

2. *NP*. 12230. Young to Lincoln, November 6, 1849.

3. *GMEM*. 45:187.

4. *SHER*. 1:116–18.

5. *MGLD*. 1:355. Gladstone to his wife, February 22, 1850.

6. *GMEM*. 6:207.

7. *PGRA*. 2:90. Peel to Graham, December 19, 1849.

8. An undated letter from Peel to Brougham probably dates from 1850. Peel had been visiting an estate in Lancashire and had observed the condition of British agriculture through a train window. "I wish Protectionists would take

As of the last year of his life that burning question was not completely answered. By 1850 the economic climate of Britain had changed markedly from that of the 1840s. Shipbuilding and other industries were busy again, exports to the United States and to the Asian nations were booming, and the national economy had a busy, even cheerful, appearance—the economy, that is, except agriculture. Agricultural income was depressed and had been for so long that its plight became the major issue of the early part of the 1850 session.

Before proceeding to analyze the important divisions of 1850, some note must be made of the minor changes in the two divisions of the Peelite section. Three of the Original Peelites, including Richard Godson, Charles W. W. Wynn, and Sir Robert Peel himself, died during 1850, reducing their number to 61 members. Among the Miscellaneous Conservatives, George R. Robinson, who had voted with the Conservatives most of the time, passed away, reducing their numbers to 45; and there seems to be no good reason to add any of the newer Uncommitted Conservatives to the list.[9] By the end of the session, then, the strength of the combined section was 106 members.

There were two very important economic-political divisions during this session which caused some of those in the Peelite section who were becoming dubious about the free trade dogma to commit themselves one way or the other. An amendment to the address on February 1 traced the agricultural depression in part to "recent legislation"—clearly an attack on free trade, while on May 14 a Whig named Grantley Berkeley actually proposed that the laws regarding grain importations be reconsidered. Those who voted for these propositions could hardly continue to be associated with the Peelites.

---

a special Train and see what *Protection* has done for agriculture through the whole of the district," he wrote. "I will consent to be hanged on the highest Ladder which the Protectionists subscribe to raise for the Ceremony—if in five years competition will not have done more for agriculture—and for *agricultural Labourers*—than Protection has done during the last two hundred" (*BP*. Peel to Brougham, Wednesday night).

9. A check of the voting patterns of Thomas Conolly (Donegal), a "Conservative," William J. Evelyn (Surrey West), a "Fair Play Conservative," Edward A. J. Harris (Christchurch, an "unpledged Conservative," and Edward H. Stanley (Lyme Regis), a "Conservative," showed them voting so consistently with the Protectionists that there is little purpose in including them as Miscellaneous Conservatives. It should be noted that Francis R. Haggitt, the "Tory" from Herefordshire, adopted the name "Wegg-Prosser" in 1850, and thereafter appears as "Francis H. Wegg-Prosser."

The following is a list of the Original Peelites and Miscellaneous Conservatives who once again confessed their faith in free trade:

William Beckett
Edward Cardwell
Francis Charteris*
Sir George Clerk
Thomas S. Cocks*
Henry L. Corry
William Cubitt*
Henry Currie*
George L. Damer
Edmund B. Denison*
Sir Charles Douglas
Marquess of Douro
Viscount Drumlanrig*
Henry H. Drummond
John Duncuft*
James B. Estcourt*
Henry Fitz-Roy
William E. Gladstone*
Henry Goulburn
Sir James Graham
Thomas Greene
Sir John Hanmer

James Heald*
Sidney Herbert
Ld. Alfred Hervey
James W. Hogg
William B. Hughes
Earl Jermyn
Viscount Jocelyn
Sir John Johnstone
William Keogh*
Richard Kerr*
George C. Legh
James Lindsay*
William A. Mackinnon
Viscount Mahon
Charles W. Martin
John Masterman
Hamilton K. Morgan*
Edward L. Mostyn
William Mure*
Alexander Oswald
Sir John Owen
Roundell Palmer*

John W. Patten
Frederick Peel
Jonathan Peel
Sir Robert Peel
William H. Plowden*
George A. Reid
George Sandars*
Joseph Sandars*
Alexander Smollett
George P. Smythe
Henry Stuart
John M. Sutton
Sir Frederic Thesiger
Frederick Tollemache
George J. Turner*
Viscount Villiers
Charles B. Wall
John Walter*
Ld. Charles Wellesley
James S. Wortley
John Young

Thus, in 1850 there were 44 Original Peelites voting for free trade, supported by eleven Free Trade Conservatives, five Uncommitted Conservatives, three Liberal Conservatives, one Moderate Conservative, and one Liberal Tory, for a total of 65 votes.

It would appear on the surface—from the results of these divisions —that the Peelite section was still as united on a vital political-economic issue as it had ever been in the past, but the results noted above are very deceptive. John Young in January, 1850, had written that the old Conservative party now existed in four fragments, the die-hard Protectionists who hated the Peelites, the conciliatory Stanleyites, the conciliatory Peelites, and the Peel-Graham group which would not think of reconstruction.[10] An examination of some other divisions will point up the growing disunity within a section which had never been characterized by solidarity.

10. *GP.* BM 44237. Young to Gladstone, January 15, 1850.

As might have been expected, the section split on the Factories Bill on June 14,[11] but what was not to be anticipated was their reaction to Disraeli's motion for a committee on agricultural distress on February 21. The division in 1849 on the special burdens on the land had not attracted a single Original Peelite vote; this one found them split 26-18 against the motion, and the Miscellaneous Conservatives voting 20–5 in favor of it. Even more important were some of the names found supporting Disraeli's motion—Henry L. Corry, William E. Gladstone, Viscount Jocelyn, John W. Patten, Sir Frederic Thesiger, and even the Peelite "Whip," John Young.[12]

Even this split, serious though it was, was mild in comparison to the full-scale rebellion that took place on May 31 when a motion was made that it was "unjust and impolitic" to expose the free-grown sugar of the British West Indies to the competition of slave-grown sugar by removing the last of the preferential tariffs. Sir John Pakington, a Protectionist member, showed that British West Indian sugar production had declined from 205,000 tons in 1831 to 142,000 tons in 1849 and predicted that the removal of the last preference would ruin the sugar growers and reduce the Negroes to destitution. Dogmatic Free Traders insisted that the West Indies needed more African labor and improved methods of cultivation, not a preferential tariff, and their views prevailed; but not before the Original Peelites and Miscellaneous Conservatives had reversed the stand taken by the Peelite section in 1846. The Original Peelites split 28-13

---

11. *Hansard* records the ayes and noes on only one major division on this well-known Ten Hours Bill on a motion made by Lord Ashley to spell out even more clearly the hours of the day during which children could be employed in the factories. Ashley's motion was opposed both by Lord John Russell and Sir Robert Peel, and lost by a single vote. On the division 19 Original Peelites, including Sir Robert Peel and Sir James Graham, and 4 Miscellaneous Conservatives, including William E. Gladstone, voted against Ashley; and 7 Original Peelites and 16 Miscellaneous Conservatives voted with him. The names of the latter deserve to be recorded: Lord Ashley, Henry J. Baillie, William Beckett, Stephen Blair, A. Baillie Cochrane, Thomas S. Cocks, William Cubitt, Edmund B. Denison, John Duncuft, James Heald, Henry A. Herbert, John Hornby, Sir John Johnstone, Richard Kerr, James Lindsay, John Masterman, Roundell Palmer, George Sandars, Alexander Smollett Jr., Frederick C. Villiers, Sir Henry P. Willoughby, and James S. Wortley.

12. Herbert believed that if an election were held at this time it would give the English counties back to the Protectionists (*NP.* 11940. Herbert to his wife, January 17, 1850). This popular feeling probably made itself felt in Parliament.

in favor of the motion; and the Miscellaneous Conservatives, 23-7.
Peel and Graham again upheld this aspect of the free trade doc-
trine; but Edward Cardwell, William E. Gladstone, Henry Goulburn, Sidney Herbert, and Jonathan Peel divided against their leaders, whose example was overwhelmingly ignored.

The measure which caused the most concern to Lord Stanley, as
leader of the Conservative party, was the Parliamentary Voters (Ireland) Bill—a measure to lower the qualification for the franchise,
and one which he believed could ruin the political position of the
Conservative party there.[13] Thus the issue, as Stanley saw it, was the
future of the Conservative party. Were the Peelites interested in its
future? As it turned out, they were—up to a point.

The two divisions in the Commons found nineteen Original Peelites and seventeen Miscellaneous Conservatives voting against the
measure, and only seventeen of the former and seven of the latter
supporting it. Among those who aided the Conservatives were Sir
George Clerk, William E. Gladstone, Henry Goulburn, Lord Jocelyn,
James S. Wortley, and many others generally identified as Peelite
stalwarts. Gladstone actually gave advice to Stanley before the division on the Third Reading on May 10,[14] and began to warm up toward Disraeli.[15] Graham considered that Gladstone was practically
lost to the Peelite section.[16] While such a judgment was obviously
premature, it is clear that Gladstone and Young were actually recruiting support for the Conservatives and entering vaguely at least
into their plans.[17]

Lord Stanley was obviously the center around whom the movement for reconciliation revolved. Gladstone had always maintained a
warmer attitude toward him than many of the other Peelites and
readily accepted the role of his liaison with the Peelite section in the

13.   *AP.* BM 43072. Stanley to Aberdeen, May 13 and 21, 1850.
14.   *DP.* Derby XII. Stanley to Disraeli, May 7, 1850.
15.   *MGLD.* 1:356. Gladstone to his wife, February 22, 1850.
16.   *GMEM.* 6:208.
17.   *GP.* BM 44237. Young to Gladstone, May 11, 1850. This is another
identification letter. Young believed that the Peelites who aided the Conservatives on the Parliamentary Voters (Ireland) Bill would support amendments
made to it in the Lords. He added that "Sir R. P.'s friends" who had been absent—Henry B. Baring, Sidney Herbert, George C. Legh, Duncan McNeill, Viscount Mahon, George Sandars, and Viscount Villiers—would also do so.

Commons; and in the Lords the Aberdeen-Stanley reconciliation which had begun the preceding year attained its most flourishing state during the 1850 session.

Aberdeen's quickened interest in cooperating with Stanley did not spring primarily from his desire to reunite the Conservative party but rather from his opposition to Palmerston's conduct of foreign policy and Peel's reluctance to support him. When the details of Palmerston's high-handed activities in support of Don Pacifico reached England and an article in the *Globe* implied that Peel approved it, Aberdeen attempted to induce Peel to take some notice of the incident;[18] but both Peel and Graham were disinclined to attack the Government.[19] Aberdeen was dissatisfied but inactive until he learned that Palmerston had also offended France, and then he contacted Stanley.[20]

Stanley was quite ready to accept Aberdeen's advice on foreign affairs, but his main interest at the moment was to raise the franchise qualification in the Paliamentary Voters (Ireland) Bill from £8 to £15 and to strike out a compulsory registration clause in the Commons version of the measure. Although both Aberdeen and Stanley stressed the importance of reconciling the two wings of the former Conservative party, it is clear that they both had more immediate and tangible objects in view when they met (Buccleuch was also present) on June 3. The Peelites promised support in revising the voters bill,[21] and Stanley agreed to lead an attack on Palmerston's foreign policy in the Lords.

For Aberdeen everything worked out as planned. A resolution was moved condemning the Government for its "unjust and exorbitant demands" on Greece, Stanley made a spirited speech, and Aberdeen had an opportunity to tell the House and the world that he disap-

18. *PPE.* 3:535. Peel to Graham, April 2, 1850.

19. Ibid., pp. 538–39. Peel to Graham, April 6, 1850. *PP.* BM 40452. Graham to Peel, April 3, 1850.

20. *AP.* BM 43072. Stanley to Aberdeen, May 13, 1850.

21. Buccleuch's attitude both toward the voters bill and Stanley is clear from his letter to Aberdeen, which read, "I cannot look upon this solely as a Party question . . . & tho' out of personal feeling and friendship toward Stanley, I would make a great sacrifice, the more I consider the point the more convinced do I become in my own conscience that he is wrong both as to the present policy and future result" (*AP.* BM 43201. Buccleuch to Aberdeen, June 3, 1850).

proved of Palmerston's methods. The combination emerged victorious when the votes were counted on June 17.

Russell and Palmerston accepted the censure calmly enough and proposed to meet it with a counterresolution in their own House. They had good reason to be calm, and Peel and Graham had equally good reason to change their minds and to voice their criticisms of a policy they cordially disapproved. Both reasons are summed up in a memorandum by Gladstone, which stated: "Voting with him [Disraeli] was disagreeable enough, but this with his strong aversion to the Palmerstonian policy Peel could not avoid, besides which, it was known that Lord Palmerston would carry the division."[22]

Not only did the Peelites join the attack, they dominated it,[23] despite Stanley's attempts to rouse the suspicious Disraeli into action. The latter was ready to welcome most of the Peelites back into the party, but not at the cost of giving up his position to Goulburn, whom, he feared, Stanley was actively seeking.[24] Under these circumstances the Protectionist leader delivered a flaccid and spiritless speech, while Gladstone especially distinguished himself among the Peelites. Palmerston, of course, carried all before him and secured a 310–264 division in his favor.

This was Peel's last division, and it was a most important one because it proved that the Peelite section had a bond of unity beyond an allegiance to a reluctant leader and an attachment to the free trade dogma. About 70 percent of the original Peelites were present and voting to sustain Aberdeen's approach to foreign relations, and 52 percent of the Miscellaneous Conservatives rallied to the same cause, while less than 17 percent of the former[25] and about 15 percent of the latter supported Palmerston. Did the Peelite section have a foreign policy? It did, and that policy was Aberdeen's.

23.   Frederic Thesiger used Stanley's speech in the Lords as a model for his own. By this time Thesiger was leaning toward the Conservatives, whom he was eventually to join. See *DP*. Derby XII. Stanley to Disraeli, June 22, 1850.

24.   *M&BDIS*. 1:1076. Memorandum by Disraeli, unknown date.

25.   This division indicated the political direction of five of the ten Original Peelites (William Bowles, Robert H. Clive, Sir John Hanmer, Lord Jocelyn, William A. Mackinnon, Charles W. Martin, Edward L. Mostyn, Sir John Owen, Frederick J. Tollemache, and Charles B. Wall). Hanmer, Mackinnon, Martin, Owen, and Tollemache later joined the Liberal party. Bowles was Palmerston's brother-in-law.

As the Peelites did not desire to carry the censure in the Commons, the outcome of the whole affair was an unqualified success and had provided them with a splendid opportunity to voice their dissent. But for Lord Stanley it was gall and wormwood—the former being the compulsory registration clause in the Parliamentary Voters (Ireland) Bill; and the latter, the £12 franchise that was eventually adopted. True to their promise, the Peelites in the Lords had helped Stanley eliminate the first and lower the second, but the Commons would not go along; and when the bill came to the Lords a second time, Aberdeen was absent and the other Peelites provided the votes necessary to carry the measure. So the Peelites helped Stanley once, but quickly deserted him. It was at this moment that Stanley, in a letter to John Wilson Croker, called the Peelites the "most dangerous men" in political life. "They are themselves powerless for good," he wrote, "they have never failed to give the Government a helping hand, when, but for them we could have neutralized, or mitigated the mischief of their measures."[26] Stanley was a moody man, sometimes in high spirits and occasionally depressed. This interpretation of the Peelite influence found him in the latter mood, which reflected his chagrin over the outcome of the Irish franchise measure, one whose effects he greatly overestimated. Certainly, the Peelites had given support to some of the liberal measures, but their liberalism had been confined within modest boundaries.

Sir Robert Peel did not live to learn the outcome of the dispute over the Irish franchise. A lung injury sustained during a fall from a recently purchased horse resulted in his death shortly after midnight on July 2. Peel's passing by no means marked the end of an era in British history as such, for, although he was born in the eighteenth century and had been in public life since the Napoleonic Wars, he was essentially a statesman of the Victorian age, whose high moral atmosphere his manner of living and thinking helped to create. But, in the history of the Peelites, his death certainly was a dividing line. No longer were his former followers bound to the baseless hope that Peel would once again return to office, and they now were free to cut their own path through the tangled wilderness of British mid-century politics.

26. Croker, *The Correspondence and Diaries of the Late Right Honourable John Wilson Croker*, 2:411. Stanley to Croker, August 15, 1850.

PART 3

The Peelites
without Peel
1851-1854

CHAPTER 16

THE FIRST OPPORTUNITY FOR OFFICE

At the time of Peel's death, the Peelite section, although restless and more disunited than ever, was still fairly numerous. The division of May 14 to reconsider previous legislation regarding the admission of foreign corn had not weakened it severely. Two Original Peelites, John Benbow and John Hornby, repudiated their previous position and thereby became regular members of the Conservative party; and so did Stephen Blair, George Dundas, Henry A. Herbert, Richard Kerr, and Sir Edmund C. Macnaghten. Among these, Benbow and Hornby, by virtue of their voting records in 1846, must be classed as true Peelites; these five Miscellaneous Conservatives had been attached only loosely to the section and would hardly rate inclusion in a Peelite list. As it turned out, Henry A. Herbert was to once again reconsider his position, and in 1852 and after he was a dependable member of the section.

There were a number of other reductions and additions to the list of Miscellaneous Conservatives during 1850–51. Lord Lincoln's father died in January, 1851, which elevated him to the dukedom of Newcastle and brought him an estate bordering upon bankruptcy. Much of his time in 1851 was necessarily devoted to private matters.[1] Sir George H. Smyth resigned his seat in 1850, Hamilton K. Morgan switched in 1851 to the Liberal party, and David Urquhart adopted so stationary a political position that his inclusion among the Miscellaneous Conservatives no longer seems warranted.[2] Among this group Lincoln certainly was a true Peelite, and for Morgan it was a stage through which he passed en route to Liberalism. The others were merely irregular Conservatives.

The nine members lost to the Miscellaneous Conservatives were to some extent replaced by new recruits. The new Sir Robert Peel made his debut as a Free Trade Conservative and represented his

1. *NP.* 11881, 11882, 11883, 11886. Lincoln to Bonham, September 25, October 19, and November 26, 1850; Newcastle to Bonham, January 26, 1851.

2. Urquhart was to head an attack on the Government on May 9, 1851 with the support of Disraeli. Like Disraeli, he favored Jewish Relief, but his statement in *Dod* described his position as virtually static.

father's old constituency at Tamworth. Herbert W. W. Wynn, who replaced his deceased uncle, Charles W. W. Wynn, at Montgomeryshire, listed himself merely as a Conservative. Sir John B. Duckworth (Exeter), George W. Heneage (Devizes), and Lord Norreys (Oxfordshire) were former Protectionists who had seen the light in 1850, modified their position against tariff cuts, and thereafter occupied true Miscellaneous Conservative positions.

So nine Miscellaneous Conservatives had been lost, and five new ones had been gained, which reduced the 1850 total of 45 to 41 in 1851. Added to the 59 Original Peelites, the Peelite section had a potential of an even hundred votes in 1851.

The death of Peel naturally forced upon the Peelite leaders a reconsideration of their whole position. The alternatives would be to dissolve the section and let its members join one of the regular parties or to continue to occupy their nebulous political position under a new leader. Very little sentiment was present to adopt the former course; Peel's death, indeed, seems to have rallied rather than discouraged the Peelite leaders. Graham leaned definitely toward the Whigs—this is clear from his replies to Russell and Londonderry, both of whom attempted to recruit him early in 1851.[3] Gladstone, Ellenborough, and Goulburn talked of Conservative reunion. Ellenborough hoped that Gladstone might lead a reunited Conservative party in the Commons,[4] and Gladstone stressed reunion, while realizing that the obstacles to it were very great.[5] Goulburn still hoped that eventually the Conservatives would reunite with their old leaders.[6]

The position of Lord Aberdeen at this time was very important and was to become increasingly more so. Like Graham, he was an "elder statesman" of the section; but, unlike Graham, he had shown a desire to assume leadership, at least in foreign affairs. Early in June, 1850, the prospects for Conservative reunion, guided by Stanley and Aberdeen, had been brighter than at any time in the past, but these prospects came to an end with the growing season.

3. *GMEM*, 6:263–65. *PGRA*, 2:123–24. Graham to Londonderry, January 31, 1851.

4. *EP*. PRO 30/12–21. Ellenborough to Clare, July 5, 1850.

5. *MGLD*, 1:373–74. Gladstone to his Father, July 9, 1850.

6. *CP*. PRO 30/48/8–50. Goulburn to Cardwell, October 5, 1850.

As of August, 1850, Aberdeen acknowledged that his lack of "extreme opinions" might qualify him to be the agent of reunion, but the project seemed too arduous and its outcome too doubtful for him to attempt to fill that role.[7] Aberdeen was a statesman not without honorable ambition, and his political senses must have told him that his chances for securing the prime ministership would evaporate if he joined the Conservative party. The rank and file of that party were Stanley's, and his alone. On the other hand, Lord John Russell was losing popularity, and the leadership of the "movement" was in a state of flux. Whether or not such thoughts passed through Aberdeen's mind, by the end of the year his stand on the Ecclesiastical Titles Bill made reunion with the Conservatives utterly out of the question.

The story of Lord John Russell's political blunder in proposing legislation to counter the so-called Papal Aggression in 1850 has been told many times in many places. Sidney Herbert's biographer stressed that the spontaneous and uniform reaction of the Peelite leaders against Lord John Russell's plan to enact "no popery" legislation is convincing evidence of the deep ideological ties that bound the Peelite leaders together.[8] Not only Graham, Aberdeen, Herbert, and Gladstone, but even Henry Goulburn, opposed Russell on the Ecclesiastical Titles issue;[9] and one found a religious liberalism among the leaders that was decidedly uncharacteristic of the Peelite section as a whole.

The Peelites could have hardly assumed a position that was more politically unrewarding, and it is this willingness to espouse a cause which might well injure their political prospects for a long time to come that lifts the Peelites above the level of tedious dogmatists who moralize positions that are mainly politically expedient. Herbert, Lincoln, and Gladstone were often accused of leaning toward Rome;[10] and Graham, Gladstone, Cardwell, and Goulburn must all have known that their position on the Papal Aggression question

7. Lady Frances Balfour, *The Life of George Fourth Earl of Aberdeen,* 2:159; Aberdeen to Guizot, August 5, 1850.

8. *SHER.* 1:131.

9. *RIPP.* BM 40877. Goulburn to Ripon, November 15 and December 16, 1850.

10. *M&BDIS.* 1:1088. Disraeli to Stanley, December 7, 1850; *NP.* 11943. Lincoln to Herbert, December 19, 1847.

would cause serious trouble for them at the next election. "This is an age of principles," Disraeli had noted in 1849, "and no longer of political expedients."[11] This was certainly true of the Peelites, whose habit of viewing issues in a moral light made them the avant garde of the Victorian age—the coterie of statesmen who most embodied its high idealism. As it turned out, there were two great divisions in the Commons before Russell's Ecclesiastical Titles Bill came to a vote, and both were of political significance.

Hoping to take advantage of the Protectionist trend that had showed itself within the Peelite section the preceding year, Disraeli on February 13, 1851, moved for a committee to consider the agricultural distress, which was opposed by the Government. On the division the Peelite section split approximately in half (40-37) against Disraeli. The members who voted with the Government were:

Henry B. Baring	Sir James Graham	Roundell Palmer
William Bowles	Sir John Hanmer	Frederick Peel*
John Boyd	James Heald*	Sir Robert Peel*
Ld. Ernest Bruce	Sidney Herbert	Joseph Sandars*
Edward Cardwell	Ld. Alfred Hervey	Sir Horace Seymour
Sir George Clerk	Sir James W. Hogg	Henry Stuart
William T. Copeland	Earl Jermyn	Sir F. Thesiger
Edmund B. Denison*	Allan Lockhart	Charles B. Wall
Sir Charles Douglas	William Mackinnon	John Walter*
Marquess of Douro	Charles Martin	Lord Wellesley
John Duncuft*	John Masterman	James S. Wortley
James B. Estcourt*	Edward Mostyn	John Young
Henry Fitz-Roy	Lord Norreys*	
Henry Goulburn	Sir John Owen	

Gladstone was away at the time, but fourteen of the Original Peelites voted for Disraeli's motion together with 23 Miscellaneous Conservatives. Despite this split in the Peelite section, the Peelite votes were responsible for the Government's narrow (281–267) victory.

A strong aura of partisan politics hangs over the division of February 20 on Locke King's motion to equalize the borough and county franchises. Later William Goodenough Hayter, the Government whip, explained to Russell that the experience of the previous year, when 99 Peelite and Protectionist votes had turned aside a similar

11. *Hansard*, 3d ser., 102:98.

motion, had prompted him to contact the Protectionist whips—but apparently not John Young of the Peelites—with a request that they be present on the division. As it turned out only seventeen Peelites and Protectionists divided in support of the Government, and it suffered a stinging defeat. Later Stanley told Hayter that his followers had learned the Government was not in earnest in opposing the motion and had therefore stayed away;[12] but it remains to be explained why all of the Peelite leaders and all but five Original Peelites and Miscellaneous Conservatives boycotted the division. It had the appearance of a Peelite-Protectionist plot to bring on a cabinet crisis.

Evidence of collusion between the two is lacking, but bring on a crisis they certainly did, and it lasted from February 21 to March 3. There is no point in recounting in detail the comings and goings of those days—suffice it to say that Russell resigned; Stanley was called in but would not try to form a government unless it were clear that a Whig-Peelite coalition were impossible; and on February 22 Graham and Aberdeen were called in for a consultation.

At this conference Graham rejected any notion that he would head a coalition, which meant that the field was left clear for Aberdeen, but forming a coalition under Peelite leadership was not what Russell had in mind. Russell wanted to bring the Peelites into his own cabinet, the bait being a much modified Ecclesiastical Titles Bill, consultations with Graham and Aberdeen on the membership of the proposed cabinet, and dedication to the principles of free trade.[13] After considering Russell's offer and consulting Newcastle, who opposed coalition save under Peelite leadership, they turned down the proposition on two main grounds—opposition to precipitous action on Reform and their refusal to accept an Ecclesiastical Titles Bill in any form.[14] Following Russell's failure to enlist the Peelites, the Government was offered to Aberdeen, who noted that the Ecclesiastical Titles Bill was an insurmountable obstacle to his acceptance and advised that Stanley be called in again.

Like Russell, Stanley needed help from the Peelites. He wanted

12. *RUSP*. PRO 30/22–9C. Hayter to Russell, March 1, 1851.

13. Spencer Walpole, *The Life of Lord John Russell*, 2: 124.

14. *PGRA*. 2:129. Newcastle to Graham, February 23, 1851; *AP*. BM 43066. Aberdeen Memorandum, February 22, 1851.

in particular Aberdeen, Lord Canning, or Stratford Canning for the Foreign Office, and, if possible, Henry Corry, Lord Ellenborough, William E. Gladstone, Henry Goulburn, the duke of Northumberland, and Sir Frederic Thesiger for other offices.[15] Why he wanted Gladstone and Thesiger is very important to understanding why he continued to court them in the future. He had noted that when they broke with Peel and Graham on the divisions of 1850, they carried with them "a good many of the smaller fry" among the Peelite section,[16] and thus securing Thesiger and Gladstone would mean acquiring a fairly large number of Peelite votes. As it turned out, Aberdeen, Viscount Canning, and Gladstone refused the offer because Stanley planned a revenue duty on corn; Henry Corry, Ellenborough, and Thesiger declined because they thought a Stanley government could not stand. Only Northumberland accepted. So on February 27 Stanley had to confess to the queen his inability to form a government, and she was compelled to fall back on Russell, who resumed office.

From the standpoint of party maneuvering, the Peelites had played their hand with great skill, using the Ecclesiastical Titles Bill to fend off the Whigs and the Protection issue to keep the Conservatives at the proper distance, which meant not only that their section would continue in existence, but that their bargaining position in the future would be much enhanced. They were courted and sought after by both parties. This had happened before while Peel was still alive, but this time it was clear that they planned to take office as a section.

One wonders, if Aberdeen had been able to foresee the tragic events of 1853–55, whether he would have turned his back on Stanley at this moment. While it was quite true that he was just as "radical" on domestic issues as most of the Liberals and thus could link his fortunes with them in good conscience, in the area of foreign affairs, where his real interests lay, he belonged with Lord Stanley and not Palmerston. He would have the prime ministership eventually; but when he retired from it, he would spend his last few years a brooding and haunted man.

15. *RUSP*. PRO 30/22–9B. Aberdeen and Graham to Russell, February 24, 1851.

16. *DP*. Derby XII. Stanley to Disraeli, March 1, 1850.

CHAPTER 17

THE PEELITES IN THE 1851 SESSION

During the balance of the 1851 session, the air in the House of Commons was charged with party conflict and general uncertainty. Among the Peelites there was little talk now of party reconstruction. They watched and counted votes, and perhaps wondered just how they would eventually fit into the scheme of things.

Three divisions seem particularly worthy of study. The first came on April 11 when Disraeli moved that agriculture should be considered in any tax relief plan. Gladstone was ready to go along with the motion, as he had in similar circumstances the year before, but Graham convinced him that Russell should be kept in office until he passed a reform bill that could be expected to be more moderate than one he would advocate if out of office and trying to return to power.[1] This essentially conservative line of reasoning caused Gladstone to line up with the opponents of the motion.

The result was an impressive show of Peelite strength. Essentially the Peelite voters of April 11 were the same as those of February 13, but they increased their strength to 43 Original Peelite and Miscellaneous Conservative votes from the 40 earlier in the year. Disraeli attracted fifteen from each half of the section, his more important recruits being Henry Corry, Lord Claud Hamilton, John W. Patten, Jonathan Peel, Sir Robert Peel, and Sir Frederic Thesiger.

Graham had been right in predicting that the Peelite vote would make or break the Government, for its majority was only 13. Sir John Young refined it further and stated that Gladstone's speech and vote had saved the Government. "Had you spoken & voted the other way," he wrote, "I would have done the same, so would Oswald, which would have reduced the maj. of 13 to 7—and I think that McNeill, H. Drummond, A. Smollett, & Wegg-Prosser, who stayed away, would have in that case voted against Ministers, leaving them only 3—too narrow a margin for them to rest upon."[2] This provides an

---

1. *GP.* BM 44777. Gladstone Memorandum, April 27, 1851.
2. *GP.* BM 44237. Young to Gladstone, April 21, 1851.

incomplete inventory of Gladstone's personal following in the Commons.

Both Young and Russell were interested in whether or not Stanley could form a government. Young noted that there were five Whig Protectionists and 28 members of the Irish Brigade in the minority, none of whom would support a Stanley government; doubling their combined strength (for a total of 66) and adding the thirteen-vote Government majority, he concluded that Stanley was in a 79-vote minority. Young predicted—quite rightly—that the Conservatives could not even secure a majority at the next election. Russell had the division analyzed for him by Hayter, who counted 36 Conservatives (he did not distinguish them from the Peelites) on the Government side during the division and carefully explained why certain Government supporters had not been there. His tally raises some interesting questions regarding the exact position of some of the Peelites.[3] According to Hayter's count, there were then 334 Liberals of all kinds, and 316 Conservatives of all connections in the Commons. Without Peelite support, Stanley could not possibly form a government.

The next important trial of strength came on May 29, when the *soi-disant* Original Peelite, Henry J. Baillie, moved that certain punishments inflicted on the Ceylon rebels after a revolt were excessive. Despite the fact that the motion involved a humanitarian issue moved by a Peelite, Graham regarded it as a Protectionist attack on the Government; not so Gladstone, who voted with Baillie.

3. *RUSP.* PRO 30/22–9C. Hayter Memorandum, April 11, 1851. See also ibid. Hayter Memorandum, May 29, 1851, which dealt with the Ceylon division. Both memorandums have the appearance of having been drawn up with some care, as might be expected, for they were for the eyes of the prime minister. The problem which comes up in connection with them is this—the first memorandum in listing the "Conservatives Voting with Government" omits the names of Sir John Hanmer, William A. Mackinnon, Charles W. Martin, Edward L. Mostyn, Lord Norreys, Sir John Owen, Frederick J. Tollemache, and Charles B. Wall, all of whom supported the Government on this occasion. The memorandum on the Ceylon division identifies Tollemache as a Conservative, but once again omits the names of the others, who once again were present and voting. Why? The reason becomes clear if we go back to the Don Pacifico division in 1850, which found Hanmer, Mackinnon, Martin, Mostyn, Owen, and Wall voting with the Government. Save for Owen, who appears to have voted with whatever Government happened to be in power, these members seem to have been no longer regarded as Conservatives, despite their classifications in *Dod*. Hanmer, Mostyn, and Wall had begun to look increasingly to Russell for leadership.

Most of the Original Peelites apparently adopted Graham's view, for they divided 24-9 against the motion; but the Miscellaneous Conservatives were undecided on the issue and split 12-12 on it.

When the controversial Ecclesiastical Titles Bill came to debate in the Commons, the subsequent divisions displayed both the strength and the weakness of the Peelite section. It became a party issue when David Urquhart, supported by Disraeli, moved that the Pope's recent action in establishing the Roman Catholic hierarchy in Britain had been encouraged by the Russell Government. From the combined section, Disraeli attracted only thirteen votes and an overwhelming 46 went against him. But on the division of May 12, which involved the principle of the measure and thus raised the religious question, Disraeli voted with the Government, and the combined section split 28-8 in favor of the bill. Disraeli could find little encouragement in the fact that only three members of the combined section (Samuel Christy, Sir Frederic Thesiger, and Frederick C. Villiers) followed his lead on both divisions; but the Peelite leaders were forced to face the hard fact that the great majority of the section did not agree with their religious policy. Only Henry Currie, William E. Gladstone, Sir James Graham, William Keogh, Alexander H. Oswald, Frederick Peel, George P. Smythe, and Francis Wegg-Prosser voted against the measure; and Keogh— according to Hayter's memorandum—was a member of the Irish Brigade.

It is virtually impossible to compile a meaningful list of the members of the Peelite section for the latter part of the session of 1851. If we began with the eight members who voted against the Ecclesiastical Titles Bill, we should lose Keogh, Oswald, Smythe, and Wegg-Prosser on the May 9 division on the same issue, for they voted against the Government, and Gladstone would leave the group on the Ceylon division. Currie had broken with the Peelites earlier in the year to support Disraeli's motion on the agricultural distress, and Frederick Peel was left as the only consistent supporter of Graham; but even in his case there is a serious question whether he was voting with the Peelites or with the Government. On straight political issues, however, the section could muster 43 or even more votes, and its members showed a strong reluctance to vote with Disraeli.

So much for the Lower House in 1851. In the Lords the main event of the session was Lord Aberdeen's attempt to use his new-found leadership to vote down the Ecclesiastical Titles Bill—an almost quixotic project when one considers the Church-oriented nature of the Upper House. He and Graham both worked hard to secure the powerful debating services of Lord Brougham[4] as well as those of some other legal minds, but their efforts met with meager success. Brougham gave his proxy but not his voice against the bill; Lord Lyndhurst both spoke and voted in its favor. Aberdeen nevertheless bravely moved its rejection on July 21, and with the aid of such Peelite Peers as Newcastle, Canning, and St. Germans, he kept the debate going for two nights; but, as in the Commons, the Peelites as a section did not endorse his brand of religious liberalism. Argyll, DeGrey, Hardinge, Harrowby, Heytesbury, Lyndhurst, Ripon, and Wellington all rallied in support of the measure; and Aberdeen was routed by a 265-38 margin. Staging this fight certainly hurt Aberdeen's position[5] and even lost him some followers, such as Lord Londonderry, who decided that the Peelite section offered no further attraction to him and thereafter "resolutely" supported the Conservative party.[6]

His difficulties in the Commons encouraged Russell to press even more strongly his efforts to secure strength among the Peelite section. In the spring he met with some modest success: Duncan McNeill, an Original Peelite, accepted a judgeship on the Supreme Court in Scotland and passed from the political scene; George J. Turner, from the Miscellaneous group, accepted the position of vice chancellor. Turner had been a steady vote for the Peelites on political and economic issues, especially during 1848–49, and probably should be numbered among them. A third enlistee was Sir James Graham's protégé,[7] Frederick Peel, who, after receiving noncommittal advice from Graham,[8] accepted the position of undersecretary for the Colonial Office.

---

4. *BP.* Aberdeen to Brougham, (?) 1851; Graham to Brougham, July 19, 1851.

5. The issue very temporarily alienated Aberdeen and Argyll. See Sir Arthur Gordon, *The Earl of Aberdeen*, pp. 202–3.

6. *RIPP.* BM 40877. Londonderry to Ripon, July 20, 1851.

7. *DP.* Derby XII. Derby to Disraeli, October 26, 1851.

8. *AP.* BM 43190. Graham to Aberdeen, October 21, 1851.

But Russell was out for bigger game. He made a gesture toward Newcastle in April;[9] and his Chancellor of the Exchequer, Charles Wood, sought to establish connections with Gladstone, Herbert, and possibly Goulburn.[10] Graham turned down another Russell offer in September, the reason (or excuse)—bungling on Reform[11]—and refused him still again in mid–January, 1952.[12] About the same time the duke of Newcastle used Russell's New Zealand policy as an excuse for not entertaining an offer.[13] The duke, who had strongly deplored Frederick Peel's decision to join Russell,[14] was one of the strongest of all advocates of continued Peelite independence.

While the younger men, such as Gladstone, Herbert, and New-castle, often discussed their political prospects, and even complained about their lack of a formal leader,[15] it is clear to one who reads the correspondence at this time that the reins of the section were in the hands of Aberdeen and Graham, both of whom expected that a cabinet crisis could not be far distant. Their only point of differ-ence concerned the correct Peelite posture while waiting for the call to office. "When the crisis comes," Graham wrote Aberdeen in January, 1852, "you are the natural adviser of the Queen; and, as arbiter between Parties and rival claims, you . . . must carefully preserve an impartial and neutral position."[16] Graham therefore re-fused to attend a preparliamentary meeting planned by Newcastle and induced Cardwell also to stay away, lest they should give the appearance of plotting against the Government.

Aberdeen evidently did not accept Graham's reasoning in this matter. At any rate, he, Viscount Canning, Lord Lyttleton, Goulburn, Gladstone, and Young met at Newcastle's residence in January where they discussed at length the complexities of the contemporary political situation—complexities to which their behavior, it must be added, contributed not a little.

9. *RUSP.* PRO 30/22–9C. Newcastle to Russell, April 26, 1851.

10. *GOP.* II-23. Herbert to Goulburn, May 14, 1851.

11. *PGRA.* 2:134–35. Graham to Russell, September 20, 1851.

12. Ibid., pp. 150–51. Russell to Graham, January 14 and 17, 1852.

13. *NP.* 12699b. Newcastle Memorandum, January 7, 1852.

14. Ibid. 12348. Newcastle to Hayward, October 27, 1851.

15. Ibid. 11888. Newcastle to Bonham, September 2, 1851. *GP.* BM 44262 Gladstone to Newcastle, October 22, 1851. *SHER.* 1:145–46. Newcastle to Her-bert, October 27, 1851.

16. *AP.* BM 43190. Graham to Aberdeen, January 10, 1852.

CHAPTER 18

THE FIRST DERBY ADMINISTRATION

When Parliament assembled in February, 1852, Russell faced the quiet hostility of the Palmerstonian Whigs and Liberals, the vocal anger of the Irish Brigade, the indifference of the Radicals who disliked his Militia Bill and failure to deal with reform, and the watchful waiting of Peelites and Protectionists, who hoped to come to power. His fate was sealed. The end came on February 20, when Palmerston, aided by many sections of the Commons, carried an amendment to his Militia Bill by a 136-125 margin.

The turnout of the combined Peelite section on this vote was very light—13 supported Russell and 18 voted against him. Graham did not vote, but Gladstone and Herbert did, so the "official" Peelite position on this division was against the Government. On the other hand, those from the combined section who supported Russell when Peelites, Palmerstonians, and Protectionists were voting against him, might be regarded as very close to the liberal party. A general analysis of the section will be made at the session just before the dissolution.

Although Derby did not waste time negotiating with the Peelites while the tariff question was still pending,[1] he managed to secure the active aid of some of them in his Government. Lord Hardinge became master general of the Ordnance; the earl of Jersey, master of Horse; the earl of Rosslyn, master of Buckhounds; and Lyndhurst was bound to the Government with an earldom. The duke of Northumberland became lord high admiral. Lord Derby was less successful in securing members from the Peelite section in the Lower House, but Henry J. Baillie became the secretary of the Board of Control; Sir Frederic Thesiger, the attorney general; Lord Claud Hamilton, a treasurer of the Household; and Sir Fitzroy Kelly, an Original Peelite who had given up his seat in 1847, became solicitor general. Lord Shaftesbury (until 1851, Lord Ashley) visited with Derby, but would not accept office under him.[2]

1. Derby explained this to Aberdeen. See *AP*. BM 43072. Derby to Aberdeen, February 29, 1852.
2. Edwin Hodder, *The Life and Work of the Seventh Earl of Shaftesbury*, 2:379.

Derby's accession to power forced the Peelites to take a more definite position. Lord Aberdeen assured Derby that nothing of a "factious or obstructive course will be attempted" before the dissolution;[3] and Gladstone, who contacted Derby through Lord Hardinge, assured him that the "body of Peelites" would support the Government through the session, provided that only necessary measures would be introduced, a dissolution would take place in the summer, and a new Parliament would meet in November.[4] Derby did not enter into a formal engagement with Gladstone, as he had no "majority" to offer, but he assured him that he intended to follow the course Gladstone outlined.[5] So Derby's minority Government rested on two outside props, the Peelites, and the Palmerstonians.

Their seating arrangements in the Commons would now indicate to the world their relationship to the new Government, with whose members they had previously been juxtaposed on the Opposition side. Gladstone's biographer told how Graham and Cardwell decided to sit on the Opposition benches near Lord John Russell, indicating their Whig sympathies, but how Herbert and Gladstone and almost 40 other Peelites took their seats below the gangway on the Opposition side, which stressed their ambiguous position.[6] Young was rather surprised to learn that Gladstone had decided to sit below the gangway on the Opposition rather than the Government side, but he faithfully followed him.[7] A part of one of Gladstone's letters that he quoted would indicate that his leader was even further from Derby than his new geographical position suggested. "I am so stupid," he wrote, "I have not guessed what you allude to as talking of our being in at the death, and qualifying 'by opposition' to share in the spoils."[8]

Two divisions enable us to secure a clearer insight into the political positions of the various Peelites during the balance of the 1852 session. Lord John Russell launched an ill-advised attack upon the Government's Militia Bill on April 26 in order to satisfy his Radical followers, who believed that it would strengthen the influence of the

3. *AP*. BM 43072. Aberdeen to Derby, March 1, 1852.
4. *DP*. Derby XII. Derby to Disraeli, March 18, 1852.
5. Ibid.
6. *MGLD*. 1:422–23.
7. *GP*. BM 44327. Young to Gladstone, March 6, 1852.
8. Ibid. Young to Gladstone, March 1, 1852.

Lords Lieutenant and the landed aristocracy. Although some of the Peelites and Miscellaneous Conservatives might have voted with Russell at this time because they disliked the measure, it seems probable that those members of the section who did so were expressing their political sympathies more than their opinion of the measure. Only seven members of the section came to Russell's support, while 43 Original Peelites and 27 Miscellaneous Conservatives took their cue from Gladstone, Disraeli, or Palmerston—all of whom voted for the Government's bill. Despite their positions close to Russell, neither Graham, who was absent, nor Cardwell, who voted with the Peelites, aided him in this attack.

The division of May 10 can hardly be classified as other than a political division. Some provision had to be made for the seats of St. Albans and Sudbury—which had been disfranchised—before the general election that summer. Writing to Gladstone, Derby explained that if he did not make such a provision, he would be accused of keeping the question open until a more Conservative Parliament could deal with it.[9] But Gladstone decided that this was not a "necessary measure" within the terms of his bargain with Derby, and he concerted his plan with Hayter and Russell for an attack on the Government.[10] If Gladstone did this to show his strength, the result was quite satisfactory—37 Original Peelites and Miscellaneous Conservatives voted with him. We are on fairly firm ground, on the other hand, if we assume that the ten Original Peelites and nine Miscellaneous Conservatives who voted with Disraeli in an attack supported by Gladstone, Russell, and Palmerston showed a strong bent toward the Conservative party.

Using these three main divisions of 1852, as well as those of 1851, as a guide and adding the information secured from some of Young's letters, it is possible to make a fairly accurate inventory of the Peelite section for the 1851–52 period, although it is very important to emphasize that so interested and involved an observer as Young was not quite sure of the political positions of some of the members of the section. At this point, it will be convenient to abandon the previous designations "Original Peelite" and "Miscellaneous Peelite," and replace them by three other categories—Liberal Peelite, Peelite,

9. *GP.* BM 44140. Derby to Gladstone, May 9, 1852.
10. Ibid. BM 44372. Gladstone to Hayter, May 5, 1852.

and Conservative Peelite—for the balance of the narrative. The one hundred Original Peelites and Miscellaneous Conservatives of the 1851–52 sessions might be divided as follows:[11]

The Liberal Peelites

Edward Cardwell	Sir John Hanmer	Lord Norreys
Francis Charteris	Sir James W. Hogg	Frederick Peel
Sir Charles E. Douglas	William Keogh	Sir Horace B. Seymour
Henry Fitz-Roy	William A. Mackinnon	George P. Smythe
Sir James R. Graham	Charles W. Martin	Charles B. Wall
Thomas Greene	Edward L. Mostyn	John Walter

The Peelites

Henry B. Baring	Egerton, William T.	Roundell Palmer
William Beckett	William E. Gladstone	John W. Patten
John Boyd	Henry Goulburn	Sir Robert Peel
Ld. Ernest Bruce	Sidney Herbert	Edward D. Pennant
Sir George Clerk	Lord Alfred Hervey	Joseph Sandars
Henry Corry	William B. Hughes	Alexander Smollett
Henry Currie	Earl Jermyn	Viscount Somerton
Edmund B. Denison	Sir John V. Johnstone	John M. Sutton
Lord Douro	George C. Legh	Frederick J. Tollemache
Viscount Drumlanrig	Allan E. Lockhart	Francis R. Wegg-Prosser
Henry H. Drummond	Viscount Mahon	Frederick R. West
John Duncuft	William Mure	James S. Wortley
James B. Estcourt	Sir John Owen	John Young

The Conservative Peelites

Charles B. Baldwin	A. Baillie Cochrane	James Heald
Henry J. Baillie	Thomas S. Cocks	George W. Heneage
Francis Baring	William T. Copeland	Henry T. Hope
Adm. William Bowles	William Cubitt	Viscount Jocelyn
Ld. John Chichester	George D. Damer	James Lindsay
Samuel Christy	Sir John B. Duckworth	John Masterman
Robert H. Clive	Lord Claud Hamilton	Alexander Oswald

11. The three lists include 94 Original Peelites and Miscellaneous Conservatives. The other six members are accounted for as follows: Lord Ashley became the 7th earl of Shaftesbury in June, 1851 and went to the Upper House; Viscount Newry and Morne died in 1851; Viscount Northland resigned his seat the same year, and so did Viscount Brackley. As we have seen above, Duncan McNeill and George J. Turner took governmental positions and resigned their seats. McNeill and Northland, of course, were Original Peelites, and Viscount Newry and Lord Ashley were also identified with the section quite early. On the basis of their voting records, Turner probably should be classified as a Peelite during 1847–50, but Brackley was simply a Conservative irregular.

Jonathan Peel	Viscount Seaham	Lord Wellesley
William H. Plowden	Thomas Sidney	Thomas C. Whitmore
Ld. William Powlett	Henry Stuart	Sir Henry Willoughby
David Pugh	Sir Frederick Thesiger	Herbert W. Wynn
George A. Reid	Frederick C. Villiers	
George Sandars	Viscount Villiers	

This distribution of the Peelites and Miscellaneous Conservatives in 1852 points up the importance of including the latter in any discussion of the Peelite section, for in the final tally the proportion of Peelites to Miscellaneous Conservatives among the group called Peelites was 27-12, among the Liberal Peelites, 13-5, and among the Conservative Peelites, 17-20. The Original Peelites showed a stronger "liberal" bent than did the Miscellaneous Conservatives as a group; but in the final analysis both groups represented all shades of opinion.

CHAPTER 19

THE ELECTION OF 1852

The election of 1852 was held under circumstances quite different from those of 1847. Britain was now entering upon the "Golden Age" of British capitalism during which the influx of gold from America and Australia brought a restrained inflation as a stimulant to business.[1] As demonstrated during the Great Exhibition of the preceding year, Britain had emerged as the world's leading industrial power, and by this time the working classes were sharing in this economic victory. Wages had risen; the cost of food had remained stable or declined; and the various factory acts had restricted the working day and provided some time off during weekends. Chartism lay in the past—if not wholly forgotten, at least slumbering. Save for relatively minor colonial and diplomatic problems, with which Britain had long since learned to live, the empire was peaceful, and the international scene free from crises. Only in the agricultural areas, where corn prices were to remain depressed until 1853, was there unrest and dissatisfaction. So the mood of the country was fairly content, which probably worked in favor of the party in power.

There were charges during and after the election that the contests did not deeply involve the Protection question, or any discernible issue, except in certain places, that of religion. Certainly there was some truth in this charge. Disraeli had long been convinced that Protection was a political liability in most constituencies, and he would have abandoned it officially before the election had not Derby insisted that the Conservative party remain committed to it until it was patent that the cause was lost. Hence, in some constituencies the Derbyites campaigned as Protectionists, in others, as Free Traders. Protection of the Protestant faith and the Established Church was probably more consistently emphasized by the Derbyites than was the tariff issue.

In examining the results of the election, we might first ask: To what extent were the choices of the Peelite section confirmed at the polls; that is to say, which of the three groups had judged most ac-

---

1. See G. D. H. Cole and Raymond Postgate, *The British People, 1746–1946*, section 6.

curately the wishes of their constituents? It would appear that the
Peelites were the most successful in this respect. Seven of them did
not stand, and five were beaten for a 30 percent loss.[2] Among the
Conservative Peelites, four did not stand and ten lost for a 38 percent attrition.[3] The Liberal Peelites made out worst of all: two
retired and six were beaten, for a 44 percent loss.[4] If the election
proved anything to the Peelites, it was that the mid-position was
the safest of all. The voting public thus did little to discourage the
Peelite movement at this stage of its history.

After the election, as we shall see, considerable bitterness sprang
up among the Peelites against the Conservatives for having made
political war on their section at the polls, but only two members of
the regular Peelite group, Sir George Clerk and Frederick J.
Tollemache, were defeated by Derbyites; and Lord Douro,[5] Viscount
Mahon, and Joseph Sandars lost out to a Reformer, a Liberal, and a
Whig. The Conservatives made greater inroads against the Liberal
Peelite group. Edward Cardwell, William A. Mackinnon,[6] Lord
Norreys, and George P. Smythe were all beaten by Derbyites, while
Thomas Greene and Charles W. Martin lost to a Liberal and a
Reformer. The losses of these two Peelite groups, however, were
only slightly larger than the ten defeats suffered by the Conservative
Peelites,[7] eight of whom lost out to Liberals, one (Alexander Os-

2. Those who did not stand were John Boyd, Henry Currie, Henry H.
Drummond, James B. Estcourt, Roundell Palmer, Viscount Somerton, and Francis H. Wegg-Prosser.

3. The Conservative Peelites who did not stand for reelection were Admiral William Bowles, Lord Chichester, George A. Reid (died in 1852), and
Thomas C. Whitmore. Henry Whitmore acquired his father's seat in the Derbyite
interest.

4. Sir Charles E. Douglas and Sir Horace B. Seymour did not contest their
seats.

5. Douro explained his defeat as follows: "There is little or no doubt that
the law was broken in many ways at the Norwich election; and it is hardly to
be imagined that candidates are to be permitted to spend £1000 in tea parties
& processions etc. at all of which voters and their families were employed and
paid munificently to carry banners and saucers, when it is forbidden to treat or
give inducements to vote. . . . I see Damer now and then. He cares much more
for his defeat than I do" (*BP*. Douro to Brougham, July 24, 1852). The death of
Wellington shortly transferred Douro to the Lords.

6. William A. Mackinnon's son, who bore the same name, won at Rye in
the Liberal interest, but was unseated; and his father replaced him in 1853.

7. The defeated Conservative Peelites included Charles B. Baldwin, A.

wald) to a Conservative, and the other (Viscount Villiers) to a Whig. The available statistics do not support the idea of a general assault by the Conservatives upon the Peelites, but the former may have had a hand in many elections whose results do not readily reveal the nature of the battles that actually took place.

Certain members from each found it wise to give up their seats and to seek new constituencies—some successfully, others unsuccessfully. Among the Peelites, William Beckett secured Graham's seat at Ripon, and Henry H. Drummond moved to Surrey; but Sir George Clerk's contest for Dover and Joseph Sandar's for Bewdley both ended in defeat. Sir James Graham, among the Liberal Peelites, headed the poll at Carlisle, while Frederick Peel won narrowly at Bury in Lancashire; Edward Cardwell was beaten twice—first at Liverpool, then at Ayrshire. The Conservative Peelites did more seat hunting than either of the others. William J. Powlett went to Ludlow, Sir Frederic Thesiger to Stamford, Francis W. Villiers to Rochester, and Lord Wellesley to Windsor; but A. Baillie Cochrane, George L. Damer, Alexander Oswald, and Thomas Sidney were all defeated in their attempts to find new seats. The Conservative-Peelite split may have figured in many of these contests.

If the Conservatives might be criticized for their ambiguous stand on the Protection issue, the voting public might also have been confused regarding the political postures of some of the Peelites. Sir James Graham, Charles B. Wall, and William Keogh all ran as Liberals; and the first, of course, was the elder statesman of the Peelites in the Commons. Who represented Peelism, Graham or Gladstone? The latter was certainly not returned as a Liberal,[8] and neither was Goulburn.[9] The difference of political position among these leading Peelites was so obvious that Gladstone induced Aberdeen to repudiate Graham's Liberal position on behalf of the Peelites in general.[10]

Baillie Cochrane, William T. Copeland, George L. Damer, James Heald, Henry T. Hope, Alexander Oswald, William H. Plowden, Thomas Sidney, and Viscount Villiers.

    8.   *MGLD.* 1:427.

    9.   *GOP.* II–24. Goulburn to Gladstone, February 4, 1852.

    10.   *MGLD.* 1:420. See also *GP.* BM 44163. Gladstone to Graham, March 27, 1852.

Once the election was over, the guessing game began. Derby believed that it had been "favourable" to his party;[11] so did most observers, but the question remained, How favorable? The *Illustrated London News*, which made a distinction between the Peelites and the Ministerial Free Traders,[12] counted 38 of the former and 29 of the latter in the new Parliament. It is clear, however, that nobody really knew the extent of the Conservative victory.

John Young and Francis Bonham, the two best authorities on Peelite matters, despite the aid of a list slipped to them surreptitiously by a prominent Conservative agent,[13] could not agree as to the strength of the postelection Peelite section. Young's letters at this time, which are an important source of Peelite information, are quoted at length in appendix 3, and there is no point in discussing them in detail, save to note that Bonham believed there might be as many as 50 Peelites in the new Parliament, while Young could count no more than 31 or 34 if Mostyn, Hanmer, and Milnes, who were actually Whigs, were added. "Twenty of this 31 or 34," he warned Gladstone, "might go with you (by you I mean Newcastle, S. Herbert, & yourself) in the event of your splitting with Lord Derby & joining the Whigs, but several of these would not like it."[14]

The trend of Young's and Gladstone's thought, as revealed by this letter, is even more evident in those of Lord Aberdeen and Newcastle, who were extremely bitter over the manner in which the Conservatives had conducted the election. Aberdeen thought their proceedings dishonest;[15] Newcastle thought that a Conservative offer to the Peelites would be "little short of an insult."[16] Graham joined their indignation by stressing the "ruthless" attacks made by Conservatives on Peelite candidates,[17] and Young charged the Conservatives with involving the Admiralty and misusing secret service funds for election purposes.[18]

11. *DP*. Derby XII. Derby to Disraeli, August 3, 1852.

12. *Illustrated London News*. July 17 and August 7, 1852.

13. This was Edwin Clofer (?). *GP*. BM 44327. Young to Gladstone, August 10, 1852.

14. Ibid.

15. *AP*. BM 43197. Aberdeen to Newcastle, July 25, 1852.

16. Ibid. Newcastle to Aberdeen, August 2, 1852.

17. *PP*. BM 40616. Graham to Bonham, July 18, 1852.

18. *GP*. BM 44327. Young to Gladstone, July 27, 1852.

Thus a regular chorus of Peelite protests arose from the election, and Lord Aberdeen was its coryphaeus. Whether or not their charges had much basis in fact need not concern us, except to note that Gladstone, who was the most reluctant to break with the Conservatives, believed that their conduct during the election had been no more shifty or blameworthy than that of Russell and the Whigs in the past.[19] Perhaps the major point of interest in this development is the demonstration once again of the strong tendency of the Peelites to moralize their behavior. They knew they would break completely with the Conservatives, and they obviously preferred that their action should have some sort of moral basis that would eliminate, or cover up, any political motives they may have entertained at this moment.

19. *MGLD.* 1:428–30.

CHAPTER 20

THE FORMATION OF ABERDEEN'S GOVERNMENT

After he had been defeated in December, Lord Derby was to charge that his government had been the victim of a factious coalition. How true his charge was can be gleaned from a short narrative of the events that led to the ousting of the Conservatives from power.

As early as July, Graham and Russell were exchanging letters looking toward the formation of a new government. When Russell asked if Gladstone and Herbert would act with the Whigs and Radicals,[1] Graham replied that they would help defeat Derby but would not join a Russell government. He therefore suggested that Russell lead in the Commons for a prime minister (presumably Aberdeen) in the Lords.[2] This Russell was most reluctant to do and indicated he would give only out-of-office support to an administration he did not head.[3]

Later the same month the busy Russell sought Lord Aberdeen's cooperation, and the latter quickly contacted Newcastle. He explained that, although the time had come to cooperate with Russell and the Whigs, he feared many statesmen would object to serving under the former premier.[4] Newcastle agreed and ruled out Russell as the future head of the coalition government.[5] The original movers of the coalition, it is clear, were Russell, Graham, Aberdeen, and Newcastle.

It appears that Graham somewhat exaggerated the readiness of Gladstone and Herbert to join in an anti-Derby movement at this time. Early in August, Gladstone wrote Aberdeen that honor would compel him to resign his seat at Oxford if he took the position that Russell should replace Derby[6] and he wished to wait until events

1. *PGRA.* 2:165–67. Russell to Graham, July 19, 1852.
2. *RP.* PRO 30/22/10. Graham to Russell, July 22, 1852.
3. *AP.* BM 43190. Graham to Aberdeen, July 24, 1852.
4. *AP.* BM 43197. Aberdeen to Newcastle, July 25, 1852.
5. Ibid. Newcastle to Aberdeen, August 2, 1852.
6. See *GP.* BM 44372. Rev. George Trevor to Gladstone, July 5, 1852.

clarified the situation. One of Herbert's letters of a later date also indicated a reluctance to attack the Conservatives.[7] Of course, all would be changed if Aberdeen, a Conservative, were heading the Government, for they could not then be accused of abandoning their position in order to secure office.

Years later, when the fading Peelites recalled this moment in the history of their section, some of them seem to have forgotten how strongly they clung to the Conservative connection in 1852. Indeed, they leaned heavily upon it as the chief means of strengthening their own bargaining position. Lord Aberdeen's case is perhaps the most interesting. "Whig and Tory have become titles without meaning," he wrote Goulburn early in September, "and I am almost inclined to think that Conservative and Radical are growing to be cant terms, better suited to the language of the Clubs, than accurately descriptive of any great divisions of the political world."[8] But later in the month, when the question of naming the prospective political coalition and its policies came up, Lord Aberdeen thought rather differently. Russell insisted that "Whig" expressed in one syllable what "Conservative Liberal" did in seven and that the phrase "Conservative Progress" was synonymous with "Whiggism."[9] Thinking it over, Aberdeen wrote to Graham: "I cannot altogether renounce my Conservative character. I think you told the electors at Carlisle that you ceased to be a Peelite at Peel's death. Now this event makes no change in me. . . . Progress must be Conservative in principle. You may fall back upon Whiggism, in which you were bred, but I was bred at the feet of Gamaliel, and must always regard Mr. Pitt as the first of statesmen."[10]

Despite his previous commitments, both in his seating arrangements in Parliament and the party designation that he bore during the election, Graham seems also to have had second thoughts regarding the old Conservative connection. In October he was ready to cooperate with Russell as an "Opposition ally" rather than as a

---

Ross to Gladstone, July 6, 1852. Gladstone's constituents were strong supporters of Lord Derby's Government.

7. *AP. BM* 43197. Herbert to Aberdeen, October 22, 1852.

8. *AP. BM* 43196. Aberdeen to Goulburn, September 2, 1852.

9. Walpole, *Russell*, 2:156.

10. *PGRA*. 2:179–80. Aberdeen to Graham, September 27, 1852.

member of his party.[11] These were the major developments in the coalition movement before the meeting of Parliament in November.

The last act of the Free Trade–Protection drama was rapidly played out, and the mighty economic struggle ended on a note of pettiness and semantics. Charles P. Villiers gave notice of an amendment to the address in which he traced the current prosperity to the "wise, just, and beneficial" free trade legislation. Disraeli, still spokesman for the depressed agricultural interest, could not accept these "three odious epithets" and drew up an amendment to the amendment, which was unacceptable to the Free Traders. Graham and Russell proposed another, and Palmerston still another which was based on the queen's speech and the Villiers and Disraeli amendments.[12] Gladstone accepted the Palmerston version as well as did the Commons by an overwhelming majority after a lengthy debate which permitted the Free Traders to purge themselves of a seven-year accumulation of resentments against the Protectionists. Because the division had the support of Palmerston, the Peelites, and the Government, it is virtually valueless from the standpoint of revealing definite political commitments.

Once the Protection issue had been laid to rest, the Derby government was permitted to present its program for the approval or disapproval of the House. Producing a budget that would promote the free trade system and at the same time provide some relief to suffering agriculture was a most difficult undertaking, and Disraeli was unable to accomplish it. He balanced a reduction of the Schedule D income tax rates—an adjustment generally popular with the Liberals—against a halving of the malt and hops taxes, a boon to agriculture; but the plan was denounced by Gladstone as the "least conservative budget" he had ever known.[13] Thus, the leader of the Peelite section in the Commons posed as an authority upon the principles not of liberalism, but of conservatism.

When the Disraeli budget came under the close scrutiny of the House in December, it rapidly became apparent that the chances for its survival, and for that of the Conservative government, were

11. *AP.* BM 43190. Graham to Aberdeen, October 25, 1852.

12. *GP.* BM 44271. Palmerston to Gladstone, November 21, 1852; Gladstone to Palmerston, November 21, 1852.

13. *MGLD.* 1:436–38.

poor. Lord Aberdeen therefore met with Russell and Lord Lansdowne on December 15 and decided that, in the event of a crisis, Aberdeen and Lansdowne would consult with the queen.[14] To this extent the "factious coalition" charge later made by Lord Derby had a basis in fact. The Peelites and Liberals were prepared to form a government. What remained to be decided was the distribution of offices between the two groups.

The following night Gladstone delivered a massive attack upon the budget, which was followed by a 305-286 division against the Government. Under these circumstances, definite political commitments had to be made by the voting members; and, if the Conservatives of all descriptions had turned out for the division, a definitive list of Peelites might be constructed. But, unfortunately, 29 of them did not vote.[15] Those who voted against the Government, but still called themselves by some sort of modified Conservative title were as follows:

A'Court, Charles H. (Wilton)	Fitz-Roy, Henry (Lewes)
Baring, Henry B. (Marlborough)	Gladstone, William E. (Oxford Univ.)
Bruce, Ld. Ernest (Marlborough)	Goulburn, Henry (Cambridge Univ.)
Charteris, Francis (Haddingtonshire)	Graham, Sir James C. (Carlisle)
Clinton, Ld. Robert (Notts. - North)	Hamner, Sir John (Flint Dist.)
Denison, Edward B. (West Riding, Yorks.)	Harcourt, George G. V. (Oxfordshire)
Drumlanrig, Viscount (Dumfriesshire)	Heneage, George F.[16] (Lincoln)

14. Walpole, *Russell*, 2:160.

15. The absentees were Francis Baring, Thomas Baring, Thomas Bateson, Philip Bennet Jr., Henry Bruen, Lewis W. Buck, George M. Butt, Charles R. Colvile, Henry C. Compton, George Dundas, Viscount Emlyn, Sir Edward Gooch, Howel Gwyn, William W. Hawkes, Henry G. Liddle, Walter Long, William F. Mackenzie, Charles A. Moody, Sir George Montgomery, Sir Robert Peel, William E. Powell, John G. Smyth, John Stuart, Sir James E. Tennant, Frederick R. West, and Basil T. Woodd. Among the Original Peelites, John W. Patten, Edward D. Pennant, and Henry Stuart, missed the division.

16. George F. Heneage, who appears as a Protectionist and Derbyite in *Dod*, and George H. W. Heneage, identified there as a Conservative, both sat in

Herbert, Henry A (Kerry Co.)	Mostyn, Edward L. (Flintshire)
Herbert, Sidney (Wilts - South)	Mure, William (Renfrewshire)
Hervey, Ld. Alfred (Brighton)	Peel, Jonathan (Huntington Bor.)
Hogg, Sir James W. (Honiton)	Sutton, John M. (Newark)
Jermyn, Earl (Bury St. Edmunds)	Vernon, Granville H. (Newark)
Johnstone, James (Clackmannon)	Vyvyan, Sir Richard B. (Helstone)
Johnstone, Sir John V. (Scarborough)	Walter, John (Nottingham Bor.)
Legh, George C. (Cheshire - North)	Wickham, Henry W. (Bradford)
Lockhart, Allan E. (Selkirkshire)	Wortley, James S. (Buteshire)
Milnes, Richard M. (Pontefract)	Young, Sir John (Cavan)

Nineteen of these were survivors of the original 112. Fifteen others from that group voted to support Derby.

Even this small group of 34 members occasioned some dispute as to their exact political identities. Lord John Russell contended that the Peelite section consisted of only 30 members,[17] a figure he probably arrived at by subtracting Hanmer, Milnes, and Mostyn from this list (Sir John Young also identified them as Whigs), and either Henry Fitz-Roy or John Walter, both of whom had shown themselves to be strongly opposed to the Conservative government. But he was omitting from consideration a number of irregular Conservatives who might well support a Peelite-led Government.

Lord Derby realized this and probably had it in mind when he raised the "factious coalition" charge, which might discourage Conservatives from supporting the Peelites. Sir James Graham had this very much in mind when he wrote, "The severance of the more liberal portion of the Conservative county members from Lord Derby and Disraeli was of vital importance, and this was the time,

---

this Parliament. Because of the description of the former, the authors cannot bring themselves to include him among the Peelites.

17. *AP.* BM 43066. Russell to Aberdeen, December 24, 1852.

and Gladstone the person, for effecting so great a good."[18] The importance of the Conservative connection was abundantly clear to the Peelite leaders at this time. "The Cons. are strong in the country," Young warned Gladstone. "Look at what they did in the last Election. . . . Another Election with the Peelites merged in the Whig Party . . . will result in their complete triumph."[19] Aberdeen, Gladstone, Goulburn, and Herbert especially stressed the Conservative nature of their outlook and that of the Peelite section.

Thus, the situation in late 1852 would have seemed to be that the Peelites had 30 or 31 regular members and a very large potential for support among the more regular Conservatives. There were ten members who acted as regular Peelites in 1852, but who either voted with the Government in 1852 or missed the division. These included William Beckett, Henry L. Corry, William T. Egerton, William B. Hughes, Sir John Owen, John W. Patten, Sir Robert Peel, Edward D. Pennant, Alexander Smollett, Frederick R. West. Among these, Hughes and Owen showed a strong tendency to vote with whatever Government happened to be in power.

Adding these to the 31 Peelites would make a total of 41. Then there were some other irregular Conservatives, most of them new men, who called themselves just Conservative or Free Trade, Moderate or Liberal Conservative, who might be included. Neither Young nor Bonham knew quite what to expect from them, and some of the cases were wholly in doubt. For example, there was William Stirling, whom Young put in Derby's camp, but whom Bonham hoped might vote with the Peelites.[20] Another was Sir Edward S. Hayes: "Hayes' case is peculiar," Young wrote. "He is entirely with us in feeling, but has been forced by his constituents . . . to take a line much more favourable to the Govt. than he otherwise likes."[21] Young also noted that Henry L. Corry's constituents demanded that he pursue a course friendly to the Government. There were perhaps a score of these who would probably vote with the Peelites on occasion.

To these 61 must also be added some of those Conservative ir-

18. *PGRA.* 2:191–92. Graham's Journal, December 19, 1852.
19. *GP.* BM 44237. Young to Gladstone, December 13, 1852.
20. *GP.* BM 44237. Young to Gladstone, September 21, 1852.
21. Ibid. Young to Gladstone, August 10, 1852.

regulars whom we have dropped from the lists in previous years. All things considered, the Peelite leaders probably would not have been far wrong if they claimed up to sixty votes in the Commons.

Such was the state of affairs when on December 19 Lord Aberdeen, owing to the illness of Lord Lansdowne, alone visited the queen and discussed the situation created by Derby's resignation. Given the opportunity to try his hand at forming a Government, he promised "not a revival of the old Whig Cabinet," but a "liberal Conservative Government in the sense of that of Sir Robert Peel."[22]

Aberdeen was quite aware that he would have to secure the services both of Palmerston and Russell, for to exclude either one would court utter disaster. So it was that the chief critic of Palmerston's foreign policy eagerly sought his assistance at the Home Office. Palmerston at first refused, but after a conference with Clarendon decided to accept the offer. Negotiations with Russell were much more wearing, lasting as they did from December 18 to 23. Keenly disappointed at this turn of affairs that had excluded him from the highest office, Russell talked of giving out-of-office support or, at most, sitting in the cabinet without portfolio; but Aberdeen and Graham were determined that he actually take office and submit himself to his electorate. Finally, Russell agreed to accept the Foreign Office on a temporary basis with the understanding that he could relinquish it whenever he chose, and with the further understanding that he would have the succession to the headship of the Government. During all his trials ahead, Aberdeen seems never to have ceased to be grateful to Russell for reaching this agreement.

Aberdeen fulfilled his promise not to re-create a Whig Government by giving generous recognition to the Peelite section. Having a choice among several offices, Graham took the Admiralty, where he had served during 1830–34; Gladstone pleased himself and the queen[23] by taking the Exchequer from whence he had lately driven his rival Disraeli. Newcastle went to the Colonial Office, the duke of Argyll took the Privy Seal, and Herbert became secretary-at-war with a seat in the cabinet. Thus, by a curious turn of fate, the peace-loving Peelites were to bear the major responsibility for conducting naval and military operations in the Crimean War.

22. *B&EVIC*. 2:503. Memorandum by Albert, December 19, 1852.
23. *MGLD*, 1:448.

Although Aberdeen was inclined to let Russell "have his way" in the distribution of minor offices,[24] the Peelites certainly were not ignored on the below-cabinet level. Edward Cardwell became president of the Board of Trade, and Viscount Canning received the Post Office. Henry Fitz-Roy became undersecretary of state for the Home Department, and Lord Alfred Hervey and Francis Charteris became lords of the Treasury. Ireland received its quota of Peelites—the earl of St. Germans became lord lieutenant; John Young, the chief secretary; and William Keogh, now a decided Liberal rather than a Peelite, became solicitor general of Ireland. In the royal household were the duke of Wellington (lately Lord Douro), Viscount Drumlanrig, Lord Ernest Bruce, and Viscount Sydney. William Monsell, who had some Peelite support, became clerk of the ordnance.[25]

Some statesmen who had been Peelites or had hovered on the edges of the section had to be overlooked simply through lack of jobs to distribute. Aberdeen offered the duke of Buccleuch, who had been president of the Council under Peel, the mastership of the Horse, and met with a friendly and perhaps not unexpected refusal.[26] Ellenborough, who had held the Admiralty under Peel for a short time, was not offered a position, and this may have turned his thoughts once again to the Conservative party.[27] Brougham may have anticipated a call to duty. If so, it never came. Aberdeen asked Clarendon to mollify Brougham, who in the end adopted a friendly attitude toward the new Government.[28]

Accepting office in the Government meant that the Commons

24. *B&EVIC*, 2:516. Memorandum by Albert, December 25, 1852.

25. See *GP*. BM 44237. Young to Gladstone, Wednesday, 1852. Monsell was a spokesman for the Roman Catholics, and seems to have had the support of Gladstone, Newcastle, and Young.

26. *AP*. BM 43201. Aberdeen to Buccleuch, December 30, 1852; Buccleuch to Aberdeen, December 31, 1852 and January 21, 1853.

27. Ibid. Aberdeen to Ellenborough, December 30, 1852; Ellenborough to Aberdeen, December 31, 1852. In his letter Ellenborough provided an interesting review of his political career. He noted he had never been a Radical and had not been attached to the Whigs since their adventure with Canning in 1827. Among the Conservatives, he had been a conciliator and had never participated in the Peelite councils.

28. *BP*. Aberdeen to Brougham, January 7, 1853. *AP*. BM 43188. Aberdeen to Clarendon, February 8, 1853.

members had to submit themselves for reelection. Graham pleased his constituents at Carlisle, who returned him without opposition;[29] but Herbert had to reassure his Wiltshire South constituents that the new Government gave the best security for the "permanent conservation" of British institutions.[30] Edward Cardwell, beaten in the general election, managed to secure without opposition the Oxford City seat vacated by John Page Wood—a seat which carried with it the obligation to follow a very liberal line in his political conduct. Gladstone faced the stiffest test at Oxford and for a time seemed to be losing the contest, but hard work and the support of the Whigs pulled him through.[31] Thus, Gladstone and Herbert were discouraged from identifying themselves with the Liberal cause, while Graham and Cardwell found that posture politically expedient. Some of the former Peelites now identified themselves as out-and-out Liberals, but Graham and Cardwell even under these new circumstances kept a tenuous connection with the Conservative party.[32]

29. *PGRA.* 2:203–4. Graham to Dunfermline, January 2, 1853.

30. *Illustrated London News*, January 1, 1853.

31. *GP.* BM 44373. Hayter to Gladstone, January 10, 1853.

32. Cardwell was still a "Free Trade Conservative;" Graham a Conservative leaning toward the Liberal party. Sir John Hanmer, Edward L. Mostyn, Charles B. Wall, and William A. Mackinnon called themselves Liberals.

CHAPTER 21

THE PEELITES IN THE COALITION GOVERNMENT, 1853–54

During the 1853 session there was still a strong focus on concerns other than the Eastern Question, and the divisions of that year permit us to make a fairly accurate appraisal of the strength of the Peelite section in the coalition government. Eight divisions might be selected to cull the Peelites who voted together on economic, colonial, and religious questions—in that order.

The Conservative party concentrated its opposition upon two points in Gladstone's financial scheme—his extension of the income tax, upon which there was a division on May 2, 1853, and his succession duties, upon which there was a major division on June 13. The latter especially was the bête noire of Lord Derby, who regarded it as an unjust attack upon real property, already overburdened with rates.[1] During 1853, however, he seems to have encountered difficulties in calling Disraeli into action, and the Conservative opposition was not effective.

The following group of Peelites and Miscellaneous Conservatives voted with the Government on either or both of the budget divisions:[2]

Charles H. A'Court	Ld. Robert P. Clinton	William E. Gladstone
Henry B. Baring	Edmund B. Denison	Henry Goulburn
William Beckett	Viscount Drumlanrig	Sir James Graham
Lord Ernest Bruce	Edward C. Egerton	George V. Harcourt
Henry Austin Bruce	William T. Egerton	George W. Heneage
Edward Cardwell	William S. Fitz-Gerald	Henry A. Herbert
Francis Charteris	Henry Fitz-Roy	Sidney Herbert

1. Jones, Lord Derby, pp. 190–91.

2. At this point it is very difficult to devise a check list for the Peelites in the Commons because there were now many Free Trade Derbyites, and the terms "Free Trade Conservative" and "Liberal Conservative" carry little meaning. As the main reason for these lists is to try to screen through the Conservative irregulars in search of those connected with the Peelites, all of the irregulars who were previously screened out were omitted from further consideration, and as many new members as possible were added. An exception is Henry A. Herbert. He appeared as a Protectionist in 1850, but had a change of heart and was therefore returned to the list.

Lord Alfred Hervey	William Mure	John Pritchard
Sir James W. Hogg	Lord Norreys	Alexander Smollett
William B. Hughes	Sir John Owen	John M. Sutton
Earl Jermyn	John W. Patten	Granville E. Vernon
James Johnstone	Sir Robert Peel	John Walter
Sir John V. Johnstone	Edward D. Pennant	Henry W. Wickham
George C. Legh	John H. Philipps	James S. Wortley
Allan E. Lockhart	Robert J. Phillimore	John Young

Among the new names on this list, perhaps the one most entitled to be associated with the Peelites was John Pritchard (Bridgnorth, 1853), who called himself a Conservative who supported Peel's policy.

Passing on to the divisions on colonial issues, one of these involved the government of India, which found the parties hopelessly confused. Derby approved the Government's measure as favorable to the East India Company—a "good Tory group," he called it—but his son, Edward Stanley, with some Radical support, moved on June 30 that the Government lacked sufficient information to legislate on the subject. None of the members on the list above came to Stanley's support, and he was overwhelmed. On the other colonial issue—the Clergy Reserves in Canada—Lord Derby took a very firm stand against the measure brought in by the Government.

The Canadian legislature sought control of the Clergy Reserves, and the conciliatory colonial policy then being followed by all parties in England would have dictated acquiescence to their request; but Derby and many other Conservatives feared that these church lands might be secularized if such permission were granted. The Conservatives, therefore, moved an outright rejection of the Government's measure both on March 4 and April 11. The Peelite section responded by casting 39 votes for the Government; only five of its members voted with the Conservatives. Obviously the section did not believe that the secularization of these lands was injurious to the Church's interests.

The religious attitudes of the 1853 Peelite section were clearly revealed in the divisions relating to the Maynooth College grant and the Jewish Relief Bill. Opposition to the granting of funds to the Roman Catholic Maynooth College had not been in the Conservative tradition—Peel had continued such grants, and Lord Derby himself in 1853 was not prepared to abandon them; but in the post–Papal Aggression atmosphere in Britain, the Maynooth policy was not popular, and the more extreme Protestants decided to meet the issue head-on by proposing a repeal of the Maynooth grants. The only consistent Peelite to vote for repeal was James S. Wortley, but some Peelites obviously felt it politically wise to avoid the division. As it was, 25 Peelite votes were cast to sustain the Maynooth system, certainly not a very heavy turnout.

There were two divisions on the Jewish Relief measure, on March 11 and April 15, both of which involved its outright rejection. As many Peelites voted against as for the the measure and proved once again that religious liberalism was not characteristic of the Peelite section as a whole.

If we use the 25 Peelites who voted for Jewish Relief as a base and add the members who usually voted with them on other issues (marked with an asterisk), the Peelite section in 1853 would appear as follows:

(2)	Charles H. A'Court*	(1)	Sir James W. Hogg
(1)	Henry B. Baring	(2)	William B. Hughes*
(1)	Ld. Ernest Bruce*	(1)	Earl Jermyn
(1)	Henry Austin Bruce*	(1)	Sir John Johnstone
(1)	Edward Cardwell	(1)	George C. Legh*
(2)	Francis Charteris	(1)	Allan E. Lockhart
(2)	Ld. Robert Clinton	(2)	William Mure
(4)	Viscount Drumlanrig	(3)	Lord Norreys
(1)	William T. Egerton*	(3)	Sir John Owen
(2)	William Fitz-Gerald	(1)	John W. Patten*
(1)	Henry Fitz-Roy	(1)	Sir Robert Peel*
(2)	William E. Gladstone	(1)	Robert Phillimore
(1)	Henry Goulburn	(5)	John Pritchard*
(2)	Sir James Graham	(1)	John M. Sutton
(3)	George V. Harcourt	(2)	Granville E. Vernon
(3)	George W. Heneage*	(2)	John Walter
(1)	Henry A. Herbert	(2)	Henry W. Wickham
(1)	Sidney Herbert	(1)	James S. Wortley
(1)	Ld. Alfred Hervey	(1)	John Young.

The numbers preceding the names provide a key to their identifications in *Dod*.[3] Although these 38 members were the reliable Peelites

3. The above numbers may be interpreted as follows: (1) "Free Trade Conservative"; (2) "Liberal Conservative"; (3) "Conservative"; (4) "Liberal Tory";

of the 1853 session, it must be stressed over and over again that they often had Conservatives of various descriptions voting with them on the divisions, so that their strength exceeded this modest number.

Before and during the 1854 session the Peelite section experienced some gains, and there was one name change which must be noted. Francis Charteris became Lord Elcho in 1854 but stayed in the Commons. A former Peelite, Thomas Greene, managed to find a seat at Lancaster late in the 1853 session and was on hand for the divisions of 1854, as was Roundell Palmer, another fairly dependable Peelite, who was returned to Parliament for Plymouth in June, 1853.[4] The earl of Dalkeith (Edinburghshire), Sir Michael H. Hicks-Beach (Gloucestershire - East), Henry Thomas Liddell (Liverpool), John Robert Mowbray (Durham City), and Jonathan Joseph Richardson (Lisburn) were returned under various irregular Conservative labels which might indicate their Peelite potential; but in most cases, it was not realized.

The session of 1854 was, of course, dominated by the Crimean War; and if party warfare were not called off altogether, it appears to have been abated considerably, and the divisions of the year were of considerable interest, but not of overriding importance. There was a minor political issue raised on March 20, 1854, when Disraeli opposed granting leave to bring in a bill to prevent bribery at the Canterbury city elections. It was not an important division, and the Peelite section turned out only 20 votes for the winning majority; but one might assume that those irregular Conservatives who would join Disraeli on a division of this nature could hardly be classed as Peelites.[5]

Who would pay for the war? How would it be paid for? These were much more important questions, involving as they did Peelite

---

(5) "Peelite Conservative." The first three of these titles were borne also by such members as George M. Butt (1), Robert Laffan (2), and Sir Edward S. Hayes (3), all of whom voted against the Government on almost every occasion they cast their votes.

4. As *Hansard* usually did not distinguish Roundell Palmer from another member with the same initials, it is often impossible to be sure how he voted in 1854.

5. These would include James Baird, Sir Michael Hicks-Beach, Sir Edward C. Dering, Thomas B. Horsfall, Henry G. Liddle, Henry T. Liddell, John R. Mowbray, and Basil T. Woodd [sic].

concepts of finance; and the two divisions on this general issue are of help in identifying the members of the Peelite section in 1854. The first of these came on May 9 when Disraeli opposed a 50 percent increase in the Malt Duties, which would press on the agricultural interest, already burdened with rates. The second was an attempt to limit the issue of Exchequer Bonds, which occurred on May 22. These divisions permit the culling of members of the section who approved Gladstone's finance proposals. The 46 are as follows:[6]

Charles H. A'Court	Sir James Graham	John W. Patten
Henry B. Baring	Thomas Greene	Sir Robert Peel
William Beckett	George W. Heneage	Edward D. Pennant
Lord Ernest Bruce	Henry A. Herbert	John H. Philipps
Henry Austin Bruce	Sidney Herbert	Robert J. Phillimore
Edward Cardwell	Lord Alfred Hervey	Jonathan J. Richardson
Ld. Robert Clinton	Sir James W. Hogg	Alexander Smollett
Earl of Dalkeith	William B. Hughes	William Stirling
Edmund B. Denison	Earl Jermyn	John M. Sutton
Viscount Drumlanrig	James Johnstone	Granville E. Vernon
William T. Egerton	Sir John Johnstone	John Walter
Lord Elcho	George C. Legh	Henry W. Wickham
William S. Fitz-Gerald	Allan E. Lockhart	James S. Wortley
Henry Fitz-Roy	William Mure	John Young
William E. Gladstone	Lord Norreys	
Henry Goulburn	Sir John Owen	

They were substantially the same group who had upheld the Government the previous year on its budget.

The Peelite section approached the reform of Oxford University gingerly. There were two divisions on the same night (May 1), the first of which involved naming the members of a proposed commission, mainly a party question; and they provided 32 votes in support of the Government. But when the Conservatives raised the question of selecting, rather than electing, the Hebdomadal Council, the Peelites furnished only 21 votes for the elective principle. By and large, however, party differences over this particular reform were adjusted quietly enough.

6. Curiously, four of the irregular Conservatives—Edward C. Egerton, Thomas B. Horsfall, Henry G. Liddle, and John R. Mowbray—refused to support Disraeli on the Malt Duties division, but voted with him against the Exchequer Bonds. This seems to divorce them completely from the agricultural interest.

Religious divisions had in the past often left the Peelite section raw and bleeding, and those of the war year were no exception. On February 28, the coalition government opposed a motion to inquire into the increasing number of monasteries and convents in Britain, which the mover contended were hostile to free government. The Government was beaten by a thumping 186-119 margin, and in the majority were not only Peelite names often associated with a cautious religious policy, such as Alexander Smollett and James S. Wortley, but simon-pure Peelites such as Henry Fitz-Roy and Sir John V. Johnstone. The division seemed to bring out a latent conservatism still present in some of the more consistent Peelites.

Later in the year the Commons was called upon to vote on a major revision of the parliamentary oath designed to remove objections raised both by Jews and Catholics. The former Peelite Sir Frederic Thesiger declared that the revision was detrimental to the Protestant constitution and the supremacy of the Sovereign, and the House followed him by a 247-251 margin. Among those who agreed with Thesiger were Thomas Greene, a faithful Peelite, and two newer Peelites, George W. Heneage and John H. Philipps, who had become regular voters with the section. Their rejection of a bill of this nature caused *The Times* some amusement.[7]

Once again, if we are to describe a Peelite section of any size in 1854, we must overlook the votes of a large number of the group on these religious divisions. Indeed, if we were to limit membership in the Peelite section to those who had been present and voting against the convents and monasteries motion and in favor of the Oaths Bill, their ranks would be thin indeed.[8] But if we disregard irregularity or absence on these divisions, the Peelite section appears to have increased from 38 members in 1853 to 49 in 1854. To the 46 names listed above as voting together on the financial divisions should probably be added those of John Pritchard and George G. V. Harcourt, who were often absent, and that of Roundell Palmer, whom *Hansard*

7. The newspaper noted: "Instead of the Jews falling into the hands of the Norman barons, they have met their fate from the Saxon churls of the Lower House. . . . We are concerned for the Lords. What will they do without their annual pastime?" *The Times*, May 26, 1854.

8. Such a list would include Lord Ernest Bruce, Henry A. Bruce, Lord Elcho, William E. Gladstone, Sir James Graham, Sidney Herbert, Earl Jermyn, Jonathan J. Richardson, and John Young.

did not often enough distinguish in its lists from Robert Palmer, a Conservative. Many other irregular Conservatives, perhaps more or less friendly to the Peelite government, often voted with the section; and, while it did not appear to be developing into a major party, it provided vital voting strength for the Government on many important divisions.[9]

According to Trevelyan, Peel and Gladstone introduced into British public life a conscientious and liberal tone, which was neither Tory nor Whig and which "still survives" at Whitehall."[10] This Peelite approach to administration, which made them in the eyes of their contemporaries the most brilliant administrators of their day, was a major reason for their political prestige and made them welcome additions to any government.

Just how capable were the Peelites in the field of administration? A recent study deals with the coalition in detail,[11] and there is no need to go over it again, but a brief consideration of this important question could hardly be avoided in a study of this nature.

The duke of Argyll, who was welcomed by the Whigs because of his connection with the Sutherland family and his debating ability,[12] took the office of Privy Seal, which, he noted, had "absolutely no ad-

9. Some reference must be made to the much more "Liberal" list of Peelite members which appears in Conacher, *The Aberdeen Coalition*, pp. 556–57, and which is based on voting records and perhaps some other unidentified sources. Many names appear on both lists, and the differences should be explained briefly. Conacher includes Sir John Hanmer, Sir Thomas Franklin Lewis, Robert B. Lowe, Richard B. Milnes, Viscount Monck, Edward L. Mostyn, Frederick Peel, and Charles B. Wall, all of whom (save for Milnes) appear as Liberals in *Dod* during 1853–55 and were therefore omitted from the list furnished herein. On the other hand, Conacher includes George Feschi Heneage, who was not included, because in 1853 he was identified in *Dod* as a general supporter of Derby, and who during the whole 1853–55 era mentioned his censure of Free Trade—the binding force of the Peelite movement—in November, 1852. The list in this book also contains a number of Original Peelites and irregular Conservatives, who, like Goulburn, voted with the Government on economic and financial matters but showed a tendency to desert on the religious divisions. Our list, therefore, is much more "Conservative" than that of Conacher and reflects the basic assumption that the Peelite movement was an aspect of British Conservatism rather than Liberalism. Thus former Peelites are dropped whenever they seem to have severed their last ties with the Conservative party.

10. Trevelyan, *The Nineteenth Century*, p. 269.

11. Conacher, *The Aberdeen Coalition*, passim.

12. Ibid., p. 22.

ministrative duties."[13] His services to the Government were limited to offering advice on such diverse subjects as the East India Company Charter, the income tax, and the projected peace terms with Russia;[14] but after the break-up of the coalition, it would not be unfair to say that he had yet to establish his reputation in the field of administration.

The details of Edward Cardwell's administration of the Board of Trade are also given effectively enough elsewhere.[15] Like other Peelite administrators, Cardwell would intervene in business affairs to promote efficiency and the public interest, but preferred to leave most matters to local jurisdictions rather than to extend the powers of the central government. His term at the Board of Trade was distinguished by the huge Merchant Shipping Act of 1854, which placed the supervision of merchant ships and seamen under the Board of Trade and gave Britain its first code of maritime law. His Railway and Canal Traffic Act of 1854 has been described as a rather innocuous piece of legislation, which, while useful, failed to protect the public in railway accidents. Unusually conscientious attention to minute details established Cardwell as an effective administrator, but his accomplishments were not of a showy sort, and only Graham seems to have appreciated fully his work in the cabinet.[16] It might be added, however, that his "business as usual" policy during the Crimean War, which permitted trade even between Britain and Russia, was popular with the Radicals, who deplored the trade interruptions occasioned by national conflicts.

Professor Conacher accepts the traditional view that Gladstone's budget of 1853 was one of the great budgets of the century,[17] and there is no reason to contest this decision, even though Gladstone had some distinguished predecessors.[18] In drawing up his scheme Gladstone had some help from Goulburn, whose health prevented

13.   Duchess of Argyll, ed., *George Douglas, Eighth Duke of Argyll*, 1:372.
14.   Ibid., pp. 418–20, 385–86, 488–94.
15.   Arvel B. Erickson, *Edward T. Cardwell: Peelite*, pp. 12–20.
16.   Erickson, *Cardwell*, p. 19.
17.   Conacher, *The Aberdeen Coalition*, p. 77.
18.   Certainly Frederick John Robinson's pioneer budget of 1824 must also receive a high ranking. This is mentioned because Gladstone was reluctant to acknowledge any debt to Robinson (then Ripon) when the latter was his superior at the Board of Trade. See Jones, *Prosperity Robinson*, p. 241.

his joining the Government,[19] and from Cardwell as well as a special committee on which Argyll served. It was a splendid example of Peelite daring, ingenuity, and capacity for detail—especially the first —for in his budget Gladstone ignored the wishes of political friend and foe alike. On the one hand, he angered business and professional people by refusing to admit the distinction between "precarious" and "permanent" incomes in the income tax; and, on the other, he affronted the landed interest by extending the succession tax— heretofore confined to personal property—to real property. With more optimism than prescience, he provided for the reduction of the income tax by stages until it would be abandoned in 1860, which pleased the Conservatives. The Free Traders were attracted by his elimination of a large number of tariffs, while the poor benefited by the lowering of the tea tax and the abolition of the tax on soap. Gladstone labored hard to force his budget first through the cabinet, then through the Commons,[20] only to have all of his calculations upset the following year by the increased expenses of the war. Gladstone believed that the practical expenses of fighting acted as a check on the ambitions of conquerors,[21] and he brought home the financial waste of the war to the British people by instituting a "pay-as-you-go" type of war financing, which doubled the income tax and raised the taxes on spirits, sugar, and malt.

Sir James Graham had established his reputation as an administrator during his previous term at the Admiralty, which he turned into a "model department" in comparison with the War Office.[22] Curiously, his Admiralty budget, presented on February 18, called for increased wages, victuals, and naval stores and had a "preparedness" aura around it, while that of Gladstone, submitted later in the session, was very definitely a peacetime budget. The explanation of this queer sequence of events seems to be that Graham prepared his estimates during a period of tension with France, which was over late in March,[23] and that Gladstone's budget was drawn up before the East-

19.　GOP. II–24. Gladstone to Goulburn, March 17, 1853.

20.　See *MGLD*, 1:457–75, and Conacher, *The Aberdeen Coalition*, pp. 58–78.

21.　Philip Magnus, *Gladstone*, p. 115.

22.　K. B. Smellie, *A Hundred Years of English Government*, p. 61.

23.　"Walewski was over here," Clarendon wrote, "& cd. not help admitting

ern Question became menacing.[24] Unless some such explanation is
accepted, one must draw a contrast—painful to devotees of Gladstone—between the abilities of these two statesmen to prepare for
future contingencies.

The details of Graham's work at the Admiralty during this period
can be found elsewhere;[25] suffice it here to note that he passed his
test as an administrator with flying colors. From the standpoint
of mobilizing a striking force for war purposes, Graham's record was
nothing short of brilliant;[26] and there were on hand early in 1854 two
splendid fleets of unsurpassed strength for that day and age,[27] but
there was little he could do to control the employment of the
naval arm once it had passed into the war zone. The commander in
charge of operations in the Black Sea area in 1854 was aging Admiral
Dundas, whom Graham did not appoint or even approve;[28] and
in the Baltic theater of operations, Graham had to choose between
Sir Charles Napier and two others, one of whom was in failing health,
and the other was one year away from being an octogenarian. The
meager results of their operations could hardly be charged to mis-
takes of Admiralty administration, but public expectations of brilliant
victories had been aroused by the press; and Graham to some extent
shared in the widespread disapprobation of the conduct of naval
operations.

Because of the difficulties he encountered in his conduct of the
Crimean War, the policies and services of the duke of Newcastle at

---

that his Govt. have behaved foolishly for themselves, & improperly towards us"
(*AP*. BM 43188. Clarendon to Aberdeen, March 25, 1853). This probably
marked the end of the tension with France.

24. "It was not till the 26th of April 1853 that we received a despatch,"
Argyll wrote, "which at last left no doubt that Russia was deliberately deceiving
us" (Argyll, *Duke of Argyll*, 1:444). This helps pinpoint the onset of the Eastern
crisis.

25. Erickson, *Graham*, pp. 336–39; Conacher, *Aberdeen Coalition*, pp.
251–56.

26. See *The Times*, January 23, 1854, and the *Standard*, August 30, 1854.
Graham was not only a highly effective administrator, but displayed the customary Peelite concern for saving money.

27. Charles D. Yonge, *The History of the British Navy from the Earliest
Times to the Present Time*, 3:290.

28. *PGRA*, 2:251. Graham to Aberdeen, October 7, 1854.

the Colonial Office have received little emphasis in the past.[29] As the colonial secretary he faithfully carried out a number of policies— disengagement in areas of peripheral importance to the empire, economy in colonial administration, and, closely related to both, the extension wherever possible of self-government—a project long dear to the heart of his colleague, Sir William Molesworth.

Newcastle struck the economy-in-government theme in his colonial budget of 1853-54, which made modest increases in funds for emigration purposes and gave some succor to poverty-stricken Gambia, but slashed expenses in many areas for a saving of £15,000. Some of his cuts may seem picayune in the free-spending twentieth century, such as discontinuing the allowances of the bishop of Quebec for visits to the Magdalen Islands in the St. Lawrence[30] and discontinuing the presents traditionally given to the Indians of the Six Nations and Port Credit;[31] but another economy decision—the abandonment of the sovereignty over the Orange River Boer State in South Africa—had far-reaching consequences.

Newcastle listened willingly to colonial requests for increased self-government, which meant shifting to local shoulders many of the expensive and tiresome responsibilities hitherto borne by the Mother Country. One case of this nature that came before Newcastle involved Newfoundland, a poor fishing colony inhabited by 106,000 people, half Protestant and half Catholic, scattered over a wide area. When their assembly demanded responsible government in January, 1853, Newcastle recognized the difficulties inherent in the situation;[32] but he was ready to grant their request, provided that Newfoundland reorganized its government along the lines of that in Prince Edward Island. As it turned out, Newfoundland did not act on his suggestion,[33] and responsible government was not granted. The wisdom of his caution was later to be demonstrated when the island received responsible government and went bankrupt.

A request in 1853 by the Canadian Assembly to make the legisla-

---

29. The only available biography of the Duke is by John Martineau—*The Life of Henry Pelham, 5th Duke of Newcastle, 1811–1864.*

30. CO. 42–390 (Canada). Rowan to Newcastle, December 21, 1853.

31. CO. 42–594 (Canada). Rowan to Newcastle, February 4, 1854.

32. CO. 194–139 (Newfoundland). Newcastle Minute, January 31, 1854.

33. CO. 194–141 (Newfoundland). Hamilton to Newcastle, June 14, 1854.

tive council elective provides an excellent example of Newcastle's thinking regarding colonial self-government.[34] As he saw it, Britain might grant the request in one of two ways—the Canadian Assembly might pass a law which would be reviewed by Parliament, or Parliament might pass an act granting the Assembly power to deal with the Legislative Council as they chose. Newcastle chose the latter course because "it would imply greater confidence in the Colonial Legislature. It would remove the possibility of future antagonism between the Imperial & Colonial Parlts."[35] He was most anxious to maintain the principle "of non-interference in the domestic legislation of the Colony by the Parliament of Great Britain."

Noninterference, however, did not mean lack of interest or noninvolvement in the problems of the colonies. Newcastle obviously approached these problems with an open mind, as in the case of New Zealand, which was required by law to pay certain sums to the defunct New Zealand Company. How to enforce payment? The new New Zealand government, whose constitution had come into operation on January 17, 1853, refused to pay; and Newcastle considered the problem down to his last day at the Colonial Office. "The Colony will certainly resist, and we have no power to enforce," he wrote, "—and in my judgement the grievance is a very real one. . . . I fear no settlement can be effected without a demand on the Imperial Exchequer."[36]

In the West Indies, Newcastle was no more successful in coping with the economic and racial problems than his predecessors had been, but his failure was not due to lack of attention. Having lost their slave labor through emancipation in 1833 and their preferential market in Britain with the adoption of free trade, the planters there had difficulty in competing with other sugar-growing areas. The standard solution to the problem (not a very effective one) proposed by the Free Traders was to increase the labor supply; and Newcastle, sharing in this view, passed the Passenger Act of 1853, which substantially reduced the cost (borne by the planters) of Indian labor brought into the West Indies via Hong Kong. The same year he

34.   CO. 42–589 (Canada). Elgin to Newcastle, July 1, 1853.

35.   CO. 42–390. (Canada). Newcastle's Notes on Rowan to Newcastle, December 31, 1853.

36.   CO. 209–122 (New Zealand). Newcastle's Minute, June 12, 1854.

projected a comprehensive reform of the Jamaican government, but granting responsible government at the time did not seem practicable; and in the immediate future the course of the West Indies was in the opposite direction.

On one of those rare occasions when Newcastle chose to ignore a colonial problem, the result was to link his name with one of the more dramatic incidents in early Australian history. The gold rushes in New South Wales and Victoria had brought many adventuresome and politically-minded fortuneseekers to these colonies; and the two colonies were frequently at odds regarding the digging fees to be imposed upon them, which encouraged the miners to resist paying them. On a dispatch from the governor of New South Wales, noting that the lieutenant governor of Victoria had proposed the abolition of fees, Newcastle wrote: "The evils are unavoidably great & inseparable from the system of Govt. but they might be mitigated by the judgement & intercommunication of the Governors."[37] Then, on a later dispatch, he observed: "The less written upon the subject the better."[38] The next year the exploited miners of Victoria staged their short-lived but historic Bakery Hill rebellion.

These glimpses of Newcastle at work in the Colonial Office reveal an earnest and conscientious administrator, and this impression is confirmed when one goes through the dispatches and discovers that the colonial secretary read and commented upon almost all of them. Only rarely did he leave this time-consuming work to his subordinates Frederick Peel and Herman Merivale. On one such occasion involving charges brought against a New Zealand judge, Newcastle wrote: "With my present duties, it is obviously impossible for me to read through such a case as this, and I feel I may approve of Mr. Merivale's and Mr. Peel's Minutes without attempting it."[39] This "case" ran through a hundred pages of evidence!

This attention to detail, sympathy for the problems of the colonists and their desire for responsible government, and eagerness to improve the administrative structure of the empire confirm Stanmore's

37. CO. 201–466 (New South Wales). Newcastle's Notes on Fitzroy to Newcastle, October 4, 1853.

38. CO. 201–467 (New South Wales). Newcastle's Notes on Fitzroy to Newcastle, November 17, 1853.

39. CO. 209–117. (New Zealand). Newcastle's "Note on Grey" to Newcastle, October 4, 1853.

conclusion that Newcastle was an "excellent Colonial Minister."[40] Had he chosen in 1854 to give up the War, rather than the
Colonial, Office, Newcastle would have gone down in history as an
exemplary Peelite administrator; but he was the most bellicose of the
Peelite high command and an early member of the "war party" in
the cabinet. So Newcastle made the wrong choice and gave up the
colonies. His troubles began the moment he ceased ideologically to
be a Peelite.

Smellie's brief description of the administrative structure of the
War Office illuminates the situation which led to the Crimea debacle
in the winter of 1854–55.[41] General control of the army and even its
military strategy was vested in the secretary of state for war and the
colonies, and his civilian assistants. But the secretary at war (at this
time, Sidney Herbert) drew up the estimates for army expenditures;
the master general and Board of Ordnance supplied matériel upon
the request of the secretary for war or the chancellor of the Exchequer; the Commissariat provisioned the army when it was living
abroad; the Board of General Officers clothed the infantry and
cavalry; the commander-in-chief was responsible for army discipline
inside Britain; and the home secretary was responsible for the use
of the army at home. This chaotic division of responsibility existed
when the Crimean War broke out in 1854.

Newcastle bore the ultimate responsibility for the operations of
the army in the Crimea, and Sidney Herbert merely checked expenditures. The latter, however, could make reforms and innovations and
exercise administrative authority in carrying them out, so it is in this
area that the historian must delve to secure his impression of Herbert
as an administrator. What did Herbert do to make the army a more
effective fighting force? His biographer notes that he secured the
early adoption of the Enfield rifle, created the first permanent en-
campment for the training of troops, expanded the educational opportunities of both officers and men, and in 1854 began to abandon
the brevet system of promotions, so that ability as well as seniority
might be weighed in certain cases.[42] These were obviously salutary
reforms, for in 1853 the army was in desperately poor shape, led by

40. *SHER.* 1:224.
41. Smellie, *English Government*, pp. 59–61.
42. *SHER.* 1:175–78, 231–33.

officers who had purchased their commissions, often inexperienced in battle or even war games.

Given Herbert's strictly limited areas of responsibility, his record at the War Office seems fairly impressive, but some other aspects of his administration tend to place evidence on the debit side of the ledger. His budget of 1853 stressed economy, asked for no increases in manpower, and was in no sense a preparedness budget. When, during the debate on the budget, Joseph Hume suggested that a single minister should be responsible for the whole department, Herbert replied that this was both impossible and undesirable.[43] Although his budget of 1854, submitted on the eve of actual hostilities, provided for a 11,000-man increase in the army, Herbert's major interest —laudable enough under other circumstances—was in educating the soldiers and improving the lot of enlisted men. At this same moment, in the Lords, Newcastle discouraged discussions of the condition of the army and its plans. Neither Herbert nor Newcastle seems to have provided dynamic leadership in preparing the army for the tasks ahead.

When the war actually broke out, Herbert's position was a false one—he helped direct the war effort without sharing the responsibility for success or failure.[44] But as late as April, 1854, Newcastle opposed any changes in the cumbersome system while the war was in progress.[45]

At the very time Newcastle was upholding the old system, Lord John Russell was trying to induce Aberdeen to make major changes in it, changes which would strengthen the position of the Whigs in the government. In May he proposed that Newcastle should keep the Colonies, give the War Office to Palmerston, and that Lord Grey should succeed Palmerston in the Home Office.[46] When Aberdeen suggested that Newcastle be mollified by receiving the Garter, Russell replied that Lord Grey was as much deserving of that honor and to award it to Newcastle would be an "affront to the Whig Party"[47]— evidence that in Russell's mind no "fusion" of parties had taken place.

43. *Hansard*, 3d ser., 124:670 ff.
44. *SHER*. 1:226.
45. *Hansard*, 3d ser., 132:639 ff.
46. *AP. BM* 43068. Russell to Aberdeen, May 29, 1854.
47. *AP. BM* 43068. Russell to Aberdeen, May 29, 1854.

In this situation Aberdeen made the wrong choice. He let Newcastle remain at the War Office and gave the Colonies to Sir George Grey.[48]

This long-overdue splitting of the two offices was accomplished in June, 1854, but it was merely half a reform, for Herbert remained in the ambiguous position of secretary at war. Russell was still not satisfied and in November of the same year sought to have Palmerston replace Newcastle and to abolish the office of secretary at war.[49] What major changes in domestic politics might have resulted from the acceptance of this proposition by Aberdeen! No one, not even Palmerston, could have warded off the disaster that struck the Crimean Army that same month; but the obloquy would have fallen on Palmerston rather than Newcastle, and one can hardly doubt but that the future prime minister's whole career would have been adversely affected by it.

One of the more effective defenses of the activities of the War Office during 1854 is provided by Stanmore.[50] He presented evidence to prove that the Crimean Army was well fed, that a temporary shortage of warm clothing stemmed from the unavoidable loss of certain transports in a hurricane, and that the chief difficulty did not lie in lack of supplies, but in transport. As one member of Parliament observed, supplies aplenty were shipped 3,000 miles; but they were needed 3,006 miles away, and the breakdown in the system lay in transporting them from the port at Balaklava to the camp six miles inland. Stanmore noted that this deficiency was due partly to the starvation of horses, which, in turn, was traced in part to Gladstone's ignoring a suggestion to ship out an extra 2,000 tons of hay.[51]

But when all explanations are considered and allowances are made, the chaotic manner in which war supplies were embarked from England and the even more confused distribution system that existed in the Crimea, not to mention specific shortages, called into question the administrative abilities of Newcastle and Herbert and left a strong

48. Palmerston was quite willing to relinquish some of the home secretary's control of army matters to the new secretary for war. See ibid. BM 43069. Palmerston to Aberdeen, July 8, 1854.

49. *NP.* 10295. Russell to Aberdeen, November 17, 1854.

50. *SHER.* 1:271–330.

51. *SHER.* 1:293–94.

impression of ineptitude in the very area in which the Aberdeen administration had been expected to excel.[52]

52. This brief survey of the administrative accomplishments of the Peelites necessarily omitted some reforms and improvements in which other cabinet officers shared. Conacher provides an effective coverage of such major reforms as the India Act of 1853, civil service reform, and the Oxford University Reform Act in his recent work on the Aberdeen coalition. Another work which deals with the origins of the civil service in Britain is by J. Donald Kingsley: *Representative Bureaucracy*, pp. 52 ff.

CHAPTER 22

LORD ABERDEEN AS PRIME MINISTER

Even more than the unfortunate duke of Newcastle, Lord Aberdeen has been stigmatized as an administrative failure. If one examines some of the better-known texts in British history, he is likely to find Aberdeen damned with faint praise by some but rejected as a failure by others. Marriott was kind enough to notice his high endowments and unimpeachable character before adding that Aberdeen "failed to overcome the difficulties of a difficult situation and a critical time."[1] Woodward noted that Aberdeen was not master of his cabinet and, being vacillating and irresolute, depended on the advice of others.[2] Keith Feiling has called him "weak and pacific,"[3] and Arnstein noted that under his leadership Britain drifted quietly into war.[4] Conacher correctly observed that Aberdeen had the misfortune to head the first British wartime administration that operated under the glare of newspaper publicity and sometimes adopted a more sympathetic attitude toward the prime minister, but he concluded that Aberdeen was neither naturally a man of business nor a war leader.[5] Certainly this last observation is proved beyond doubt, but there are still facets of the Aberdeen story that deserve stronger emphasis if full justice is to be done to him both as a leader and a figure in British history.

Although some writers have stressed that major decisions within the cabinet did not reveal divisions according to party lines,[6] one might raise a serious question regarding the extent to which the coalition actually coalesced; and this is of decisive importance in any interpretation of Lord Aberdeen's qualities of leadership. Although Newcastle, Argyll, and Aberdeen at times noted that harmony existed in the cabinet, there were two unbridgeable divisions—one political,

1. Marriott, *England Since Waterloo*, pp. 224, 237–38.
2. Woodward, *Age of Reform*, pp. 262–64.
3. Keith Feiling, *A History of England*, pp. 907–8.
4. Walter L. Arnstein, *Britain Yesterday and Today*, pp. 96–98.
5. Conacher, *Aberdeen Coalition*, pp. 550–53.
6. Ibid., p. 232.

the other ideological—that were to sharply circumscribe Aberdeen's freedom of action and to constantly thwart his efforts to exercise the leadership to which his position entitled him. During the whole period of his administration, Lord John Russell, leader of a section far more numerous than Aberdeen's own, stood at his elbow, impatiently awaiting his retirement, which would return leadership to the Whigs. He was at all times alert for opportunities to advance the Whig interest.

The ideological conflict was one which Aberdeen had realized ever since the Maine Boundary aftermath, if not before. Although historians tend to make Palmerston more bellicose than he actually was and Aberdeen more yielding than was really the case, there can be no question but that they differed sharply regarding the proper use of threat and menace in the conduct of international affairs. Aberdeen certainly knew this. If so, then why did he ever decide to sit in a cabinet with Palmerston? The answer seems to be simple enough —he desired to be prime minister; and as of late 1852 Aberdeen had no reason to anticipate that such a crushing issue in foreign policy would shortly arise.

This would seem to lead to another important question, When this unanticipated issue arose in acute form, why did not Aberdeen retire from his untenable position? The answer to this is that he probably did not consider his position untenable, for it was buttressed by three factors—his own considerable prestige in international affairs, his belief that Russia was not seeking a war and would compromise, and the support he had a right to expect from the Peelites in his cabinet. Feeling as he probably did that his resignation would undermine the chances for peace, Aberdeen stayed on and lived out a pathetic story of a pacifist being forced by circumstances beyond his control into war.

When the dispute between Russia and France over the Holy Places reached some intensity in March, 1853, Aberdeen advised Clarendon that Britain would give no commitment to France and would try to preserve Turkish integrity only as one of the powers bound by the general treaty.[7] Clarendon from the first put the worst possible interpretation upon Russian motives and guessed that she "clearly intends

---

7. *AP.* BM 43188. Aberdeen to Clarendon, March 21, 1853.

to humiliate L. Napoleon as well as the Sultan."[8] Only five days later the foreign secretary noted he had been wrong. Russia had opened friendly communications with France, and the latter admitted she had acted foolishly.[9] Later in the month Aberdeen advised Clarendon that he should try to promote close relations with Austria as well as with Russia and France.[10]

In May the well-known quarrel between Russia and Turkey over the former's "ancient rights" to protect the Christians in the Turkish Empire entered an acute phase, which led to the Russian ambassador's departure from Constantinople on May 21. This act of diplomatic coercion found the cabinet in doubt as to Russia's intentions. Following the line he had adopted earlier in the year, Aberdeen urged multilateral negotiations in which Prussia and Austria would also be involved as the best means of clarifying Russian intentions. But Russia's act had reawakened deep suspicions among the more warlike members of the cabinet, who looked with favor upon the French policy of escalation of the crisis by employing the fleets of the two nations as a bilateral threat. In an undated letter, perhaps written on May 23, Clarendon suggested that Admiral Dundas be ordered to join the French fleet at Salamis, so that the two could cruise toward Turkish waters. "I recommend this as the least measure that will satisfy public opinion," he added, "& save the Govt. from shame hereafter if, as I firmly expect, the Russian hordes pour into Turkey on every side."[11]

Aberdeen was reluctant to go along: "I cannot yet believe that it will be necessary to do so [resist Russian demands] by war," he wrote on May 30, "if the Emperor should hitherto have been acting in good faith; if his whole conduct should have been a cheat, the case is altered."[12] A cabinet meeting was duly held on the subject of the fleet movement, and at this meeting Aberdeen was overborne —all he could obtain was the shadow of a compromise. "The Cabinet, or at least a portion of it," he wrote on June 1, "appears to wish that the fleet should sail without waiting to know on what footing Russia

8.   Ibid. Clarendon to Aberdeen, March 20, 1853.
9.   Ibid. Clarendon to Aberdeen, March 25, 1853.
10. Ibid. Aberdeen to Clarendon, March 29, 1853.
11. *AP.* BM 43188. Clarendon to Aberdeen, Monday night.
12. Ibid. Aberdeen to Clarendon, May 30, 1853.

& the Porte have been placed by the rupture of the negotiation. I do not object to this; but I think you should communicate frankly to Russia the motive and spirit of our movement. It is possible that the step we shall have taken may not destroy our salutary influence as much as I fear."[13] Aberdeen's great difficulty was his inability to present to the cabinet indicative proofs of the pacific intentions of Russia. Perhaps these would be forthcoming later; then he might have his way. Meanwhile, he was forced to go along with the escalation; otherwise, Palmerston, Russell, Landsdowne, Clarendon, and Newcastle would have resigned from the cabinet and ousted him both from power and from the position in which he might yet prevent the outbreak of war. So the fleet on June 2 was dispatched to Besika Bay outside the Dardanelles.

In the early summer of 1853 the escalation continued. On July 2 the Russians occupied the Principalities, not as an act of war, they insisted, but as a guarantee that their just demands on Turkey would be met. This action on the part of Russia had long been expected; but Palmerston, who was alert to the changing mood of the general public,[14] demanded on July 4 that the Anglo-French fleets be ordered to group in the Bosphorus and that Stratford de Redcliffe, the British ambassador to the Porte, be given discretionary powers to order the fleet into the Black Sea if this seemed necessary for the protection of Turkish territory.[15] Aberdeen replied to Palmerston in a thoughtful letter the same day. Pointing out that sending the fleet into the Bosphorus would breach a treaty, that the cabinet had previously decided that the mere occupation of the Principalities would not justify calling up the fleet, and that they could not be sure of the tsar's intentions until a formal proposal had been made to settle his differences with Turkey, Aberdeen refused to make such a warlike move merely to satisfy public opinion. "In a case of this kind I dread popular support," he confided. "On some occasion, when the Athenian Assembly vehemently applauded Alcibiades, he asked if he had said anything particularly foolish!"[16]

13. Ibid. Aberdeen to Clarendon, June 1, 1853.
14. The charge that Palmerston helped excite public opinion is said to rest purely on "circumstantial" evidence. See Herbert C. F. Bell, *Lord Palmerston*, 2:91.
15. *AP*. BM 43069. Palmerston to Aberdeen, July 4, 1853.
16. Ibid. Aberdeen to Palmerston, July 4, 1853.

Russia, behaving at times like an irresponsible bully, certainly did little to strengthen Aberdeen's position. Shortly after Aberdeen had calmed Palmerston, Nesselrode issued an arrogant circular defending Russia's occupation of the Principalities, which galled the touchy viscount and caused him to renew his demand for action.[17] Once again Aberdeen's reasoning was effective in calming Palmerston, who even went so far at this time as to admit the virtue of Aberdeen's waiting policy.[18]

That policy was arguable only so long as Russia had not rejected a compromise solution of her demands upon Turkey that was drawn up by the Great States of Europe. Aberdeen realized the extreme importance to peace of the so-called Vienna Note agreed upon by Britain, France, Prussia, and Austria; and before it was ever presented to Turkey, he urged Clarendon to make it wholly clear to that country that her rejection of it would be interpreted by Britain as evidence of a Turkish determination to go to war.[19] Britain, he reasoned, had already put pressure on Russia by moving her fleet; now it was time to exercise strong pressure on the Porte, who might otherwise be encouraged to use British involvement to achieve her own political objectives. Aberdeen thought that a general war would destroy the Turkish Empire and that they should be told as much; Russell and Clarendon, on the other hand, seem to have believed "a successful war wd. give new life to Turkey."[20] At any rate, there was again a delay, and Clarendon did not advise Turkey that the note must be accepted until August 3.[21]

When Russia, on August 5, accepted the Vienna Note as a solution to her quarrel with Turkey, Aberdeen's strategy was at high noon; and when she even agreed to a slight modification of it to make it more acceptable to Turkey, his trust in that nation's peaceful intentions seemed to have been vindicated. If Lord Stratford now used his reputed influence with the Turks to accept the note, then the crisis would have passed by and Lord Aberdeen probably would have been heralded by later historians as the great peacemaker, a title to which his Anglo-American diplomacy already had given him strong claims.

17. *AP.* BM 43069. Palmerston to Aberdeen, July 12, 1853.
18. Ibid. Palmerston to Aberdeen, July 15, 1853.
19. *AP.* BM 43188. Aberdeen to Clarendon, July 16, 1853.
20. Ibid. Clarendon to Aberdeen, July 28, 1853.
21. Ibid. Clarendon to Aberdeen, August 3, 1853.

Aberdeen obviously did not trust Stratford. As early as June 1 he opposed giving him powers to call up the fleet,[22] and as the crisis unfolded, Aberdeen's distrust of him became ever deeper. When on August 20, the Turks amended the Vienna Note making it unacceptable to Russia, both Aberdeen and Clarendon were strongly inclined to put the blame on the British ambassador. Stanmore found Stratford guilty of not carrying out his instructions properly;[23] a recent study dubbed him the "chief instigator" of the "unjust war of conquest" against Russia.[24] On the other hand, Harold Temperley concluded that the Turks were beyond his control, and he was unjustly blamed for the rejection of the Vienna Note.[25] The truth might well be that it would have taken firm Franco-British pressure on the Porte to secure acceptance of the note; pressure of this intensity was certainly never generated in France, and Aberdeen was unable to call it up in England. So Turkey followed her own selfish interests and brought the roof down on three other nations.

By late 1853 Aberdeen concluded that Lord Stratford was not even "honest."[26] Feeling as he did, why in the world did he not remove the noble lord from his strategic position in current international affairs? The explanation is to be found once again in the divided Government—the coalition that did not coalesce. If Aberdeen had recalled Stratford, Russell and Palmerston would have resigned, and his Government would have been broken up; so the prime minister faced the choice of retaining Stratford or leaving his office.[27] The agonies of doubt and dread he must have experienced in such a situation do not show up in the correspondence.

Even if Russia had remained conciliatory, Aberdeen's position in the cabinet would have been undermined by the Turkish rejection of the Vienna Note, but Russia blundered anew on September 17 by releasing her own interpretation of the note, which gave her rights far beyond those contemplated by the powers who had indited it. It was now virtually worthless as a means of conciliation.

22. *AP.* BM 43188. Aberdeen to Clarendon, June 1, 1853.
23. *SHER.* 1:196–97.
24. M. V. Nechkina, ed., *Russia in the Nineteenth Century*, p. 409.
25. Harold Temperley, *England and the Near East: The Crimea*, pp. 347–48.
26. *AP.* BM 43188. Aberdeen to Clarendon, November 9, 1853.
27. *MGLD.* 1:488.

Failure followed failure. That same month the tsar and the emperor of Austria conferred at Olmütz, seeking a substitute for the Vienna Note. Russia seemed in a pacific mood, and a substitute was eventually framed; but France rejected it, and so did the British cabinet. Meanwhile on October 4, Turkey, bent on war, ordered the Russians to leave the Principalities; and the question thereafter was not one of preventing war, but of localizing the Russo-Turkish War and bringing about a cease-fire. Aberdeen tried his best to restrain Turkey, and he spent much of October helping to devise diplomatic notes that would force that nation to pause before the fighting actually got underway.

The harassed prime minister now wished to inform Turkey bluntly that any future support by Britain would depend upon her acceptance of two propositions—the cessation of hostilities while negotiations with Russia took place and a promise that she would accept British advice regarding any future solution of the quarrel with Russia. Aberdeen proposed to inform Turkey that the British government "cannot permit themselves, in consequence of unfounded objections, or by declaration of war which they have already condemned, to be drawn into the adoption of a policy inconsistent with the peace of Europe, as well as with the true interests of Turkey itself."[28] But Palmerston would not go along with instructions of this character, and those sent to Stratford were a weak substitute for Aberdeen's virtual ultimatum.[29] Bell concludes that Palmerston came "nearest to incurring direct responsibility" for the outbreak of the war when he altered Aberdeen's note calling for a suspension of hostilities.[30]

On November 1, Palmerston wrote a strong letter to his superior, outlining his views in the new situation. "It seems to me that our Course is plain, simple and straight," he observed. "That we must help Turkey out of her difficulties by negotiations if possible and that if negotiation fails, we must by Force of arms carry her Safely through her Dangers."[31] In his reply, Aberdeen reviewed his whole policy and concluded: "If the Turks should reject our advice, I confess I am

28. *AP.* BM 43188. Aberdeen to Clarendon, October 12, 1853.
29. *SHER.* 1:213–14.
30. Bell, *Palmerston*, 2:89.
31. *AP.* BM 43069. Palmerston to Aberdeen, November 1, 1853.

not disposed to be dragged into a war by a Government which has lost . . . controul its own subjects. . . . Be this as it may, I should be perfectly prepared to oppose, even to the extremity of war, the possession by Russia of Constantinople and the Dardanelles."[32]

Russia and Turkey had fought wars before without involving the other nations of Europe, and Aberdeen hoped the present conflict might be localized if Britain and France continued to stand aloof from it. Alas for his hopes! War hysteria in Britain had risen to such a peak that the destruction of the Turkish fleet by the Russians late in November at Sinope, a "perfectly legitimate act of war,"[33] was regarded in Britain as the Massacre of Sinope; and even Clarendon was impressed by the "frightful carnage" on that occasion.[34] The weight of the British press strongly buttressed the development of the popular war psychology.[35]

Aberdeen might have taken the easy way out of his dismal situation by resigning when Palmerston retired temporarily from the Government over the reform issue in December, but he continued at his post doggedly seeking some means of avoiding the looming catastrophe. Midway in that month the cabinet approved Stratford's decision to move the fleet into the Black Sea as a means of preventing future Sinopes and to protect Turkey while new solutions were being considered. Some new possibilities were projected at Vienna; but, with war preparations being discussed at the various capitals, these proposals had little chance of being considered seriously. On February 4, after failing to receive acceptable explanations for the presence of the Anglo-French fleets in the Black Sea, Russia withdrew her ambassadors from London and Paris. Even in the face of these unpromising circumstances, Aberdeen could still write on February 12: "I still say that war is *not inevitable*; unless, indeed, we

32. *Ibid.* Aberdeen to Palmerston, November 4, 1853.

33. Barbara Jelavich, *A Century of Russian Foreign Policy, 1819–1914*, p. 120.

34. *AP.* BM 43188. Clarendon to Aberdeen, December 18, 1853.

35. That stanch Tory-journalist, who had sometimes helped Aberdeen in the past, John W. Croker, tried to defend Aberdeen's policy in the *Quarterly Review*, only to find "that my influence was not sufficient to induce the adoption of your own views—not, I ought to add—from any reluctance . . . to defending you *personally*, but because public opinion ran so strong against *any* mediating policy that the Editor was on the whole afraid to encounter it." *AP.* BM 43196. Croker to Aberdeen, February 10, 1854.

are determined to have it, which perhaps for aught I know may be the case."[36] The following month war was declared.

By the opening of 1854 all of the buttresses upholding Aberdeen's position had been removed. It seems not unfair to state that it was his international prestige, used in the interests of peace, that kept the fruitless negotiations going so long; but, after the failure of the Vienna Note, his influence in his own Government was undermined, and the reins slipped from his hands. His contention that the Russians would accept a peaceful solution was undermined periodically by their hasty and irresponsible decisions beginning in May, 1853, with the severing of relations with Turkey and progressing to the removal of their ambassadors from London and Paris in February, 1854.

Finally, his supporters in the cabinet deserted him one by one. Newcastle was the earliest defector from Peelite policy. Herbert seems to have been caught in the Sinope hysteria,[37] and so was Graham, who thereafter considered war with Russia to be inevitable.[38] Gladstone still supported Aberdeen as late as December 22,[39] but two months later he was trying to convince the prime minister that the coming war with Russia was actually a defensive measure.[40] Aberdeen seriously considered resignation, but Gladstone persuaded him to stay on.

The following year Aberdeen looked back on the period just before the declaration of war and noted: "We have a gloomy prospect before us, for which I cannot help feeling myself to be deeply responsible. I clearly foresaw all these consequences, and although unsupported, I ought more firmly to have resisted the final decision."[41] This seems to indicate that Aberdeen was completely alone when that decision was taken. Some years later Gladstone also looked back on that moment. "It is true," he wrote, "that Lord Aberdeen always lamented his assent to the Russian War. It is also true . . . that Sir James Graham in his latest years changed his opinion on the subject

36.   *AP.* BM 43188. Aberdeen to Clarendon, February 12, 1854.
37.   *SHER.* 1:216.
38.   *PGRA.* 2:226. Graham to Dundas, n.d.
39.   *MGLD.* 1:491. Wood Memorandum, n.d.
40.   Ibid., pp. 491–92. Gladstone Memorandum, February 22, 1854.
41.   *GP.* BM 44089. Aberdeen to Gladstone, October 4, 1855.

of that war."[42] Unfortunately, Gladstone did not give the details of his own part in the coming of the war.

It would seem to be proved beyond reasonable doubt that Aberdeen explored not only every avenue, but every country road and footpath in his search for peace between April, 1853, and March, 1854. The question remains, however, whether this was the right way to go about finding it.

Palmerston would have adopted a much firmer policy toward Russia in the spring of 1853. Clarendon later seemed convinced that this would have been much more effective in preventing the growth of the crisis. "We are now in an anomalous & painful position," he wrote in November, "& . . . I have arrived at the conviction that it might have been avoided by firmer language & a more decided course 5 months ago. Russia wd. then, as she is now, have been ready to come to terms, & we shd. have exercised a control over the Turks that is now not to be obtained."[43] This line of reasoning, so destructive of Aberdeen's reputation as a statesman, finds an ultimate expression in a biography of Palmerston, which traces the origins of the war to the peace party in the cabinet.[44]

The evidence accumulated to buttress this thesis includes Aberdeen's well-known pacifism; his former friendly relations with the tsar, who came to believe he would not oppose a settlement of the Eastern Question; his strongly expressed dislike of Turkey; and, finally, the claims the tsar believed he had established for Austria's friendship during the revolutions of 1848–49. These factors led the tsar to conclude that the British, who were primarily interested in moneymaking,[45] would not actually go to war to protect Turkey. But if Palmerston had been premier—so runs the argument—the tsar would have been rapidly disabused of such a notion.

There seem to be certain valid objections to this line of reasoning. In the first place, it was not Russia but Turkey that caused the trouble. Aberdeen was quite successful in putting the tsar into a conciliatory mood, but—largely due to the objections of his colleagues—he was unable to force Turkey to accept a settlement. The tsar seemed to

42. *GP.* BM 44136. Gladstone to Cobden, December 13, 1861.
43. *AP.* BM 43188. Clarendon to Aberdeen, November 4, 1853.
44. Bell, *Palmerston,* 2:85.
45. Peter Gibbs, *Crimean Blunder,* p. 27.

respond to the velvet glove approach, but otherwise he matched defiance with defiance. Thus, when Britain and France sent their fleets to Besika Bay, the tsar carried out his threat to occupy the Principalities; after Turkey rejected the Vienna Note, the Russians proclaimed their distorted interpretation of it. After the Turks declared war, the Russians responded by destroying their fleet at Sinope; after the French and British ordered their fleets into the Black Sea, the tsar recalled his ambassadors from London and Paris. On the basis of this reconstruction of events, it would seem that a firm line might have merely brought about war sooner rather than later, and at a time when both the British public and their armed services were less prepared than they were to be in 1854.

The final answer to this Palmerston versus Aberdeen controversy would seem to lie in a profound psychological study of Nicholas II to determine just why he acted as he did. Meanwhile, the sterling courage of Lord Aberdeen to maintain his position in defense of peace while the war spirit was growing daily more intense, while his colleagues and friends one by one deserted him, while the newspapers raised the hue and cry against all pacifists, cries out for scholarly acknowledgement. Where was the weakness? What is the substance of courage?

PART 4

Years of Disintegration 1855-1857

CHAPTER 23

THE CHANGE OF GOVERNMENTS

During the parliamentary recess at the year's end, newspaper accounts of incredible mismanagement of affairs in the Crimea made the headlines, and the Aberdeen Government rapidly lost the confidence of the nation. No sooner had Parliament assembled on January 23 than the Radical leader, John Roebuck, moved for a committee to inquire into the condition of the army in the Crimea; and Lord John Russell dealt the Government a grievous blow by handing in his resignation. Shaken but loyal, his colleagues rejected Newcastle's offer to fill the role of scapegoat and resign, and they tried to unite their forces in opposition to the motion.

It turned out to be an impossible task. The Parliament faithfully reflected the public mood of disappointment and impatience; and Radicals, Conservatives, and some Liberals united on January 29 to put the Government into a decisive 305–148 minority on the question of the investigating committee. Aberdeen had no alternative but to resign.

One might reason that all Conservatives who voted to sustain the Government on January 29 were Peelites; and, by and large, he would not be far from wrong. But as one surveys the list of loyal supporters, he encounters such members as Sir Thomas D. Acland, who took pride in his stanch conservatism, and Viscount Emlyn, James F. Freshfield, Charles S. Hardinge, Sir William Heathcote, and Loftus T. Wigram, all of whom were faithful Conservatives. Their votes on this occasion might be explained by a reluctance to change the Queen's Government in the midst of a war. Then there were a number of other quite reliable Peelites, such as George W. Heneage and Jonathan J. Richardson (not to mention Sir James Graham), who were absent from the division; so if it is considered to be a list of the Peelites in 1855 without making additions and deletions, it could hardly be accurate. Even a corrected list can be contested in some details.

Bearing these observations in mind, one might offer the following as the Peelite section of early 1855:[1]

1. The absentees on the January 29, 1855, division are marked with an

A'Court, Charles H.
  (Wilton)
Baring, Henry B.
  (Marlborough)
Baring, Thomas
  (Huntingdon)
Bruce, Ld. Ernest
  (Marlborough)
Cardwell, Edward
  (Oxford City)
Clinton, Ld. Robert
  (Sandwich)
Dalkeith, Earl of
  (Edinburghshire)
Denison, Edmund B.
  (West Riding, Yorks.)
Drumlanrig, Viscount
  (Dumfriesshire)
Egerton, William T.*
  (Cheshire - North)
Elcho, Lord
  (Haddingtonshire)
Fitz-Roy, Henry
  (Lewes)
Gladstone, William E.
  (Oxford Univ.)
Goulburn, Henry
  (Cambridge Univ.)
Graham, Sir James R.*
  (Carlisle)
Greene, Thomas
  (Lancaster)

Harcourt, George G.
  (Oxfordshire)
Heneage, George W.*
  (Devizes)
Herbert, Henry A.
  (Kerry Co.)
Herbert, Sidney
  (Wilts - South)
Hervey, Ld. Alfred
  (Brighton)
Hogg, Sir James W.
  (Honiton)
Hughes, William B.
  (Carnarvon Dist.)
Jermyn, Earl
  (Bury St. Edmunds)
Johnstone, James
  (Clackmannon)
Johnstone, Sir John
  (Scarborough)
Legh, George C.
  (Cheshire - North)
Lockhart, Allan E.
  (Selkirkshire)
Lushington, Charles M.
  (Canterbury)
Mure, William*
  (Renfrewshire)
Owen, Sir John
  (Pembroke Dist.)
Palmer, Roundell
  (Plymouth)

Patten, John W.
  (Lancashire - North)
Peel, Jonathan
  (Huntingdon Bor.)
Peel, Sir Robert
  (Tamworth)
Pennant, Edward D.*
  (Carnarvonshire)
Philipps, John H.*
  (Haverford - West)
Phillimore, Robert J.
  (Tavistock)
Richardson, Jonathan J.*
  (Lisburn)
Smollett, Alexander*
  (Dumbartonshire)
Stirling, William
  (Perthshire)
Sutton, John M.
  (Newark)
Vernon, Granville H.
  (Newark)
Wickham, Henry W.
  (Bradford)
Wortley, James S.
  (Buteshire)
Young, Sir John
  (Cavan)

The section, after an initial jump at the time of the fall of the Derby administration, seems to have held at a fairly steady level—about 38 in 1853, and 49 in 1854, and 46 in 1855.

There was, however, some change in membership which might be noted. Four Peelites of 1854—William Beckett, Henry A. Bruce, William S. FitzGerald, and John Walter—voted against the Government. Beckett and FitzGerald became more dependable Conservatives

---

asterisk. The name of Robert Stephenson might be added; but, like George F. Heneage, he was a die-hard Protectionist and thus does not seem to belong on a Peelite list.

thereafter, while Bruce and Walter became fairly steady supporters of the Palmerston Government. Lord Norreys went to the Upper House as the earl of Abingdon late in 1854. The places of these five were taken in 1855 by Thomas Baring, George G. Harcourt, and Jonathan Peel, who were conservative Peelites; Roundell Palmer, whose voting record is discernible in *Hansard* at this time; and Charles M. Lushington, who was elected to Parliament in August, 1854.

After this momentous division, Lord Aberdeen resigned; and Lord Derby was given an opportunity to form a government but Derby realized that the general public wanted Palmerston and without the popular viscount his chances for success were dim. As it turned out, Palmerston would accept only if Clarendon, Herbert, and Gladstone[2] would also join; and, being unable to secure the services of this group, Derby, who probably believed that Palmerston would be unable to form a government on his own,[3] temporarily gave up his commission.

As it turned out, Derby was quite wrong in his judgment of Palmerston's prospects. As it had been Russell, not Palmerston, who had scuttled the Aberdeen Government, the Peelites were hard pressed to find a valid excuse not to join him, especially at this time of national emergency. Aberdeen urged them to join, but would not at first express his own confidence in the Government. Finally, the former prime minister satisfied his friends that their confidence would not be entirely misplaced; and Graham, Gladstone, Argyll, Viscount Canning, St. Germans, and Sir John Young resumed their previous duties. Herbert went to the Colonial Office. The most warlike of the Peelites, the duke of Newcastle, was made the scapegoat for the Crimean debacle, excluded from office, and replaced at the War Office by Lord Panmure.

The question might be raised: Was this another coalition government? The weight of evidence supports the contention that it was an extension of the former coalition with a change in the headship. The queen evidently considered the Peelites to be a separate

2. Gladstone was extremely unpopular with the Conservative rank and file. See J. R. Jones, "The Conservatives and Gladstone in 1855," *English Historical Review* 77 (January, 1962).

3. *DP.* XVII. Miscellaneous Observations #43.

group;[4] Lord Aberdeen believed his followers could make any alliances they wished.[5] Gladstone told Herbert that joining Palmerston
would be a coalition, while accepting overtures from Derby would
mean reunion;[6] Graham joined Palmerston only with reluctance,
fearing that Peelite policies might be distorted or abandoned.[7] Cardwell did not favor a new coalition with the Whigs and wanted to
keep the Peelite section together.[8] The separate identity of the Peelites was generally acknowledged by others outside the Peelite ranks.
"I see," Palmerston wrote, "that the Peelite section still continues to
endeavour to make itself a little separate section."[9] The diarist, Charles Greville, also regarded them as a distinct unit in Parliament.[10]
While it is true that certain members of the section, especially Newcastle, Viscount Canning, Lord Elcho, Lord Ellesmere, James S.
Wortley, and George G. Harcourt, were drawn toward Palmerston,
only the first seems at this time to have considered himself a Liberal.

Hitherto the Peelite leaders had conducted their affairs very well
and had managed to secure a maximum political advantage out of
their separate status; but they had hardly formed the new coalition
before they made a mistake that went far to undermine their position. On joining the Palmerston Government, Graham and Gladstone
had assumed that the new prime minister would continue to oppose
the "Sebastopol Committee" to investigate the state of affairs in the
Crimea; but in February Gladstone learned this was not to be the
policy. He was deeply disturbed. How could they fall resisting this
motion under Aberdeen and then tamely accept it under Palmerston? Such a change might be interpreted by some observers as proof
that the original motion had been designed to get rid of Lord Aberdeen.[11]

Palmerston felt so sure of his own position in the country and the

4. *B&EVIC*, 3:94–95. Memorandum by the Queen, January 25, 1855.

5. *GP.* BM 44745. Gladstone Memorandum, February 3, 1855.

6. Ibid. Gladstone Memorandum, February 21, 1855.

7. Ibid. Gladstone Memorandums, February 4 and 6, 1855.

8. Ibid. Gladstone Memorandum, February 2, 1855.

9. Evelyn Ashley, *The Life and Correspondence of Viscount Palmerston*,
2:78–79. Palmerston to his brother, February 15, 1855.

10. *GMEM.* 7:118.

11. *GP.* BM 44163. Gladstone to Graham, February 15, 1855.

House that the prospect of a Peelite secession seems to have held no terrors for him. He refused to change his policy toward the appointment of the committee; and when he announced it on February 21, Graham, Gladstone, Herbert, Cardwell, Lord Alfred Hervey, Lord Elcho, Henry Fitz-Roy, and Lord St. Germans left the Government. There were a number of others who did not follow their Peelite leaders. Lord Ernest Bruce, Viscount Drumlanrig, Sir Robert Peel,[12] and Sir John Young[13] in the Commons, and the duke of Argyll,[14] Viscount Canning,[15] Viscount Sydney, and the duke of Wellington in the Lords[16] chose for one reason or another to stay on.

Once again the Peelites had adapted their course to a high ideal—loyalty to their former leader;[17] and it was another of those unusual Peelite decisions that was politically suicidal. Many members of Parliament, the newspapers,[18] and the general public professed shock that they would suddenly abandon their important positions while the war was still on. Herbert's biographer even went so far as to charge that their resignations weakened the Government in its peace negotiations, and thus prolonged the war for another year.[19] But to preserve their collective sense of honor, the Peelites did not hesitate to brave the storm of adverse public opinion.

Few would deny that they had acted wrongly if their resignations

12. Peel had become a lord of the Admiralty in February, 1855.

13. Young had been promised the position of high commissioner of the Ionian Islands, and he decided to stay and accept it (*GP*. BM 44237. Young to Gladstone, Jan. 31, 1855). This decision did not sever his connection with Gladstone, but he was removed from the Commons until 1859.

14. Argyll stayed because of "my own clear sense of what was due to the public interests in a great crisis" (Argyll, *Memoirs*, 1:538).

15. Palmerston considered Canning to be one of his regular followers by this time (George Douglas, ed., *The Panmure Papers*, 1:51).

16. Wellington was but loosely attached to the Government. "Palmerston is to *speak* to me tomorrow," he wrote. "I would rather he would write, for I fancy he intends to come to an *understanding* as to my support of his government. It lessens the chance of our agreeing, for in writing I might qualify my support" (*BP*. Wellington to Brougham, [?], 1856).

17. Herbert did not believe he should remain in office while under investigation by the committee (G. P. Gooch, ed., *The Later Correspondence of Lord John Russell, 1840–1878*, 2:192; Lansdowne to Russell, Feb. 21, 1855).

18. See *The Manchester Guardian*, Feb. 24, 1855; *The Times*, Feb. 23, 1855.

19. *SHER*. 1:268.

did, indeed, prolong the war; but this charge need hardly be taken seriously. It is based on a string of assumptions that (1) without the secession the Government would have appeared stronger in its dealings with Russia; (2) this added strength at home would have enabled Palmerston (or Russell, who conducted the abortive peace negotiations of 1855) to force the Russians to accept his peace terms; and (3) the war would therefore have ended. This interpretation omits any discussion of the peace terms themselves as well as whether the military situation then existing justified them, which certainly is germane to the argument. If Palmerston had resigned, this quite likely would have encouraged the Russians to hold out for softer terms; but the resignation of the peace-loving Peelites from the Government certainly provided no sign that the posture of the Government was weakening; indeed, it could be interpreted in quite the opposite fashion.

The decision to resign from the Government left the Peelite leaders in a position of even more than usual ambiguity for the remainder of the session. Should they support or oppose the Government of which they had been a part? Uniform support of it would have demonstrated a confidence in Palmerston which would vitiate the reasoning that had led to their resignations; uniform opposition would not only have been unpopular, but would have severed completely their former ties with the Liberals. Under these circumstances, it is not strange that the Peelites pursued an independent course, sometimes supporting, sometimes opposing, the Government.

There were six interesting divisions during the balance of the 1855 session—one relating to the Church, one to Scottish education, three to finance, and one to the conduct of the war itself. The first of these may be dismissed very briefly, as may the second. Both the Government and Disraeli opposed the Church Rates Abolition Bill of May 16, and so did the Peelite section by a large majority. Edward Cardwell was the only major defector; Gladstone opposed the measure. The Scottish Education Bill of April 27 stirred little interest; and Cardwell, Gladstone, and Herbert all supported the Government against Disraeli.

Two of the three financial divisions are of special interest because Gladstone chose to appear as financial spokesman of the section against the Government's financial plans. Disraeli's attack on the Government's Newspaper Stamp Duties Bill on March 26 failed to enlist Peelite support; but the Repayment of Loan Bill, voted upon on April 30, was supported by Gladstone. This bill provided for the repayment of the war loan in annual installments of £1,000,000 over a period of sixteen years after peace was restored. Gladstone, perhaps influenced by the fact that his own budget of 1853 had failed to forecast the financial condition of the country accurately, contended that the Government had no right to project its policies so far in the future. Sir Fitzroy Kelly, former Original Peelite now turned Derbyite Conservative, insisted that the proper procedure would be for the Government to apply surpluses to the debt's retirement whenever they were able to do so. Gladstone carried a majority of the Peelite voters with him.[20]

This victory may have encouraged Gladstone to continue his course. Disraeli provided him another opportunity for so doing on July 20 when he attacked the Government's plan to guarantee the interest payments on a £5,000,000 loan to Turkey. Gladstone believed it was quite legitimate to give direct aid to a country whose integrity they were fighting to preserve, but he did not think that a case for such aid had been established. Once again he carried more Peelites with him than voted with the Government and demostrated that the section accepted him as its financial spokesman.[21]

The major political division of the session arose on May 25 when Disraeli produced a resolution expressing dissatisfaction with the uncertain conduct of the Government with reference to every great question of war and peace. Although he toned it down by adding that the House should support the war until an honorable peace had been achieved, it was clearly a partisan attack on the Government. This was the only division of the session for which the Peelite section turned out in sizable numbers, and their votes provide almost

20. Gladstone secured the support of thirteen Peelite voters, against ten for the Government, or nine, if the vote of Lord Ernest Bruce, one of its members, is disregarded.

21. Gladstone secured an 11-5 majority of the Peelite vote on the Turkish Loan issue. Those who followed him on one or both of these divisions were: Henry B. Baring, Edward Cardwell, the earl of Dalkeith, George W. Heneage, Sidney Herbert, Lord Alfred Hervey, Earl Jermyn, Charles M. Lushington, Roundell Palmer, Jonathan Peel, Edward D. Pennant, Robert J. Phillimore, William Stirling, John M. Sutton, and Granville H. Vernon.

an inventory of the section—31 against Disraeli and only three for him. The only major defector was Jonathan Peel, who was to find his way into the Conservative party. It was clear from this division that the Peelites had no desire to be labeled an opposition peace party.

These divisions would indicate that the Peelite section was still operative, though weakened, in 1855. Cardwell, Gladstone, Graham, and Herbert almost always voted together; the majority would accept Gladstone's financial leadership even in wartime; and they eschewed a peace-at-any-price approach to the war situation. But where they would go from here was highly uncertain at the moment.

The uncertainties regarding their future course in politics caused some minor disputes among the Peelite leaders in 1855 and one desertion. The hearings of the Sebastopol Committee were less unpleasant than might have been anticipated, but Newcastle's testimony drew a strong protest from Mrs. Sidney Herbert for not "doing justice to Sidney's indefatigable exertions in the War Office."[22] Newcastle's wounded feelings were patent in his reply, which noted that he had himself assumed "the whole weight of obloquy wh. attached to the conduct of the war."[23] His bitterness in particular was directed toward certain unidentified Whigs, who, he charged, sought to "crush all Liberals who are not Whigs."[24] In his difficult situation, Newcastle found the utmost kindness and understanding in Palmerston, who in early summer asked him to go to the Crimea to report on the state of the army there. Aberdeen advised refusal, lest Newcastle meet with a hostile reception;[25] but the duke accepted the mission and subsequently prepared a lengthy report on his findings. Granville transmitted it to Clarendon and commented that parts of it were clumsy, others tiresome, and "the egotism is remarkable."[26] But Palmerston thought enough of his services to offer Newcastle the Garter, which Aberdeen advised him to accept but which he refused.[27]

Thereafter, Newcastle went into a sort of ostentatious semiretire-

22.   *NP*. 12244. Mrs. Herbert to Newcastle, April 29, 1855.
23.   Ibid., 12245. Newcastle to Mrs. Herbert, May 1, 1855.
24.   *GNP*. PRO 30/29–18. Newcastle to Granville, April 16, 1855.
25.   *GP*. BM 44089. Aberdeen to Gladstone, June 27, 1855.
26.   *GNP*. PRO 30/29–18. Granville to Clarendon, Sept. 10, 1855.
27.   *GP*. BM 44089. Aberdeen to Gladstone, Dec. 8, 1855.

ment from politics, and he seems to have declined an invitation from Herbert to attend a preparliamentary conference early in 1856. It was probably just as well, for he had now cut all ties with the Conservatives and was to all intents and purposes an unattached member of the Liberal party.

The Peelite party in the Lords was now in a more advanced state of decay than it was in the Commons. Aberdeen had had his day and had no further political ambitions, only lingering regrets and self-criticism for having led his nation into the war. The duke of Argyll, whose sympathies were still "Peelite," had remained in the Government and the Liberal movement. Despite his sympathies, remaining in the government had not been too difficult because he had never been a member of the "regular Peelite group."[28] Viscount Canning, another who had remained, acted as a sort of go-between for the Government in its dealings with the Peelite section until his appointment as governor general of India in 1856. Among the others, Ripon was ill, rarely attended Parliament, and only occasionally wrote to Goulburn or Brougham. Ellenborough had made an approach to the Conservatives in 1855, but by the end of the year he, like Newcastle, was in political isolation.[29] Brougham's last hope for office had vanished when he received no invitation to join the coalition government, and his political activity was limited to corresponding with Aberdeen, Herbert, Thesiger, and Newcastle. Lord Lyndhurst by this time was a Derbyite.

The only important professed and active Peelite in the Lords was St. Germans. When the secession had taken place early in the year, he had felt it his duty to "adhere to the friends and colleagues of Sir Robert Peel";[30] but he lacked the prestige to set himself up as the new leader of the crumbled section. Although there existed in the Lords in 1855 and after a group of liberal Conservatives upon whom Derby could not count to fight for his version of conservatism, their Peelism was scarcely distinguishable from Whiggism motivated by a desire to serve the best interests of their distinguished class.

Even in the Commons the Peelite leaders had not lived in complete

28. Argyll, *Memoirs*, 1:537–38.

29. *EP.* PRO 30/12–21. Derby to Ellenborough, Feb. 3, 1855, and Jan. 19, 1856.

30. *PGRA.* 2:267. St. Germans to Graham, Feb. 22, 1855.

harmony in 1855. When it became known that the negotiations with Russia that year had broken down over matters that seemed to go beyond the original objects of the war, Gladstone and Graham favored supporting a censure proposed by the Radical, Milner Gibson, who deplored the loss of this opportunity to end the war. But Herbert, who felt he had not been sufficiently consulted in this decision, balked and refused to go along lest it weaken the government's hand in its future negotiations with Russia. Graham accepted Herbert's view, and then it was Gladstone's turn to be offended on the same ground of insufficient consultation.[31] As it turned out, they had offended each other needlessly, for Gibson decided to withdraw his motion.

Various members of the Palmerston government were offended by the activities of the Peelites once they had left the Government. Clarendon complained to Newcastle that Gladstone, Herbert, and Graham "have really behaved very ill" and that he was particularly disgusted over Gladstone's attitude toward the Turkish loan.[32] Why Clarendon censured Graham rather than Cardwell is not clear, for Graham's voting record had not been hostile toward the Government. Gladstone was impervious to such criticism: "It is hardly possible to believe one is not the greatest scoundrel on earth," he wrote Aberdeen, "when one is assured of it from all sides on such excellent authority."[33] Gladstone knew exactly what he was doing—keeping the section together—and he had no plans to give up the attempt regardless of public opinion.

Although Lord Aberdeen believed the Peelite section was practically defunct, he helped prolong its shadowy existence by attending a preparliamentary meeting in 1856 in company with Gladstone, Graham, and Herbert.[34] If their section was in a bad way, they were not alone amid the confusion. Not long after this meeting Sir James Graham told Charles Greville that no one man in the Commons—Palmerston, Disraeli, or Gladstone—had as many as ten followers. Sir Robert Peel, indeed, had destroyed party in England, and it had virtually ceased to exist.[35]

31. *SHER.* 1:434.
32. *NP.* 12566. Clarendon to Newcastle, August 11, 1855.
33. *MGLD.* 1:549. Gladstone to Aberdeen, August 9, 1855.
34. *NP.* 12552. Herbert to Newcastle, Jan. 11, 1856.
35. *GMEM.* 7:223.

CHAPTER 24

THE PEELITE SECTION IN 1856

The description in *Dod* of the various Conservatives in 1856 fall roughly into four categories. Few identified themselves as followers of Lord Derby, and virtually none attached themselves to Disraeli. One group, however, noted that they had "censured Free Trade in 1852." This referred to the 53 members who on the second division on the night of November 26 had voted against a resolution which stated that the improved condition of the country was attributable to free trade and the removal of the taxes on food. They seem to have regarded themselves as a special clique within the Conservative party.

A much larger group of Conservatives attached themselves to the February 23, 1853, division on the Maynooth grant. They evidently believed that the revision or abolition of that grant was a worthwhile national objective, and in most cases they probably reflected the views of their constituents.

There was a third and even larger group who simply called themselves "Conservatives" without attaching themselves to a specific issue or leader. It was augmented in the 1856 edition of *Dod* by the virtual elimination of the old designation "a Conservative, but in favour of free trade" by the dropping of the second phrase. Through this process Henry B. Baring, Lord Ernest Bruce, and the earl of Dalkeith, William T. Egerton, Henry Fitz-Roy, Thomas Greene, Sidney Herbert, Lord Alfred Hervey, Sir James W. Hogg, Earl Jermyn, Sir John V. Johnstone, Allan E. Lockhart, John W. Patten, Jonathan Peel, Sir Robert Peel, Edward D. Pennant, John M. Sutton, Jonathan J. Richardson, Alexander Smollett, and James S. Wortley became plain "Conservatives"; and it is the more remarkable when one considers that Bruce and Peel were members of the Palmerston government.

The fourth group were the hyphenated Conservatives, who modified their conservatism by attaching it to some loosening adjective. Thus the elections during 1855 brought to the House Edmund Antrobus and Sir Henry J. Stracey, Conservatives who backed a number of reforms; Peter Blackburn, a Liberal Conservative; Sir Michael R. S. Stewart, a Moderate Conservative; and Sir Stafford H. North-

191

cote, a "Liberal-Progressive-Conservative" (on the basis of his voting record, Northcote interpreted that type of Conservative to be a fairly steady follower of Disraeli). Among the newcomers, only Edmund Antrobus was irregular enough in his voting habits to be classed with the Peelites.

The major political division for the session of 1856 came on May 1, on a resolution supported by Disraeli, that the fall of Kars was due "to the want of foresight and energy on the part of Her Majesty's Administration." Perhaps to demonstrate his control of certain votes, Gladstone voted with Disraeli on April 29 to prevent adjournment of the debate,[1] then divided against him and the resolution. Disregarding the former Peelites who now served in the Government, the following represent the Peelite section in 1856:

Edmund Antrobus	George W. Heneage	George C. Legh
Henry B. Baring	Henry A. Herbert	Sir John Owen
Edward Cardwell	Sidney Herbert	Roundell Palmer
Earl of Dalkeith	Lord Alfred Hervey	John H. Philipps
Edmund B. Denison	Sir James W. Hogg	Robert J. Phillimore
Henry Fitz-Roy	William B. Hughes	Jonathan J. Richardson
William E. Gladstone	Earl Jermyn	John M. Sutton
Sir James Graham	James Johnstone	Granville H. Vernon
George G. Harcourt	Sir John V. Johnstone	Henry W. Wickham

Although the Government won by a comfortable majority, and these Peelite votes did not represent the margin of victory on this division, the official position of the Peelite section in 1856—if it is admitted they had one—was a highly qualified support of the Government.

The Peelites provided some strength to the Government on three losing divisions in April and June. The April 7 division involved a resolution that the billeting of soldiers with private families in Scotland was injurious to the discipline of the men and oppressive to the Scottish people. Disraeli supported this resolution; Palmerston opposed it. Graham and seven other Peelites voted with Palmerston; but almost as many, including the earl of Dalkeith and Lord Elcho, opposed the Government, and it lost 139-116.

---

1. Those who followed Gladstone in this unusual switch were Lord Alfred Hervey, Roundell Palmer, Robert J. Phillimore, Jonathan J. Richardson, and Granville H. Vernon. Graham, Herbert, and Cardwell did not vote on this division.

There were two other losing divisions for the Government in June, one on June 17 involving a reform of Irish education and a second on June 25 on a measure to abolish the then-existing corporation of Maynooth College and to establish the Maynooth College Managers as a wholly independent body. Gladstone, Graham, and three other Peelites could not save the Government on the first of these, and Graham and eleven other Peelites failed to rescue the Government on the second. If Gladstone had attended and voted on the second of these, the Government might have won, for the margin of the loss was very narrow—174-168.

The Peelite section of 1856 followed its usual voting pattern on April 9 when a division was taken on the Oath of Abjuration Bill designed to admit Jews to Parliament. A small group, including Edmund Antrobus, Gladstone, Graham, and nine others voted for the measure; but an equal number, including Thomas Greene, William B. Hughes, Allan E. Lockhart, and Johnathan Peel, voted against it, indicating that their positions on this particular issue had not changed much during the past decade.

The Peelites voted with the Government on two other divisions, which might be described as uncontested divisions, for Disraeli also voted on the same side. The first was a motion to provide the ballot at elections—a radical idea for that time when one considers that this was the very year the true ballot was first adopted in South Australia and the American Republic had not yet adopted the custom. Only one Peelite, James Johnstone, declared his confidence in the private voter, while 15 others, including Gladstone and Graham, ran for cover.

The statesman who was to launch his later career over the prostrate body of the Irish Church thought rather differently on the subject on May 27 when a motion was made for an "impartial disendowment" of that institution. Gladstone and fourteen other Peelites linked arms with Palmerston and the Conservatives (save for Disraeli, who did not vote) and won the division by a large majority.

If we consider only these divisions, the record of the Peelite section in supporting the Government was a fairly good one—but there were others on Church-connected issues which found them in opposition. They joined Disraeli on March 5 in a futile attempt to defeat the Church Rates Abolition Bill, which would abolish the church rates imposed by parish governments. Dissenters strongly supported the bill, but Conservatives regarded it as an attack on the Church and its property. Graham, Gladstone, Herbert, and twelve other Peelites voted against the measure. Cardwell and Antrobus broke with the section on this occasion.

The Peelite leaders also supported Disraeli in opposing the Government on a curious issue involving whether or not the bishops of London and Durham should be permitted to retire in order to receive their pensions. Though a minor issue, Gladstone, Graham, and six other Peelites voted against the retirement bill on July 23.

Much more important was the national education issue that came to a vote on April 11. This involved a series of resolutions offered by the Government to create educational subdistricts in England and Wales, over which subinspectors would have supervison. After a certain period of time the county, city, and borough governments would be granted power to levy school rates so that education would be made available to the poor. In many ways an attractive plan, it foundered on the question of religious instruction. The House as a whole was convinced that schools so financed would be limited to the teaching of secular subjects. So the plan lost by more than a hundred votes, of which the Peelites furnished more than a score, including those of Cardwell, Gladstone, Graham, and Herbert.

No division of the session illustrated so vividly the remarkable degeneration of party regularity than one held on July 10 on the subject of the Appellate Jurisdiction of the Lords. In this debate the prerogatives of the Crown were thought to be involved, as well as the traditional structure of the Upper House. Palmerston and Disraeli opposed the motion, and the Peelites split—some usually thought to be conservative voted for it, others usually more liberal voted against it; and the surprising result was another loss for the Government.

Amid all this confusion and disorganization in 1856, Lord Palmerston, like Russell before him, sought to strengthen his Government by recruiting among the Peelites. His first approach was to the professed "independent" duke of Newcastle, who accepted the lord lieutenancy of Nottinghamshire, provided he did not sacrifice his "political independence" by accepting.[2] The independent member then asked and received from Graham the qualified approval of his

2. *NP.* 12602. Newcastle to Palmerston, November 18, 1856.

conduct.[3] Palmerston then offered Newcastle a committee chairman-ship, which was quickly refused. Just before the opening of the 1857 session the duke visited Aberdeen, to whom he confessed a linger-ing attachment for the Peelites, excoriated Lord John Russell, and noted that joining Derby was impossible so long as Disraeli occu-pied his position of leadership.[4] It is interesting to note that he should at this late date have thought of Derby at all.

Palmerston's eye also fell on James S. Wortley, whose voting rec-ord was not particularly favorable to the Liberals—indeed, in 1856 he had voted consistently against the Government when present, which was not very often. Offered the post of solicitor general, he consulted Herbert and Gladstone and thereafter accepted it. Glad-stone apparently told him there was no reason to refuse, providing he could stomach Palmerston's foreign policy.[5] The desertion of so important a Peelite seems to have shocked Gladstone, who wrote to Herbert that Wortley's defection provided a "warning" that brought home the difficulties of their political position.[6]

Graham was also thoroughly discouraged. In the existing political situation he could see no way of promoting "conservative Reform at home" and "non-intervention abroad," which he considered to be the basic principles of Peelism.[7] Writing to Aberdeen, the "head of Peel's surviving friends," he noted the growing weakness of their group: Cardwell might be driven into the Government camp by his con-stituents, and Gladstone might find his way to the Conservative front bench when Parliament met.[8] Losing Cardwell would be a heavy blow, but the loss of Gladstone would be catastrophic.

Graham was quite aware that Gladstone had been sounded out that spring by Sir William Heathcote, his colleague at Oxford Uni-versity, and that thoughts of Conservative reunion had not been wholly absent from his mind since that time. Graham had warned him about the "Disraeli obstacle," but Gladstone seemed to feel that his rejoining the Conservatives might not be far off.

3. *NP.* 12603. Graham to Newcastle, November 19, 1856.
4. *GP.* BM 44089. Aberdeen to Gladstone, January 24, 1857.
5. *GMEM.* 7:248.
6. *SHER.* 2:65.
7. *GRP.* Graham to Aberdeen, Nov. 11, 1856.
8. Ibid.

The position of Gladstone and the other Peelites was most discouraging at the moment. Once again they lacked a leader under whom they might take office, for Aberdeen and Graham were in the deep twilight of their careers. All of the Peelites distrusted Palmerston's conduct of foreign affairs, and Russell held no charms for them, though Aberdeen and Graham still looked upon his as a possibility. Disraeli stood as an obstacle to Conservative reunion even if the rank and file would welcome back the Peelites, which was doubtful.

This was the situation when Whitwell Elwin, editor of the *Quarterly Review*, apparently acting on his own initiative, suggested to Gladstone that Derby wished to discuss politics with him. Consulting Aberdeen, Gladstone was told he had little option but to see Derby, but the former prime minister begged him not to sit with the Opposition in the 1857 Parliament.[9] Gladstone was torn between loyalties to his friends and dissatisfaction with his present position, and ended by assuring Elwin that he would talk to Derby as an old friend, but not as a political leader.[10]

This turn of events seems to have troubled Aberdeen, who wished to prevent a preparliamentary meeting between Gladstone and Derby at all costs, so he warned Gladstone that such a meeting might force Graham, Herbert, and Cardwell to tell the Commons that they had not been parties to the concert, which would leave Gladstone in a "painful state of isolation."[11] Herbert also tried to discourage Gladstone,[12] and so did Graham, though Graham was satisfied that nothing would be arranged at such a meeting.[13] Even more than Graham, it was Aberdeen who may have not forgotten Derby's chilly reception of his own Government in 1852 and who now stood forth as the obstacle to the Conservative reunion.

Aberdeen believed that they must suggest to Gladstone an alternative to Derby, for the Palmerston government might be expected to collapse at any time and Gladstone obviously wanted to resume office again. Graham agreed with him that Russell was the man who

9. *GP.* BM 44089. Gladstone to Aberdeen, Dec. 8, 1856.
10. *MGLD.* 1:556. Gladstone to Elwin, Dec. 13, 1856.
11. *GP.* BM 44089. Aberdeen to Gladstone, Dec. 20, 1856.
12. *SHER.* 2:66–67. Herbert to Gladstone, Dec. 19, 1856.
13. *GP.* BM 44164. Graham to Gladstone, Dec. 16, 1856.

"can give the *Coup de Grace* to Palmerston,"[14] and the titular head of the section held up that admittedly shopworn political leader as the man of the future.[15]

Although Gladstone was by no means lacking in political courage, the prospect of leaving his close friends and entering the ranks of a party many of whose members disliked him intensely caused him to hesitate, then to agree to postpone his conference with Derby until after the session opened. Thus Peelite unity was preserved and the section entered upon its final battles the following month.

14. *GP.* BM 44089. Graham to Aberdeen, Jan. 20, 1857.
15. Ibid. Aberdeen to Gladstone, Dec. 30, 1856.

CHAPTER 25

THE DEFEAT OF PALMERSTON'S GOVERNMENT

The meeting between Derby and Gladstone, the anticipation of which had sent such shock waves through the Peelite world, occurred on February 4 and lasted about four hours. Derby had the largest single party at his command, while Gladstone had only a small number of personal supporters; yet the concert was as between equals. Disraeli had given notice of an attack on Palmerston's deficit spending on February 3, and Gladstone agreed that this was the issue upon which the viscount should be overthrown, but without specifying what alliances might take place after that event.

During the week following this conference Gladstone conferred with Herbert and Graham, who were prepared to attack, and helped draw up four resolutions on finance to be presented to Derby. When he saw them on February 11, the Conservative leader found he could accept only two of them,[1] so they decided to attack the budget as a whole, rather than in detail.

The crosscurrent in the negotiations was provided by Aberdeen, Graham, Cardwell, and Herbert, all of whom would utilize the Conservative attack for their own purposes but wanted to divorce themselves from the Derbyites while so doing. They pressed Gladstone to concert his attack with Russell and move his own resolutions. Although Gladstone agreed to inform Russell of developments, he steadfastly refused to enter into competition with Disraeli; and the others finally accepted his point of view. Then they brought up the question of future arrangements: Would Gladstone lead in the Commons with Russell as prime minister in the Lords? Gladstone replied that the same arrangement might be made under Derby's leadership, and Graham noted that Disraeli stood in the way. Being unable to agree upon their future course of action, his friends concluded their conference with Gladstone "vehemently deploring our position, which I said, and they admitted, was generally condemned by the country."[2] This allusion to their unpopularity was rather unusual for the Peelite leaders, who, it must be said, never had courted public opinion.

1. *GP.* BM 44140. Derby to Gladstone, Feb. 11, 1857.
2. *MGLD.* 1:560–61. Gladstone Memorandum, Feb. 14, 1857.

In the event, the Conservatives drew up their own resolution, modified slightly by Gladstone, which simply demanded that the Government adjust their estimated income and expenditures so that deficiencies would be avoided in fiscal years 1858–59 and 1859–60. One basic point at issue between the Conservatives and Peelites—whether the deficit should be made up by direct or indirect taxation[3]—was thus avoided. With these arrangements made, the great division was held on February 23.

This division proved conclusively that the Peelites simply could not deliver the vote. Of the 27 members who had supported the Government on the Kars division the preceding year, 13 supported it again and five were absent.[4] The earl of Dalkeith, Gladstone, Graham, Sidney Herbert, Lord Alfred Hervey, Earl Jermyn, Roundell Palmer, Robert J. Phillimore, and Granville H. Vernon seem to represent the total reliable Peelite force in early 1857—even Cardwell had bolted. There were six other possible Peelites who joined them on the division, but probably as much in support of Derby as of Gladstone.[5] What made it the more embarrassing was that a united section could have easily won the day.

For the Palmerston government the danger had by no means passed. Lord Derby had been preparing a second attack upon the Government for its conduct in the *Arrow* incident, which had led to war with China. The project was Derby's own, supported by the peace-loving elements in the Conservative party, but the cause attracted some Peelite and former Peelite lords, such as Aberdeen, Ellenborough, Haddington, and Lyndhurst. Despite this infusion of strength, Derby's attempt to censure the Government was voted down.

The center of interest then moved quickly to the Commons, where Richard Cobden and the Radicals raised the China issue on the same

3. For an excellent analysis of the outstanding differences between the Peelites and Conservatives, see Lord John Manners letter in appendix 3.

4. Edward Cardwell, Henry Fitz-Roy, George G. Harcourt, George W. Heneage, Sir James W. Hogg, James Johnstone, Sir John V. Johnstone, George C. Legh, Sir John Owen, John H. Philipps, Jonathan J. Richardson, John M. Sutton, and Henry W. Wickham supported the Government; Edmund Antrobus, Henry B. Baring, Edmund B. Denison, Henry Herbert, and William B. Hughes were absent.

5. This group included Thomas Baring, Lord Robert Clinton, Allan E. Lockhart, Charles M. Lushington, Jonathan Peel, and Edward D. Pennant.

day (February 26) that Derby was being beaten on it in the Lords. Conservatives in the Commons would naturally support a censure in their own House, while the small Peelite force there would take its cue from Aberdeen, so that an interesting, if unnatural, combination of Radicals, Conservatives, Peelites, and a few Liberals defeated the Government on the China issue on March 3.

Because some of the irregular Conservatives would support the attack because of its Conservative connection, others because of the Liberal element behind it, and still others because Gladstone and Graham joined in, this division is virtually valueless as a means of identifying the Peelites in the Commons at this time. Suffice it to say that all nine Peelites who had joined the Conservatives in the February 23 attack voted together on this issue, and they were joined by 14 others who may or may not, like Cardwell, have followed Peelite policy in so doing.

Charles Greville noted in April, 1857: "For a long time past it has been absurd to talk of the Peelites as a Party. There are not a dozen men in the House of Commons who could by any possibility be so designated."[6] In making this estimate, one cannot be sure just whom he had in mind. Possibly he used the nine members of the February 23 division as a base and simply added one or two others. Whatever may have been his method of calculating their numbers, the statement provides further evidence of the disintegration of the Peelite section. Its rank-and-file members, like its leaders, were feeling the political pointlessness of continuing in isolation, and perhaps they too realized that the country had no lasting love for splinter groups.

6.   *GMEM.* April 4, 1857.

CHAPTER 26

THE ELECTION OF 1857

Lord Palmerston wisely decided that the issue on which he had been defeated was not a popular one, and he therefore had the queen dissolve Parliament, so he could take his case to the people. Those who had defeated him had the same uneasy suspicion about the nature of their case, which, though humanitarian and moralistic, was not a vote getter. Gladstone therefore asked Derby whether he should try to broaden the election issues by moving some resolution before the dissolution,[1] but Derby discouraged it and tried to accomplish the same purpose by delivering a blistering attack on Palmerston on March 16, an oratorical classic which called the prime minister a political chameleon without convictions on domestic issues.

Derby and Gladstone might consult and orate, but the voting public recalled how one had refused to take the helm, and the other had quit office, during the Crimean War; and in this postwar atmosphere no explanations could counteract the widespread, instinctive belief that both the Conservatives and Peelites had lately been weighed in the balance and found wanting.

Sensing the difficulties ahead, Derby hoped to avoid such electoral clashes between Conservatives and Peelites as had occurred in 1847 and 1852, and he suggested to Gladstone that they reach agreements in areas of possible conflict. Gladstone may have accepted this offer for himself at Oxford,[2] where Derby was chancellor, but he had to confess his inability to commit the Peelites as a whole.[3] Lord Malmesbury, the Conservative leader, contacted Sidney Herbert on the same subject, only to be informed coldly that there was no such thing as a Peelite party, and that he could give no pledges whatsoever,[4] an answer which left the Conservatives wondering with whom or what they had been negotiating only a month or so before.

1. *GP*. BM 44140. Derby to Gladstone, March 7, 1857.
2. *SHER*. 2:78.
3. *GP*. BM 44747. Gladstone Memorandum, undated.
4. *SHER*. 2:78. Herbert to Malmesbury, March 6, 1857.

In the election of 1857, the positions of Gladstone and Herbert were very different indeed. Gladstone presented himself as a Liberal Conservative, and his conduct toward Derby had been sufficiently friendly in 1856 to assure an uncontested election at Oxford. Herbert, on the other hand, had to make a vital decision. Would he continue to stress the Conservative label? If so, it might inhibit his political prospects in the future. So, while still calling himself a Liberal Conservative, he stressed liberalism in his election address, including reform based on "fancy franchises" such as Derby was to offer in 1859;[5] and this brought a Conservative candidate into the field against him. Herbert nevertheless won easily and thereafter could feel free to make such political alliances as he might choose.

Sir James Graham was still a Conservative "leaning toward" the Liberal party in his electoral appeals. His platform was summed up as "Peace, Retrenchment, and Reform";[6] and he worked hard to scotch a rumor, not entirely baseless in view of his recent voting record, that he had been acting in concert with his former intimate friend, Lord Derby. As he explained it, he presently acted with the "two or three remaining colleagues of Sir Robert Peel" and stood before his constituents as one wholly free from any secret commitments. The Carlisle voters approved his course, and he was second highest at the poll.

As Graham had noted in 1856, Cardwell's constituents at Oxford (City) were in advance of him in the Liberal movement, and his voting record in past years had not been entirely free from objection. Hence he found himself taking third place in a contest for two seats; and, as in 1852, he was temporarily without a seat in Parliament.[7] But he was subsequently able to show that one of his opponents had been guilty of corrupt practices; and in the following by-election, though opposed by the author-turned-Radical-politician, William M. Thackeray, he came off the victor. There was nothing in Cardwell's electoral experiences in 1857 to lure him in a conservative direction.

The general opinion after the election was that both the Peelites and Radicals had been soundly defeated. After the votes were

5. *Ilustrated London News*, April 4, 1857.
6. GRP. Graham to Mounsey, March 6, 1857.
7. See Erickson, *Cardwell*, pp. 21–22.

counted, Derby wrote, "The Peelite and Manchester parties are obliterated";[8] and Greville noted the "complete rout" of the same two groups.[9] And *The Times* recorded an unusual obituary as follows: "The Peelite Party is no more because their ground is too narrow to stand on."[10]

The election of 1857 simply made clear to the political world what many must have suspected for some time, and especially after the division of February 23, that the Peelite section was to all practical purposes dissolved. The extent to which this disintegration had taken place can be ascertained by surveying the 1857 postures of some of the former members of the section.

There were, aside from Cardwell, Graham, and Herbert, 35 statesmen from the original "112" involved in this election. Three of these, Lord Alfred Hervey and Sir James W. Hogg, both important Peelites, and Sir George Clerk, who sought to return to Parliament for Dover, were defeated, which leaves 32 others to be accounted for.

A dozen of these campaigned as Conservatives during the election, and their subsequent records show an acceptable party regularity, including Henry J. Baillie, John Boyd, Henry L. Corry, William T. Egerton, Lord Claud Hamilton, Sir Fitzroy Kelly, Allan E. Lockhart, John W. Patten, Jonathan Peel, Edward G. Pennant, Alexander Smollett, and Sir Frederic Thesiger. On the other hand, a number of Peelites had given up the hyphenated labels and had campaigned as Liberals. These included Lord Ernest Bruce, Henry FitzRoy, Sir John Hanmer, Sir John V. Johnstone, William A. Mackinnon, Charles W. Martin, Edward L. Mostyn, Sir John Owen, Frederick J. Tollemache, George Tomline (Whig), and James S. Wortley. Five others had retained a Conservative label but leaned toward Lord Palmerston, including Henry B. Baring, William H. Gregory, William B. Hughes, Earl Jermyn, and George C. Legh; while Beriah Botfield, Townshend Mainwaring, and John J. Johnstone leaned strongly in the opposite direction. This left only one—William T. Copeland—to occupy a truly independent position.

What was true of the Original Peelites was true for some of the

8. *DP.* Derby XII. Derby to Disraeli, April 24, 1857.
9. *GMEM.* April 4, 1857.
10. *The Times,* April 3, 1857.

more prominent Peelites of a later vintage. Thomas Baring, Samuel Christy, the earl of Dalkeith, and William Stirling campaigned as Conservatives; Edmund B. Denison, Lord Elcho, Henry A. Herbert, Sir Robert Peel, John Walter, and Henry W. Wickham, as Liberals, and in both cases the labels described their political positions with fair accuracy. Then there were Edmund Antrobus, Henry A. Bruce, Lord Robert Clinton, and George G. Harcourt who retained a Liberal-Conservative label but were for practical purposes Liberals. In 1859 Bruce was to drop the Conservative designation and to campaign as a Liberal.

It is true that if one goes through the 1857 edition of *Dod*, he will find some 57 members listed as Liberal, Moderate, or Independent Conservatives; but if one checks their voting records, 32 of them appear actually to have been fairly dependable Derbyites. This would leave 25 members to become the basis for a new Peelite section.

But the picture for the Peelites was probably even more dreary than this. One of the chief reasons why many Conservatives could not quite make up their minds between Lord Derby and the Liberals was that it was by no means a choice between a conservative or liberal position, but actually between the regular Conservative leader and that former Canningite-Tory, Lord Palmerston, who showed little inclination to take up the cudgels for reforms of any nature. Thus, we can find Conservatives voting to sustain Lord Palmerston on the crucial division of February 19, 1859, and doing the same favor for Lord Derby when his Government was overthrown by the division of June 11, 1859.

The *Times* was right. The ground was too narrow for the Peelites to stand upon. Most of it, indeed, was occupied by the Derbyite conservatives and the Palmerstonian conservatives, who perhaps believed the liberal designation was more in keeping with the progress of the period.

Early in April, Granville H. Vernon sat in the quiet of the Carlton Club and penned a letter to the duke of Newcastle:

> That body of men to whom I earnestly looked—in whom I specially trusted—whom I zealously and independently followed, is now broken up. How or why it is unnecessary here to enquire. I rejoice to have been humbly associated with them. My adherence to Gladstone cost me two

years ago the office which was all but offered me, and which I confess must have gratified me. It is not for me to say whether Gladstone, Graham etc. did right in joining or leaving the Ministry. I think they did wrong in leaving it—but when they say they could not have staid consistently with their honour . . . what is to be answered? . . . It is now time I should come to my point. It is clear that, if one is to give up complete isolation & exclusion, a line must be taken—and a side. I lean to the liberal side—and Hayter is the doorkeeper. I confess I have a great repugnance to making out an application to him to look out for a seat for me—and on no account would I bond myself to a staunch acceptance of their estimates—but still I would do what is fairly consistent with the views of a man desirous of an honourable career in public life. . . . Here I am sitting for the last time in the Carlton which I never left tho' little frequented in many years, but from which I am about to take my name. Here I am without a seat (except the said Carlton chair).[11]

Letters by the rank-and-file Peelites are not numerous, and this one must be taken to represent the sentiments of many Peelites at this moment in their history—an earnest regard for the importance of their individual opinions, a sense of admiration for their former leaders, and a feeling of regret that practical politics demanded that chilly party regularity should replace casual consultations among men of like minds.

11. NP. 12287. Vernon to Newcastle, April 9, 1857. He was the son of Granville Harcourt Vernon, one of the Original Peelites.

CHAPTER 27

TWILIGHT OF THE PEELITES

During the election Herbert announced to Gladstone a determination that he did not make quite so clear to his constituents. "I am weary of the evils which the existence of a third party . . . created, and shall take my place where my opinions and predilections alike keep me—namely on the Liberal side of the House."[1] Gladstone would not argue the matter at length at that moment but replied that he could not give even qualified support to Palmerston or follow a Liberal party that had abandoned the principles of Peelism.[2]

Once the election was over a major reevaluation of their position was made by the Peelite leaders.

Gladstone began the discussion in a letter to Aberdeen on March 31. "A creditable exit seems particularly needful," he observed, "so that when we scatter . . . we shall be scattered for a reason."[3] Looking back on the events of the past four years he recalled that Graham and Cardwell had gone into opposition when Lord Derby had come to power, but the other Peelites had professed opposition only on the Protection issue. The coalition had never really achieved a fusion of the two parties. The mortar was still wet when Russell chose to blow it apart, and since that time the Liberals had been antagonistic toward the Peelite section. What should be done now? More specifically, how could the Peelites follow Palmerston, who had abandoned all their ideas on foreign policy, retrenchment, taxation, reform, education, and the Church?

Aberdeen's recollection and interpretation of the recent past proved quite different from that of Gladstone. Admitting that the Peelites had been affiliated with the Conservatives down to the election of 1852, he insisted that their behavior during that election had broken the bond; and the Peelites, therefore, had fused with the Liberal party.[4] This seems to have been more an appeal for action

---

1. *SHER.* 2:82. Herbert to Gladstone, March 18, 1857.
2. Ibid., pp. 82–83. Gladstone to Herbert, March 22, 1857.
3. *GP.* BM 44089. Gladstone to Aberdeen, March 31, 1857.
4. *GP.* BM 44089. Aberdeen to Gladstone, March 31, 1857.

at the moment than an accurate recitation of their past history, and Gladstone was quite naturally dissatisfied with it. If a fusion between the Peelites and Liberals had actually taken place in 1852, he replied, then he had been deceiving his constituents at Oxford as recently as a fortnight ago.[5] Aberdeen's rejoinder was that Gladstone, following the breakup of the coalition, had remained on the Liberal side of the House and had refrained from declaring a general hostility to the Government.[6] This, of course, proved that Gladstone was not a member of the Opposition party, but did it mean that he was actually a Liberal?

Their correspondence on this subject was then sent to Herbert for his views. Replying at length, Herbert stated that the fusion process had begun when they had decided to oppose Disraeli's budget, that it had been completed when the coalition Government had been formed, and that, after quitting the Palmerston Government, they had confirmed their position as "independent Liberals" by sitting on the Liberal side of the House.[7] Herbert failed to make clear why an "independent Liberal" should continue to call himself a Liberal Conservative and to retain his membership at the Carlton Club.[8]

When Graham was drawn into the argument, he, too, agreed with Aberdeen's interpretation of the past and added the statement: "A party we never were."[9] Aberdeen and Graham do not appear to have solicited an opinion from Newcastle, who had been probably the earliest advocate of the fusion theory, even though he had

---

5. Ibid. Gladstone to Aberdeen, April 4, 1857.

6. Ibid. Aberdeen to Gladstone, April 8, 1857.

7. *AP*. BM 43179. Herbert to Aberdeen, April 12, 1857.

8. Cardwell, Gladstone, and Herbert were still listed as members of the Carlton Club as late as 1859. By 1857 Henry B. Baring, Henry Fitz-Roy, Sir John Hanmer, William A. Mackinnon, Edward L. Mostyn, and Henry W. Wickham had left Pall Mall and registered at Brookes's Club on St. James's Street. But as of that year, Lord Ernest Bruce, William H. Gregory, William B. Hughes, Earl Jermyn, George C. Legh, George Tomline, and James S. Wortley were still listed as members of the Carlton Club; so were Edmund B. Denison, Lord Elcho, and Sir Robert Peel. Some of the Peelites were affiliated with none of the clubs. Graham in 1857 was a member of Boodles', but not of Brooke's, or the Carlton. Sir Robert Peel, on the other hand, was carried as a member of all three of these clubs.

9. *PGRA*. 2:309. Graham to Herbert, April 15, 1857.

tended to undermine it by calling himself merely an independent member of Parliament.

There is little about Peelite history that is absolutely definite and clear-cut; and no matter which side one takes in this controversy, his conclusions are open to criticism, if not refutation. Graham's statement that they never were a party was true only to the extent that they never developed party machinery; in a practical sense, they were clearly a section and were recognized as such both by contemporary statesmen and newspapers. The nature of the coalition Government can be argued one way or the other, but the important fact is that the Peelites joined it as a unit and left as a unit. Thereafter, the only leader who had a strong penchant for the Conservative party was Gladstone, while the others of the inner circle had a strong leaning toward the Liberals.

Insofar as the two great political divisions were concerned, the rank and file of the Liberal party in 1857 appears to have been friendly toward the Peelites while that of the Conservative party was hostile. Although many of the Liberal leaders feared that fusion with the Peelites would lessen their own chances for office, Derby and Disraeli would have been only too happy to have found places for them.

After the election, Herbert made a most un-Peelite suggestion— that they demonstrate to the world that the Peelite section had been disbanded by discontinuing the practice of sitting together in Parliament. This brought a roar of disapproval. "I am not sure that it is sound, or wise that friends should separate," Aberdeen observed.[10] Graham (who had followed such a course in 1852) protested: "The possibility of such a sad necessity is too painful for me to contemplate."[11] As usually happened, the older men had the last word and the opening of the new Parliament found the Peelites once again sitting together; and the history of the Peelites thus ends on a proper note both of friendship and ambiguity.

In an age which stresses noninvolvement and shrinks with a sophisticated horror at verbal or written emotional displays, the correspondence and relations among these Peelite leaders, splendid examples as they were of the purest Victorian idealism, may appear

10. *AP.* BM 43179. Aberdeen to Herbert, April 18, 1857.
11. *GRP.* Graham to Herbert, April 15, 1857.

to be embarrassingly demonstrative and sentimental. Yet, if one ignores the deep feelings of emotional attachment that existed among the Peelite leaders, he overlooks the primary bond that held them together and the wellspring of their strength to fight for their ideals without a thought for the political consequences.

After something more than a decade of fitful existence, a deepening purple shadow had fallen over the Peelite section, blotting out the last outlines of a middle party that time had failed to develop. Sitting together as political friends, Graham, Gladstone, and Herbert voted to oust Palmerston in the division of February 19, 1858. Thereafter, they sometimes played a friendly part toward the brief Conservative administration of Lord Derby. Although Graham and Herbert voted to end that administration on June 11, 1859, Gladstone, as a final gesture toward his old connection, voted with the Government.

When the Palmerston administration returned to power that year, the Peelite leaders, save for Aberdeen and Graham, who had no desire to return to office, finally made their commitment. For most of them, their existence did not long outlast the demise of their section. Aberdeen and Graham died in the fullness of their years in 1860 and 1861; Newcastle and Herbert, in 1864 and 1861, while still in their prime. Gladstone lingered on to put a firm Peelite stamp on the Liberal party until 1898, surviving even the youngest of the Peelite leaders, Edward Cardwell, who had passed away in 1886.

PART 5

The Peelites
in History

At the conclusion of a work of this nature it is customary to raise and answer certain general questions about the subject of the study as a means of placing it within the context of the period to which it belongs. Many such questions might come to mind regarding the Peelites, but from a political point of view perhaps the major one is: Were the Peelites a phase of "conservative Liberalism" or an aspect of "dynamic Conservatism?" Any answer to this question must include a consideration of why they happened to come into existence, what they tried to do, and how they fitted into the general pattern of the age.

The origins of the Peelite movement can be traced to the Reform Act of 1832 or, even further back, to the forces that called that change into existence. In a process that was to be repeated again after 1867, the immediate effect of this electoral change was to strengthen first the Liberal element in the Commons, and then, after a short period, to bring in a vastly strengthened Conservative party. Most observers agree that the Conservative party which triumphed in 1841 was the handiwork of Sir Robert Peel, who adapted the old Tory party to the changing socioeconomic situation in Britain by creating an amalgam of bourgeois and aristocratic persons and interests which was stable only as long as the fundamental economic interests of these groups did not clash. Though still land based, the party contained a liberal element of middle-class aristocrats and many from the middle class who aspired to aristocracy.

What gave the Conservative party its triumph in 1841 was not merely the reaction of middle-class and aristocratic elements to the threat of Chartism and radicalism of various types, but a feeling among its members that it was attuned to the age. Peel's "moral Government," as Bentinck called it, caught the spirit of the early Victorian age, justifying the leadership of the propertied classes on the ground that they gave moral as well as political leadership to the nation. It was this feeling, as well as their individual abilities, that made the Peelite leaders the most admired (though certainly

not the best liked) statesmen of the period and placed them in
contrast to the Tory and Whig leaders earlier in the century. But
the new Conservatism went beyond this and in its programs showed
a willingness to experiment, to reform, to cut new—if cautious—paths
through the political thicket. The Conservative of the 1841-45 period
could feel part of the movement. He believed he was adapting the
nation's institutions to the demands of "progress"—a progress that
was emphasized in the newspapers and periodicals of the time and
seemed clearly evident in the expansion of the railways, the advances of science, the continued growth of machine production, and
in the ever-more-popular statistical studies, which seemed to document the progress. The wounds that had lingered in the party since
Catholic Emancipation were healed. The members at the Carlton
Club felt united and aggressive.

Peel was able to maintain the unity of the Conservative party only
so long as he did not step across that indefinable line which separates
dynamic Conservatism from actual Liberalism, and he might well
have kept his party together had his economic program brought
prosperity to the nation; but the fact was that the measures that
had worked quite well for Frederick John Robinson in the 1820s,
scaling down prohibitive tariffs and making new trade arrangements,
failed to invigorate the sluggish economic situation of the early 1840s.
So he took a firm step across the line and turned to the Radicals for
a remedy.

Most observers today can readily understand what Peel did in
1846, but it is almost impossible to feel the reaction that swept
through the Conservative party as a result of it. For many of the
land-based Conservatives it must have seemed like the end of the
world, and even for the others this appropriation of a Radical nos-
trum could not but create nervousness and even panic. So the leadership of the party found itself deserted by most of the rank and file,
and those who remained true to them were often uneasy and silent
in their places.

This extraordinary act, this startling volte-face, brought down
upon the Original Peelites charges of political dishonesty, ostracism
from the circles in which they had been most loved, recriminations,
and general abuse. But they held their heads high during the storm.
They knew they had acted in the public good. They refused to go

down, and their mutual martydom provided the primary bond that held the section together down to 1852, by which time it was apparent to all but the die-hard "53" that the Peelites had been right both intellectually and morally.

There was a strong secondary bond which held them together during the period up to Peel's death—the pacific foreign policy of Lord Aberdeen, which was upheld in contrast to the more aggressive policies of Lord Palmerston and which turned them out in large numbers to censure the foreign secretary after the Don Pacifico debate. But, unlike the tariff question, foreign policy moved them toward a reconciliation with the Conservatives, a movement within the section which reached its flood stage in 1850.

Aside from free trade and a conciliatory foreign policy, the Peelite leaders created a number of other attitudes during the ten years of the section's existence, but these were never definite and distinct enough to set the Peelite section off sharply from the other parties and sections of Parliament. One of the main preoccupations of their leaders was economy in government, and they went beyond the Conservatives (who were more kindly toward the armed services) and well beyond the Whigs in this regard. Economic government meant lighter taxes and the availability of more money for investment in domestic and foreign trade. This attitude usually had the support of the section as a whole, but it was too materialistic an issue to stir much emotional enthusiasm.

On the subject of reform the section was too divided for it to become a rallying point. It is true that, as a whole, the section opposed the introduction of the ballot, but at that point unanimity ended, even among the Peelite leaders. Henry Goulburn accepted the middle-class infusion of 1832 as an act whose wisdom time had proved, but he feared the advance of democracy probably as much as did Lord Derby. Graham, Gladstone, Herbert, and Cardwell all believed that Britain's comparative passivity during the revolutionary years 1848–49 had shown that safety lay in a broad-based government; and, once Russell brought up the issue again in 1851, they were ready for another installment of reform. Curiously, none of them was as ready to act in this field as was Lord Aberdeen, who wrote in 1857: "I do not know what benefit is to be expected from any of the measures which are proposed, but I confess . . . I am not afraid of any experiment. It would not be easy to increase the inconsistency, contradiction, and falsehood by which it is characterized."[1]

Although they might differ as to the extent of the next measure of reform, the Peelite leaders, and probably most of the section, looked with favor upon improving the quality of administration. Efficient administration meant finding the most qualified men for governmental positions and employing experts to serve on commissions and boards of inquiry; and this, in turn, meant modifying the age-old system of patronage. Peel had set an example in 1846 of doling out rewards for merit rather than service to the party, and Aberdeen took pride in the fact that he had adopted the same policy. The alternative to the patronage system for governmental employment was to establish some means of securing talent by open competition. This was a laudable objective but, once again, not a stirring one.

The subject of religion, on the other hand, was one that held a wide emotional appeal, and a common policy in this area might have provided a strong bond of unity within the section. As a group, the Peelite leaders were deeply religious, but not theologically oriented (save, perhaps, for Gladstone). They enjoyed the ordered beauty of the service and accepted the Established Church as a vital feature of British life. But, as conservative reformers, they could not close their eyes to the fact that the favored position of the Church had created lethargy both among its clergy and laity and that abuses, such as pluralism, absenteeism, the inefficient management of Church property, and a haphazard distribution of benefices, had crept in. Earlier in his career, Peel had created an ecclesiastical commission to investigate clerical incomes. This commission had reduced the salaries of the higher-paid clerics and subdivided the larger parishes; but by mid-century the movement for further church reform lagged.

One reason for this lag was the sudden awakening of Protestant fears, in and outside the Established Church, that Roman Catholicism was posing a threat to their faith, which they associated with the British way of life. The defection of Newman to Roman Catholicism in 1845 and the Papal Aggression question of 1850 stoked

1. *BP.* Aberdeen to Brougham, August 24, 1857.

those fears. One has only to read through the descriptions many members provided for *Dod* during the 1850s to understand both the extent and intensity of this fear. Under these circumstances, further reforms of the Church might be denounced on one hand as serving the cause of popery or, on the other, as attempts to "Americanize" British institutions by introducing "voluntaryism." This helps account for the failure of the Peelites to push for Church reform.

A recent writer, however, has noted that the Peelites were the foremost champions of religious liberalism in Victorian Britain.[2] Liberalism is a vague term, which to be meaningful had to be reduced to certain elements. If religious liberalism meant conceding the right of every British subject to worship freely as he chose, not only the whole Peelite section but the Conservatives would be classified as Liberals.[3] If it meant admitting Dissenters to Anglican preserves, the Peelite leaders and many of the rank and file were more liberal than the Conservatives. If it meant abolishing the Jewish parliamentary disability, then the Peelite leaders and only a minority of the section were Liberals. If it meant sustaining the right of Roman Catholics to expand their convents and monasteries, even some of the more liberal Peelites were unsure. Even the religious liberalism of Lord Aberdeen had its limits.[4] In this area one should undoubtedly judge the attitudes of the Peelite leaders and those of the section separately, and evaluate them within the context of the times. On such a basis, the Peelite leaders were liberals, while the rank and file as a whole was conservative. This, of course, is of great importance because it meant that the Peelite leaders could not use this issue to consolidate their section.

In certain other areas, the liberalism of the Peelite leaders was scarcely distinguishable from that of the Conservatives, or even the House as a whole. Believing as they did in small, efficient government, they were unwilling to push out too far the frontiers of state

2. Josef L. Altholz, "The Political Behavior of English Catholics, 1850–1867," *The Journal of British Studies* 4 (November, 1964).

3. See Jones, *Lord Derby*, p. 146.

4. Aberdeen wrote, "I take for granted, however, that in admitting absolute freedom of religious belief and worship you would of course exclude any immoral and anti-social doctrines which might justly demand the interference of authority" (*BP*. Aberdeen to Brougham, August 19, 1855).

interference in economic and social affairs. While they would support Cardwell's Merchant Shipping Act, which was a salutary measure, they opposed—on the authority of Peel himself—such measures for the benefit of labor as the Ten Hours Act. Lord Ashley, indeed, experienced the greatest difficulties in enlisting the consistent support of any political party or section for his measures of social reform.

Nor can the attitudes of the Peelite leaders, or the section as a whole, on the subject of education be considered avant-garde. This was certainly most apparent from their voting records on the National Education resolutions of 1856, which were designed to create a decent system of public education in England and Wales, financed from local rates. One might understand the Peelite opposition to completely secularized schools—the issue is still debated today—but they weakened their position by not facing up to the problem of mass ignorance and offering some alternative to the scheme proposed in these resolutions.

The Peelite leaders were also remiss in the areas of law and court reform. Much had been done prior to 1846 in eliminating the draconian laws surviving from the eighteenth century, and Peel had earlier played a distinguished part in this reform movement; but thereafter his interest had lagged. In 1842 Graham and Lord Lyndhurst had secured the passage of a law which established courts of bankruptcy in various parts of the country, and two years later Graham took the lead in abolishing imprisonment for debt. He also saw to it that a large number of minor court officials were transferred from the fee system to salaries. In these measures Graham received little encouragement from the other Peelites or from Peel himself. As a member of the coalition government, Edward Cardwell promised to bring in a law providing for limited liability, but the concerns of the Crimean War prevented it. A real reform of the legal and courts system had to wait for the first Gladstone administration (1868–74).

Such were the primary attitudes of the Peelites. Now, what did they actually accomplish? First and foremost, they fought the battle for free trade; and this system, aided by the improvement of communications, gold discoveries, and other factors, introduced into Britain two decades of general prosperity. This battle was not entirely concluded until 1852, so that Peelite interest for six of the ten years the section existed was centered primarily in this area, and other reforms were of minor importance.

A second of the more important Peelite attitudes, the conciliatory Aberdeen foreign policy, continued to receive emphasis down to the time of Peel's death; but after that event, and especially after the opportunity for office presented itself, the Peelite leaders unwisely, as it turned out, subordinated this tenet of their faith and threw in with Palmerston and Russell. Most of the Peelites, except Newcastle, attempted to preserve this pacific attitude during the long crisis of 1853–54 preceding the outbreak of the Crimean War; but under the stress of national feeling all, save Aberdeen, abandoned it. They reasserted it—together with the Conservatives and Radicals—at the time of the China War; yet, when all is said and done, as a force for preserving the peace, they failed.

One of the more long-lasting bequests of the Peelites was the tradition of efficient public administration they had created in the various departments of British government. Their efficiency and frugality was demonstrated not only during the Peel administration but also during their membership in the coalition. Gladstone, Graham, and Goulburn were undoubtedly superior in the field of public finance to any of the Whigs or Conservatives, and in the Colonial Office the duke of Newcastle provided an economical, but friendly, administration that carefully considered the wants and needs of the colonies. Had it not been for the Crimean War, Graham, Gladstone, Cardwell, Herbert, and Newcastle would probably have all been accounted very successful administrators, and even that discrediting development did not prevent Palmerston from seeking their services in his government.

Closely tied to this emphasis on administrative efficiency was the movement to supplant the conventional patronage system with something better. The India Act of 1853 provided opportunities for higher appointments in that area by competitive examination, and the following year both Graham and Gladstone subscribed to a report drawn up by Sir Stafford Northcote and Sir Charles Trevelyan, which advocated a similar reform at home. But the Crimean War, a lack of public interest, and the opposition of Lord John Russell, who was keenly aware of the importance of patronage to a party leader, combined to postpone this reform and to carry it over—like that of the courts—until Gladstone himself came to power.

Their contributions to the expansion of the definition of religious liberty were of a persistent, if modest nature. Year in, year out, the Peelite leaders set an example for the rest of the section by voting to admit the Jews into Parliament, but just as consistently the bulk of the section ignored the votes of their leaders. Perhaps the only definite accomplishment for the Peelites in this field was forcing on Russell a modification of the Ecclesiastical Titles Bill, but in the long run this was of a minor significance.

So much for the Peelite attitudes and accomplishments of the Peelite leaders. What they were never to do was to reduce their concept of "conservative reform" to specific and identifying issues which would command the adhesion of the unattached Conservatives and more conservative Liberals, once the free trade issue had been settled. Perhaps they failed in this respect because there was so little demand for reforms during this "decent, quiet, and ordered" (as Charles Villiers called it) period of the 1850s. The more ardent Protestants were likely to join hands with Derby and Disraeli; those who desired a Liberal attachment without having to do much about it could join Palmerston. The smaller number who wanted to identify themselves with the movement (the Radicals having been discredited by the Crimean War and its aftermath, for the time being) could join Lord John Russell, as did Aberdeen, Graham, and Gladstone. So if the Peelite leaders could find no standard around which to rally their forces, it was probably more the fault of the times than of their leadership.

Except when a free trade issue arose, the members of the Peelite section often displayed more disunity than unity. Some would vote to admit the Jews to Parliament, then look with disfavor on Maynooth; others would take just the opposite stand. Some anticipated political reform with some favor; others were indifferent or hostile toward it. Some were strong pacifists; others found themselves increasingly drawn toward Palmerston's vigorous assertion of British nationalism. A few would support Lord Ashley's humanitarian reforms; the majority would not. On studying their records, one gets a vague impression that most of the Peelites wished to be identified with progress and modernity, but that they clung tenaciously to the

Conservative pier, so that they would never be swept out into deep water and could paddle around in the shallows as they wished.

This clinging to the Conservative label, even by the Peelite leaders, not to mention retaining their memberships in the Carlton Club, goes far to undermine the theory that the Peelites of this period were a part of the Liberal movement. It is significant that Gladstone rather than Graham, Herbert, or Cardwell, assumed direction of the Peelite section in the Commons once Peel had died, for he was the most tenacious in clinging to what was left of the Conservative connection. There is little reason to doubt that this attitude was not adopted merely as a political expedient or that it did not reflect his personal desires. Among the three outstanding leaders of the moment—Russell, Palmerston, and Derby—Gladstone felt closest to Derby and undoubtedly would have rejoined him had it not been for his Peelite friendships and the "Disraeli problem."

On the other hand, one could argue that Peelism was an early phase of Liberalism, distinct from the liberalism of the Whigs, which triumphed when Gladstone (who at the time still called himself a Peelite) formed his first administration in 1868. Further evidence for this point of view is the dislike many Conservatives felt for the Peelites during this decade as well as the large number of Peelites who finally joined Palmerston. It must be admitted, however, that joining Palmerston was hardly like going over Niagara into the rapids of Liberal progress.

There still remains to assess the role of the Peelite section in British politics during this period. Undoubtedly, they gave a fillip to the concept of party irregularity so extensive that Graham concluded they had destroyed party. Following their example, many members of Parliament felt they had the right whenever they chose to plead their consciences and desert their party on almost any division, except one of no confidence; and this greatly confused the political situation.

For the Conservatives the Peelite section and their influence was a decade and more of pure migraine. Lord Derby on more than one occasion complained of the "loose fish" in the Commons and the so-called independent members on whom no one could depend. This situation was certainly a factor in his refusal to take office in 1855. When he told the Lords at that time "to hold that high and responsible situation dependent for support from day to day upon precarious and uncertain majorities, compelled to cut down this measure, and to pare off that—to consider with regard to each measure not what was for the real welfare of the country, but what would conciliate a half dozen here, or obviate the objections of some half-dozen there. . . . I say this is a state of things which cannot be satisfactory to any Minister . . . to carry on with a minority is an intolerable and galling servitude as no man of honour or character would expose himself to,"[5] he was speaking from the heart.

To secure a deeper insight into what Derby had in mind, we have only to consider Disraeli's satisfaction at the results of the election of 1857, which was considered a Conservative defeat. Although the Conservatives had lost 20 seats, reducing their numbers from 280 to 260, Disraeli was more satisfied with the new group than the old, which had contained 60 unreliables.[6] Now these 60 were not Peelites but Conservatives who followed the Peelite example in cherishing their political independence and rejecting party dictation. So long as the Peelite section was extant to set an example, it was probably impossible to reconstruct a reliable Conservative party.

There can be no question but that the Peelite section exercised a distracting influence upon the Whig-Liberals, especially those in the upper echelons of the party. Those who fought the day-to-day battles for the party in the Commons and the Lords found themselves (with good reason) wondering whether or not their services would be rewarded once the prize of office had been attained, for in the wings was a glittering array of Peelites waiting to occupy an indefinite number of cabinet seats. So long as Peel lived, the Whigs could usually count on Peelite support if ever it were really needed, but after his death the Peelites became quite unreliable. They played at least a passive role in the premature upset of Russell in February, 1851, and an active one in turning him out a year later. Most Whigs believed the price for their joining the coalition was unfairly high, and they left it at the first opportunity once their own leader had retired. Thereafter, when the opportunity presented itself, they tried to overthrow Palmerston in March, 1857; and, when

5. *Hansard*, 3d. ser., 136:1333–49.
6. *M&BDIS.* 1:1476. Disraeli to Mrs. Willyams, April 13, 1857.

this proved premature, they bided their time and helped bring down the curtain on him in February, 1858.

Certainly neither the Whig leaders nor Lord Derby (who was ousted by the Peelites in 1852) could regard the Peelites as other than disorganizers. British political life, indeed, paid a high price in instability to salve the tender consciences of the Peelites.

Yet there was another side to the coin, an oft-recurring feature in the splendid democratic tradition. While granting the practical necessity for party functioning with all the discipline and rigged voting that such rule implies, the application of too-demanding regularity is likely to leave the obscure member with an isolated feeling, with the sense of being merely a cog in a machine over which he has little or no control. What recourse does he have but to try to assert his independence both as a warning to, and means of, disciplining a too arrogant directing authority in his party? Probably not since the abolition of the purchased boroughs did the members in the Commons feel so free to follow their individual ideas and consciences as during this period of Peelite disorganization. One can well imagine that many had a new sense of importance and may have even enjoyed themselves immensely. For if there was one attitude that the Peelites popularized and made fashionable, it was that even the most mute back-bencher, when it came to a division, had a duty to vote his conscience and his sense of honor.

APPENDIX 1

The following list contains the names of the members who probably composed the famous "112" who voted for the repeal of the Corn Laws on February 27, 1846. After their names are a few facts about them, including the years of their lives, their backgrounds and economic interests when available, the constituency or constituencies they represented, and their political designations as of 1857 or at the time between 1846–57 when they left Parliament.

The capital letters following many of the descriptions help link the members with certain of the major movements of the period. All, of course, were attached to free trade, so this is omitted. *J* indicates they supported Jewish Emancipation; *C*, that they usually voted for measures favorable to the Catholics; and *JC*, that they were favorable to both. An *A* means that they voted with one or more of Lord Ashley's humanitarian measures; and *S*, that they voted against removing the differential duty on West Indian sugar or supported Buxton's motion of May 31, 1850, which in most cases (if not all) indicated an interest in the continuing battle against slavery and the slave trade. *FP* means they identified themselves with Aberdeen's foreign policy by voting against Palmerston on the Don Pacifico affair. Absence of letters after a name may mean no more than that individual missed the division or divisions involving one or more of these issues.

1. Acland, Thomas Dyke, Jr. (11th Bt.) (1809–May 25, 1898). Landed interest. Oxford University. Somerset West, 1837–47. Free Trade Conservative. He ran unsuccessfully as a Conservative in 1859, then stood as a Liberal in 1865. *S.*

2. A'Court-Repington, Edward Henry (1783–1855). Royal Navy. Brother of Lord Heytesbury. Heytesbury, 1820–32; Tamworth, 1837–47. Free Trade Conservative.

3. Attwood, John (1800–1860?). Son of a gentleman. Connected with an iron works in Stafford County, and the Harwich Railway Company. Harwich, 1841–48. Election voided in 1848. Free Trade Conservative.

4. Baillie, Henry James (1804–85). West Indian proprietor, Inverness-shire, 1840–57. Joined the Conservative government in 1852 as a joint secretary of the Board of Control. *S; A; FP.*

5. Baillie, Hugh Duncan (1777–June 21, 1866). A career army officer with rank of colonel. Rye, 1830–33; Honiton, 1834–47. Free Trade Conservative. *S.*

6. Baird, William (1796–1864) of Elie Fife. An iron-master. He took the Chiltern Hundreds in April, 1846, to make way for Lord Lincoln. Falkirk Dist., 1841–46. Free Trade Conservative.

7. Baldwin, Charles Barry (1790–1859). Son of an army officer. Became a barrister and bank director. Totness, 1830–31; 1839; 1841–52. Free Trade Conservative. *S; FP.*

8. Baring, Henry Bingham (1804–69). Connected both with the army and the East India Company. Junior lord of the Treasury, 1841–46. Callington, 1831; Marlborough, 1832–59. Liberal Conservative. *J*; *FP*.

9. Baring, William Bingham (2d Lord Ashburton, 1848) (1799–1864). Banker and landowner. Served on Board of Control under Peel. Thetford, 1826–30; Callington, 1830; Winchester, 1832–37; Staffordshire - North, 1837–41; Thetford, 1841–48. Later supported the Aberdeen Coalition and then Palmerston. *J*.

10. Barkly, Henry (1815–98). Son of West Indian proprietor and merchant. Leominster, 1845–49. Appointed governor of British Guiana by Russell in 1849 and made his career in the colonial field. Liberal Conservative.

11. Beckett, William (1784–1863). A banker and businessman. Leeds, 1841–52; Ripon, 1852–57. Free Trade Conservative. *A*; *FP*.

12. Benbow, John (1769–1855). A railway director. Dudley, 1844–55. Conservative, *S. A.*

13. Bodkin, William Henry (1791–1874). Famed criminal lawyer. Rochester, 1841–47. Later a Conservative. Knighted in 1867. *S*; *A*.

14. Botfield, Beriah (1807–63). Harrow. Christ Church. Botanist and antiquarian. Landed interest. Ludlow, 1840–47; 1857. Liberal Conservative.

15. Bowles, Rear-Admiral William (1780–July 2, 1869). Royal Navy. Brother-in-law of Lord Palmerston. Launceston, 1844–52. Free Trade Conservative. *S*.

16. Boyd, John (1789–1862). Son of an Irish landowner. Coleraine, 1843–52 (Chiltern Hundreds); Coleraine, 1857. High Conservative.

17. Bruce, Lord Ernest Augustus Charles Brudenell (3d marquess of Ailesbury, 1878) (1811–86). A vice-chamberlain under Peel. Marlborough, 1832–57. Palmerstonian Liberal. *JC*; *FP*.

18. Buckley, Edmund (1780–1867). Interested in coal, iron, and the canals. Newcastle-under-Lyme, 1841–47. Free Trade Conservative.

19. Cardwell, Edward T. (1813–86). Winchester, Oxford. Barrister interested both in business and finance. A secretary of the Treasury under Peel. Clitheroe, 1842–1847; Liverpool, 1847–52; Oxford City, 1853–57. Liberal Conservative. *S*; *JC*; *FP*.

20. Carnegie, Swynfen Thomas (1813–November 29, 1879). Son of the earl of Northesk. Navy Captain. Stafford Bor., 1841–47. Free Trade Conservative.

21. Clerk, Sir George, Bt. (1787–1867). Married into the Ellenborough family. Career politician. Vice-president of the Board of Trade under Peel. Edinburghshire, 1811–32; 1835–37; Stamford, 1838–47; Dover, 1847–52. Defeated for Dover in 1857. Free Trade Conservative. *J*; *FP*.

22. Clive, Robert Henry (1789–1854). Second son of the earl of Powis. Large land holdings; chairman of two railway boards; East India proprietor. Friend of Lord Lincoln. Ludlow, 1818–32; Shropshire - South, 1832–47. Free Trade Conservative. *S*.

23. Cockburn, Sir George G. C. B. (1772–1853). Royal Navy. Portsmouth,

1818–20; Weobley, 1820–28; Plymouth Bor., 1828–32; Ripon, 1841–47. Free Trade Conservative.

24. Copeland, William Taylor (1797–1868). Owner of porcelain factory at Stoke-upon-Trent. Coleraine Bor., 1831–37; Stoke-upon-Trent, 1837–52, 1857. Liberal Conservative. *S; FP.*

25. Corry, Henry T. L. (1803–73). Second son of the earl of Belmore. Small landowner. A lord of the Admiralty under Peel. Tyrone, 1826–57. Derbyite Conservative. *S; FP.*

26. Cripps, William (1805–May 11, 1848). Son of a member of Parliament. A barrister by profession. Lord of the Treasury under Peel in 1846. Cirencester, 1841–47. Free Trade Conservative.

27. Damer, George Lionel Dawson (1788–1856). A son of the earl of Portarlington. Landed interest. Portarlington, 1832–47; Dorchester, 1847–52. Free Trade Conservative. *S; C; FP.*

28. Dickinson, Francis Henry (1813–90). Son of a general. A magistrate. Somersetshire - West, 1841–47. Free Trade Conservative. *A.*

29. Douglas, Sir Charles Eurwicke (1806–February 21, 1887). Son of a baronet. Former secretary of Lord Goderich. Warwick Bor., 1837–52. Free Trade Conservative. Returned for Banbury in 1859 as a Liberal.

30. Douro, Marquess of (Arthur Richard Wellesley) (2d duke of Wellington) (1807–84). Aldborough, 1829–31; Norwich, 1837–52. Free Trade Conservative. *C; FP.*

31. Drummond, Henry Home (1783–1867). Son of a banker. Scottish lawyer and bank director. Sterlingshire, 1821–32; Perthshire, 1840–52. Free Trade Conservative. *S; C; FP.*

32. Dugdale, William Stratford (1801–September 15, 1871). Estate owner. Trustee of Rugby, and Yeomanry captain. Shaftesbury Bor., 1830. Bramber, 1831–32; Warwickshire - North, 1832–47. Free Trade Conservative.

33. Eastnor, Viscount (Charles Somers). (1819–83). Eldest son of earl Somers, whom he succeeded in 1852. Reigate, 1840–47. Free Trade Conservative.

34. Egerton, Lord Francis (1st earl of Ellesmere) (1800–57). A son of the duke of Sutherland. Bridgewater estates; Bletchingley-Sutherland Co. Lancashire - South, 1835–46. Free Trade Conservative.

35. Egerton, William Tatton (1806–83). Large landowner. Lymington, 1830–32; Cheshire - North, 1832–57. Conservative. *FP.*

36. Escott, Bickham (1801–53). Son of a cleric. Lawyer by profession. Winchester, 1841–47. Free Trade Conservative.

37. Estcourt, Thomas Grimston Bucknall (1776–1853). Landowner, barrister, and patron of three livings. Declined a baronetcy from Peel in 1846. Oxford University, 1826–47. Free Trade Conservative.

38. Fitz-Roy, Henry (1807–59). Son of the 2d Baron Southampton. Landed interest. Lewes, 1841–57. Liberal. *JC; FP.*

39.   Flower, Sir James (1790–1850). Son of a baronet. Hertfordshire land-owner; sheriff of Norfolk Co. Thetford, 1841–47. Free Trade Conservative.

40.   Glynne, Sir Stephen Richard (1807–74). Landowner. Lord lieutenant of Flintshire. Flintshire, 1831–47. Free Trade Conservative.

41.   Godson, Richard (1797–1850). A lawyer and queen's counsel. St. Albans, 1831; Kidderminster, 1832–35; 1837–52. Free Trade Conservative. A.

42.   Gore, Montagu (1811–84). A barrister and writer. Devizes, 1832–34; Barnstaple, 1841–47. Free Trade Conservative. S.

43.   Goulburn, Henry (1784–1856). West Indian proprietor. Chancellor of the Exchequer under Peel. Horsham (1807), St. Germans (1812); West Looe, 1818–26; Armagh, 1826–31; Cambridge University, 1831–56. Free Trade Conservative. S; FP.

44.   Graham, Sir James Robert (1792–1861). Land and business. Home secretary under Peel. Carlisle (1820); Cumberland - East (1830); Pembroke Dist. (1838); Dorchester (1841); Ripon (1847); Carlisle Dist. (1852–57). Conservative leaning toward Liberals. JC; FP.

45.   Greene, Thomas (1791–August 10, 1872). Lawyer and patron of one living. Lancaster, 1824–57. Free Trade Conservative. S; C.

46.   Gregory, William Henry (1817–92). Harrow. Christ Church. Interested in horse-racing. Dublin City, 1842–47; Galway Co., 1857. Liberal Conservative leaning toward Palmerston.

47.   Grimsditch, Thomas (1786–1864). Landowner and lawyer. Mayor of Macclesfield, 1833–34. Macclesfield, 1837–47. Free Trade Conservative. A.

48.   Hamilton, Lord Claud (1813–84). A son of the marquess of Abercorn. Landed interest. Tyrone, 1835–37; 1839–57. Became a treasurer of the Household in Lord Derby's 1852 government. S; FP.

49.   Hamilton, William John (1805–67). A lawyer and chairman of a railway company. Newport, I.W., 1841–47. Free Trade Conservative. S.

50.   Hanmer, Sir John (1809–81). A Flintshire landlord. Shrewsbury, 1832–37; Kingston-upon-Hull, 1841–47; Flint District, 1847–57. Liberal. J.

51.   Herbert, Sidney (Lord Herbert of Lea, 1860) (1810–61). Half brother of the earl of Pembroke. Secretary at War under Peel. Wiltshire - South, 1832–57. Leaning toward Palmerston. S; JC; FP.

52.   Hervey, Lord Alfred (1816–75). Sixth son of the marquess of Bristol. Eton. Cambridge. Barrister. A lord of the Treasury in the coalition government. Brighton, 1842–57. Liberal. C; A; FP.

53.   Hogg, Sir James Weir (1790–1876). Bt. 1846. Barrister and East India Company Director. Beverley, 1835–47; Honiton, 1847–57. Free Trade Conservative. J; FP.

54.   Hope, George William (1808–October 18, 1863). Eton. Oxford. Son of a general. Lawyer by profession. Undersecretary for the Colonies under Peel. Weymouth, 1837–41; Southampton, 1842–47. Liberal Conservative. S.

55.   Hornby, John (1810–December 5, 1892) of Raikes Hall, Lancaster. A

lawyer by profession. Blackburn Bor., 1841–52. Free Trade Conservative. S; A; FP.

56. Hughes, William Bulkeley (1797–1882). Son of a knight. A barrister by profession. Oxford City, 1830–37; Carnarvon Dist., 1837–57. Liberal Conservative. FP.

57. James, Sir Walter Charles (Lord Northbourne, 1884) (1816–93). Son of a baronet. Oxford. Kingston-upon-Hull, 1837–47. Free Trade Conservative.

58. Jermyn, Frederick William, Earl (1800–October 30, 1864). Son of the marquess of Bristol. Bury St. Edmunds, 1830–57. Conservative. JC.

59. Jocelyn, Robert, Viscount (1816–54) Eldest son of the earl of Roden. King's Lynn. A secretary of the Board of Control under Peel. 1842–54. Free Trade Conservative leaning toward Derby.

60. Johnstone, John J. Hope (1796–July 11, 1876). Son of a knight. Royal Navy. Dumfriesshire, 1830–47; 1857. Liberal Conservative.

61. Johnstone, Sir John Vanden Bempde (1799–February 24, 1869). Baronet and partron of two livings. Oxford. Yorkshire, 1830–31; Scarborough, 1832–37; 1841–57. Liberal. A; JC; FP.

62. Kelly, Sir Fitzroy (1796–1880). Chief counsel for the Bank of London and the East India Company. £25,000 p/a. Solicitor general under Peel (1845), and Lord Derby (1852). Ipswich, 1838–41; Cambridge Bor., 1843–47; Suffolk - East, 1852–57. Conservative.

63. Kirk, Peter (1800–57). The son of a knight. Mayor of Carrickfergus. Carrickfergus, 1835–47. Free Trade Conservative.

64. Lascelles, William Sebright (1788–1851). A son of the earl of Harewood. Landed interest. Northallerton (1820); East Looe (1826); Northallerton, 1831–32; Wakefield, 1837–47; Knaresborough, 1847–51. Liberal (1847).

65. Legh, George Cornwall (1804–77). From an ancient landowning family. Cheshire - North, 1841–57. Conservative. FP.

66. Lockhart, Allan Eliott (1803–March 23, 1878). A Scottish lawyer. Selkirkshire, 1846–57. Liberal Conservative. C; FP.

67. Lyall, George (1784–1853). Merchant, shipowner, and chairman of the East India Company. London, 1833–35; 1841–47. Free Trade Conservative.

68. Macgeachy, Forster Alleyne (1809–87). The son of a mayor. Oxford. Honiton, 1841–47. Free Trade Conservative.

69. Mackinnon, William Alexander (1789–1870). Chief of Clan Mackinnon; large estates in Ireland. Insurance business. Dunwich, 1819–20; Lymington, 1831–52; Rye, 1853–57. Liberal.

70. McNeill, Duncan (1793–1874). Lord advocate and solicitor general for Scotland under Peel. Made judge of the Supreme Court of Scotland in 1851. Argyllshire, 1843–51. Liberal.

71. Mahon, Viscount (Philip Henry Stanhope) (1805–75). Landlord in Kent. Secretary of the Board of Control under Peel. Wootton Basset, 1830–31; Hertford Bor., 1835–52. Free Trade Conservative. S; FP.

72. Mainwaring, Townshend (1807–December 25, 1883). Welsh landowner and son of a clergyman. Denbigh, 1841–47; 1857. Liberal Conservative.

73. Martin, Charles Wykeham (1801–70). Estate owner. Eton. Oxford. Newport, I.W., 1841–52; West Kent, 1857. Liberal. *JC*.

74. Masterman, John (1782–1862). London banker and East India Company director. London, 1841–57. Free Trade Conservative. *S; A; FP*.

75. Meynell, Captain Henry (1790–March 24, 1865). Navy captain and groom-in-waiting to the queen. Landed interest. Lisburn, 1826–47. Free Trade Conservative.

76. Milnes, Richard Monckton (1809–85). Family in the Derbyshire cloth trade. Son of a member of Parliament. Pontefract, 1837–57. Moderate Conservative who supported Russell (1847). Liberal. *S; A; JC*.

77. Mostyn, Edward M. L. (Baron Mostyn, 1854) (1795–1884). Heir to the Mostyn estates. Flintshire, 1831–37; 1841–42; Lichfield, 1846–47; Flintshire, 1847–54. Liberal. *A; JC*.

78. Neville, Ralph (1817–86). Son of a clergyman. Windsor, 1841–47. Free Trade Conservative.

79. Northland, Viscount (Thomas Knox, 3d earl of Ranfurly). (1816–58) Heir to Ranfurly title. Eton. Dungannon, 1838–50. Free Trade Conservative.

80. Oswald, Alexander Haldane (1811–68). An Ayrshire landlord. Ayrshire, 1843–52. Free Trade Conservative inclining toward Liberals. *S; JC; FP*.

81. Owen, Sir John (1777–1861). Barrister. Lord lieutenant of Pembrokeshire and patron of six livings. Pembrokeshire, 1806–41; Pembroke Dist., 1841–57. Liberal. *A; JC*.

82. Patten, John Wilson (1st Baron Winmarleigh) (1805–92). Landowner and son of a member of Parliament. Lancashire - North, 1830, 1832–57. Conservative. *S; FP*.

83. Peel, Jonathan (1799–1879). Brother of Sir Robert Peel. Army man. Surveyor General of Ordnance under Peel. Norwich, 1826–31; Huntingdon Bor., 1831–57. Conservative. *S; FP*.

84. Peel, Sir Robert (1788–1850). Cloth manufacturer and landowner. Patron of two livings. Prime Minister, 1834–35; 1841–46. Cashel (1809); Chippenham Bor. (1812), Oxford University (1818), Westbury (1828); Tamworth, 1830–50. Independent member. *J; FP*.

85. Pennant, Edward Gordon Douglas (Baron Penrhyn of Llandegai) (1800–1886). Brother of the earl of Morton. Army. Carnarvonshire, 1841–57. Conservative. *S; FP*.

86. Polhill, Captain Frederick (1798–1848). Army. Landed interest. Bedford Bor., 1830–47. Free Trade Conservative. *A*.

87. Praed, W. Tyringham (1781–1846). A banker. St. Ives, 1838–46. Free Trade Conservative.

88. Reid, George Alexander (1823–May 12, 1852). Son of a prominent brewer. Director of London and Southwestern Railway. Windsor, 1845–52. Free Trade Conservative. *S; FP*.

89. Reid, Sir John Rae (1792–July 30, 1867). Son of a baronet and merchant. East India proprietor and West Indian merchant. Governor of the Bank of England. Dover, 1830; 1832–47. Free Trade Conservative.

90. Russell, Jesse David Watts (1812–March 7, 1879). Son of a gentleman. Oxford. Staffordshire - North, 1841–47. Free Trade Conservative.

91. Sandon, Viscount (Dudley Ryder, 2d Earl of Harrowby) (1798–1882). Heir to peerage. Tiverton, 1819–31; Liverpool, 1831–47. Free Trade Conservative. A.

92. Seymour, Sir Horace Beauchamp (1792–1851). Son of Lord Hugh Seymour. Army. Landed interest. Oxford (1820), Bodmin (1826), Midhurst (1841), Antrim (1845), Lisburn, 1847–51. Free Trade Conservative. JC.

93. Smollett, Alexander Jr. (1802–81). Son of an Admiral. Landed interest. Dumbartonshire, 1841–57. Conservative. S; A; FP.

94. Smythe, George Percy (1818–57). Eldest son of Viscount Strangford. Landlord in Penhurst area. Young England. Canterbury, 1840–52. Free Trade Conservative. S; JC; FP.

95. Somerton, Lord (James C. H. W. Ellis, 3rd earl of Normanton) (1818–96). Land. Wilton, 1841–52. Free Trade Conservative. S.

96. Stewart, John (1790–April 7, 1860). West Indian proprietor. Lymington, 1832–47. Free Trade Conservative.

97. Stuart, Henry (1804–54). Grandson of the earl of Bute. Landed interest. Bedford Bor., 1841–54. Free Trade Conservative. S; FP.

98. Sutton, John Henry Thomas Manners (1814–77). A son of Viscount Canterbury. Undersecretary for the Home Department under Peel. Cambridge Bor., 1841–47; Newark, 1847–57. Free Trade Conservative. JC.

99. Thesiger, Sir Frederic (2d Lord Chelmsford) (1794–1878). Barrister with West Indian connections. Attorney general under Peel. Woodstock, 1840–41; Abingdon, 1844–52; Stamford, 1852–57. Conservative. S; FP.

100. Tollemache, Frederick James (1804–84). Brother of the earl of Dysart. Landed interest. Grantham, 1826–31; 1837–52, 1857. Liberal. JC.

101. Tomline, George (1812–89). Son of a baronet with Church connections. A colonel. Shrewsbury, 1841–47; 1852–57. Whig.

102. Trench, Sir Frederick William (1775–1859). Major general in the army. Served in Wellington Administration. Cambridge, 1818–32; Scarborough, 1835–47. Free Trade Conservative.

103. Vernon, Granville Harcourt (1792–1879). Church connections. Retford - East, 1831–47. Free Trade Conservative. JC.

104. Villiers, Viscount George A. F. (1808–1859). Eldest son of the earl of Jersey; son-in-law of Sir Robert Peel. Cirencester, 1844–52. Free Trade Conservative. S; FP.

105. Wall, Charles Baring (1795–1853). Hampshire magistrate. Authority on art. Newphew of Sir Thomas Baring, and patron of two livings. Guildford (1818); Wareham, 1826–30; Weymouth, 1831; Guildford, 1832–47; Salisbury, 1847–53. Free Trade Conservative. JC.

106.   Wellesley, Lord Charles (1808–58). Second son of the duke of Wellington. Army. Hampshire - South, 1842–52; Windsor, 1852–55. Conservative. *FP.*

107.   Whitmore, Thomas Charlton (1807–March 13, 1865). Landed interest. A magistrate. Bridgenorth, 1832–52. Free Trade Conservative. *FP.*

108.   Wood, Colonel Thomas, Sr. (1776–1860). East India Company member and patron of one living. Brecknockshire, 1806–47. Free Trade Conservative.

109.   Wood, Colonel Thomas, Jr. (1804–October 23, 1872) Son of the above. Related both to the Londonderrys and the Graftons. Military. Middlesex, 1837–47. Free Trade Conservative.

110.   Wortley, James Archibald Stuart (1805–81). A son of Baron Wharncliffe. Landed interest. A Queen's Counsel. Halifax, 1835–37; Buteshire, 1841–57. Liberal. *A; J; FP.*

111.   Wynn, Charles Watkin Williams (1775–1850). Montgomeryshire landowner and barrister. Lifelong politician. Montgomeryshire, 1795–1850, which may be a record. Free Trade Conservative.

112.   Young, Sir John (1807–76). Son of baronet. East India Company proprietor. Secretary of the Treasury under Peel. Cavan, 1831–55. Free Trade Conservative inclining toward Palmerston, *JC; FP.*

APPENDIX 2

THE DIVISION ANALYSES IN *HANSARD*

Cons. of February 27[1]		*Cons. of March 27*[2]		*Cons. of May 15*[3]	
English Counties . .	12	English Counties . .	12	English Counties . .	12
English Boroughs .	68	English Boroughs . .	65	English Boroughs .	68
English Univs.	2	English Univs.	2	English Univs.	2
Welsh Counties . . .	4	Welsh Counties . . .	4	Welsh Counties . . .	4
Welsh Boroughs . . .	3	Welsh Boroughs . . .	3	Welsh Boroughs . . .	3
Irish Counties	4	Irish Counties	5	Irish Counties	4
Irish Boroughs	7	Irish Boroughs	3	Irish Boroughs	7
Scotch Counties . . .	8	Scotch Counties . . .	6	Scotch Counties . . .	5
Scotch Boroughs . .	1	Scotch Boroughs . .	1	Scotch Boroughs . .	1
	109		101		106

The above analyses pose a difficult problem for historians of the Peelites when used to check on the accuracy of a Peelite list for February 27, 1846. The first analysis lists only 109 Peelites, rather than the traditional 112, which makes it impossible to draw up a list for that vital division to use as a starting point. The comparison between the Peelite List furnished in this book and these analyses might be presented as follows:

The English Counties (12-12-12).—The Peelite List and the analysis agree for the division of *February 27*. The 12 English County votes were: Cheshire (W. T. Egerton and Legh), Hampshire (Wellesley), Lancashire (Lord Egerton and Patten), Middlesex (T. Wood Jr.), Shropshire (Clive), Somerset (Acland and Dickinson), Staffordshire (Russell), Warwickshire (Dugdale), and Wiltshire (Herbert). The *March 27* analysis also agrees if Christopher Turnor is substituted for Egerton, whose pair is not counted. The situation for *May 15* is the same as for March 27, but the addition of Lord Granville Somerset would raise the total to 13.

The English Boroughs (68-65-68).—The analysis for February 27 lists only 68 votes; the Peelite List in this book provides 72. The two-vote boroughs were: Bedford (Polhill and H. Stuart), Cirencester (Cripps and Villiers), Cambridge (Kelly and Sutton), Honiton (H. D. Baillie and Macgeachy), Hull (Hanmer and James), London (Lyall and Masterman), Lymington (Mackinnon and Stew-

1. Great Britain. Parliament. *Hansard's Parliamentary Debates*, 3d ser., 85 (1846): 271.
2. Ibid.
3. Ibid. 86 (1846): 726.

233

art), Marlborough (H. B. Baring and Bruce), Newport, I. W. (W. J. Hamilton and Martin), Scarborough (J. V. Johnstone and Trench), Tamworth (A'Court and R. Peel), Thetford (W. B. Baring and Flower), and Windsor (G. Reid and Neville), for a total of 26 votes. The one-vote boroughs were: Abingdon (Thesiger), Barnstaple (Gore), Beverley (Hogg), Blackburn (Hornby), Bridgenorth (Whitmore), Brighton (Hervey), Bury St. Edmunds (Jermyn), Canterbury (Smythe), Clitheroe (Cardwell), Dorchester (Graham), Dover (J. Reid), Dudley (Benbow), Grantham (Tollemache), Guildford (Wall), Harwich (Attwood), Hertford (Mahon), Huntingdon (J. Peel), Kidderminster (Godson), Lancaster (Greene), Launceston (Bowles), Leeds (Beckett), Leominster (Barkly), Lewes (Fitz-Roy), Lichfield (Mostyn), Liverpool (Sandon), Ludlow (Botfield), Lynn (Jocelyn), Macclesfield (Grimsditch), Newcastle-under-Lyme (Buckley), Norwich (Douro), Pontefract (Milnes), Reigate (Eastnor), Retford East (Vernon), Ripon (Cockburn), Rochester (Bodkin), St. Ives (Praed), Shrewsbury (Tomline), Southampton (Hope), Stamford (Clerk), Stafford (Carnegie), Stoke (Copeland), Totnes (Baldwin), Wakefield (Lascelles), Warwick (Douglas), Wilton (Somerton), and Winchester (Escott), for a total of 46 votes. Six of these 72 were absent on *March 27*, leaving 66 votes; the analysis records only 65. Five of the 72 were absent or paired on *May 15*, but James Lindsay added another vote for a total of 68. The analysis also records 68 for this division.

The English Universities (2-2-2).—Cambridge (Goulburn); Oxford (Estcourt).

The Welsh Counties (4-4-4).—Brecknockshire (T. Wood Sr.), Carnarvonshire (Pennant), Flintshire (Glynne), and Montgomeryshire (Wynn).

The Welsh Boroughs (3-3-3).—Carnarvon Dist. (Hughes), Denbigh Dist. (Mainwaring), and Pembroke Dist. (Owen).

The Irish Counties (4-5-4).—The two agree for February 27: Antrim (Seymour), Cavan (Young), and Tyrone (Corry and Lord Hamilton). But to secure five votes for the March 27 division, one must add the pair of Thomas Bunbury, and ignore that of William Verner, which might be in error. Yet, if Bunbury's vote is added to the May 15 total, the result is 5, rather than the 4 of the analysis.

The Irish Boroughs (7-3-7).—For the February 27 division the Peelite List includes Carrickfergus (Kirk), Coleraine (Boyd), Dublin (Gregory), Dungannon (Northland), Lisburn (Meynell), and Portarlington (Damer), and to secure the 7 of the analysis the pair of Lord Newry must be added. Although the analysis records 3 votes on the March 27 division, only 2 from the Peelite List (Kirk and Meynell) were present and voting. Six of the 7 were present and voting on May 15, and Kirk paired, which would agree with the 7 of the analysis.

The Scotch Counties (8-6-5).—The Peelite List and the analysis agree on the February 27 division. The eight votes were probably: Argyllshire (McNeill), Ayrshire (Oswald), Buteshire (Wortley), Dunbartonshire (Smollett), Dumfriesshire (J. H. Johnstone), Inverness-shire (H. J. Baillie), Perthshire

(Drummond), and Selkirkshire (Lockhart). For the March 27 division all but Smollett were present, yet the analysis lists only 6 votes. For the May 15 division the Peelite List and the analysis agree there were 5 voters (Drummond, J. H. Johnstone, Lockhart, McNeill, and Smollett).

The Scotch Boroughs (1-1-1).—The same borough (Falkirk) was represented on all three divisions, but Lord Lincoln replaced William Baird for the May 15 division.

APPENDIX 3

Some of the more important Peelite identification letters are as follows:

1. Sir John Young to William E. Gladstone, 4 August 1852. *Gladstone Papers*, BM 44237.

> I have looked through the returns as carefully as I could, and to me they appear as follows: Supporters of government who are nowise tainted by Free Trade or any other noxious liberality—272. Whigs and radicals—304. Remain 78. 654. With these 78 or the majority of them in the balance thus, Free Trade Derbyites, on whom the Govt. may confidently rely—25, Doubtful—18, Oldham vacant—1,[1] Firmer Free Traders who do not admit the fallacy that conservatism does not and cannot exist out of Lord Derby's ranks—34, total 78. Amongst the doubtful I reckon Patten, Egerton, Smollett, all of the new names unknown to me, Jocelyn, Beckett Denison etc.[2]
>
> I make the Govt. a present of Mr. Stuart, Masterman, W. Beckett, R. Clive, (illegible), Tennent, Stirling, S. Cocks, Baird, Christy, F. Baring, G. Sandars etc.—all of them Free Trade Derbyites, but I rank in the 34—Sir R. Ferguson, Mostyn, Mr. J. Hanmer, and Mr. Milnes.[3]
>
> Supposing a division to take place in which the 25 Free Trade Derbyites & all the doubtful went with the Govt. the numbers would be 272 & 25 and 18—315; Whigs etc. 304, giving the Govt. a majority of 11. But then the 34 are absent—if present and voting together they would convert the Govt. majority into a minority of 23 or augment it into a majority of 45. This is as near the mark as I can bring the estimate.

1. Due to the death of John Duncuft, a former Peelite member.

2. This reference probably includes: John Wilson Patten (Lancashire-North), William Tatton Egerton (Cheshire-North), Alexander Smollett (Dumbartonshire), Viscount Jocelyn (Lynn), and Edmund Beckett Denison (West Riding, Yorkshire). On the crucial 17 December 1852 division Patten was absent, Denison opposed the Government, and the others voted with Disraeli.

3. These references probably include: Henry Stuart (Bedford), John Masterman (London), William Beckett (Ripon), Robert Henry Clive (Shropshire-South), Sir Emerson Tennent (Lisburn), William Stirling (Perthshire), Thomas S. Cocks (Reigate), James Baird (Falkirk District), Samuel Christy (Newcastle-under-Lyme), Francis Baring (Thetford), George Sandars (Wakefield), Sir Robert Ferguson (Londonberry), Edward L. Mostyn (Flintshire), Sir John Hanmer (Flint District), and Richard M. Milnes (Pontefract). In a letter Young classified Hanmer, Mostyn, and Milnes as Whigs, but in *Dod* they were classed as Free Trade or Moderate Conservatives. By and large, Young's classifications proved correct, but Ferguson was to vote with Disraeli in December.

2. Sir John Young to William E. Gladstone, 10 August 1852. *Gladstone Papers,* BM 44327.

The classification of such men as Col. Lindsay, Evelyn, A. E. Lockhart & H. Corry in the same list as Lowe, Fitzroy, Ld. Clinton, Sir J. Johnstone, Sir T. Lewis[4] will in my opinion lead to erroneous calculations on our part. Of these fifty I should say that Heneage, Willoughby, Fitzgerald, Dering, Jocelyn, W. Beckett, Col. Lindsay, Evelyn, A. Lockhart, and H. Corry[5] i.e. *10* will be found voting with the Govt. on all occasions. Those of them who were in the last parliament sat with the ministerial party, never with us, and if I am not mistaken all voted against or positively refused to vote for your motion as to the nonallocation of the vacant seats.[6] Hen. Corry has been forced by his constituents to promise general support to the Government. Then again I must question whether we can depend upon Colvile, H. Stuart, Hogg, G. Harcourt, Sir Robert Peel, B. Denison, W. B. Hughes, Smollett or Hayes—9 more.[7] H. Stuart has been much with [illegible] & W. Forbes & will no doubt be influenced by the companionship. Hogg will vote precisely as suits his own views of his own interest and advancement. No reliance can be placed even for a day on either B. Denison, or W. B. Hughes. The former has little courage or self-reliance; the latter was promised something by Sir Robert Peel, what I know not, and the hope

4. Young was undoubtedly correct in this interpretation. The references were probably to James Lindsay (Wigan), William J. Evelyn (Surrey-West), Allan E. Lockhart (Selkirkshire), and Henry Corry, all of whom were to vote with Disraeli on 17 December 1852. Among the others, Robert Lowe (Kidderminster) and Sir Thomas F. Lewis (Radnor District) were Liberals, and Henry Fitz-Roy (Lewes), Sir Thomas F. Lewis (Radnor District) were Liberals, and Henry Fitz-Roy (Lewes), Lord Robert R. P. Clinton (Notts-North), and Sir John V. Johnstone (Scarborough) were Liberal Conservatives who were to vote against the Conservatives on that division.

5. These references are probably to George H. W. Heneage (Devizes), not the other George Heneage, Sir Henry P. Willoughby (Evesham), William R. S. Fitzgerald (Horsham), Sir Edward C. Dering (Kent-East), Viscount Jocelyn (Lynn), William Beckett (Ripon), James Lindsay (Wigan), William J. Evelyn (Surrey-West), Allan E. Lockhart (Selkirkshire), and Henry Corry (Tyrone). All of these members voted with the Conservatives in December.

6. His memory failed him. Henry Corry voted against the Government on that division.

7. These references were probably to: Charles R. Colvile (Derbyshire-South), Henry Stuart (Bedford), James W. Hogg (Honiton), George G. V. Harcourt (Oxfordshire), Sir Robert Peel (Tamworth), Edmund B. Denison (West Riding, Yorkshire), William B. Hughes (Carnarvon District), Alexander Smollett (Dumbartonshire), and Sir Edmund S. Hayes (Donegal). Young was not so accurate in his analysis of the views of his particular group. Denison, Harcourt, and Hogg opposed the Conservatives in December, and Stuart and Peel missed the division.

of attaining this object is what has really kept him with us. Otherwise there is no reason to mark him differently from E. Pennant, who can at any time command Mr. Hughes' vote.

Smollett's vote will be influenced by what he thinks his constituents wish. Hayes' case is peculiar. He is entirely with us in feeling, and opinion, but has been forced by his constituents and the country gentlemen of Donegal to promise to take a line much more favourable to the Govt. than he otherwise likes. These nineteen off—the list is reduced very much to what I put it at in my last letter to you—viz. 31. I stated 34, but then I added Mostyn, Hanmer, Milnes. I am inclined to reckon Whitmore and E. Pennant as much more with us than Bonham seems to do.[8] I know the latter's opinion well unless it has been altered since or by the election.

Twenty of this 31 or 34 might go with you (by you I mean Newcastle, S. Herbert, & yourself) in the event of your splitting with Lord Derby & joining the Whigs, but several of these would not like it. What has kept the members together so long has been mainly the adherence to the principle of Sir R. Peel's commercial policy, and the hopes of seeing you, i.e. those who served in Sir R. Peel's cabinet, called to power, and enabled to dictate alliances & their policies to rival parties. The commercial policy is now out of point and the hope above alluded to has I fear been much chilled by Graham's defection to the radicals and the defeats our friends met at the recent election. However, I should add we must not lay too much stress on names without considering the question on which we may be called to vote. For instance, I am told that if Lord John Russell proposes a want of confidence early in the session, he or anyone else doing the same will be beaten. If the Address is ambiguous on commercial policy, an amendment could be carried against them by a great majority.

3.   Sir John Young to William E. Gladstone, 21 September 1852. *Gladstone Papers*, BM 44327.

He questions my placing H. Stuart, Dering, Willoughby and Wm. Beckett as decided Derbyites—but they will be found so, three at least times out of four. Johnstone of Clackmannon he reckons decidedly hostile to the Govt. Whitmore decidedly with Govt. Stirling doubtful. Fitzgerald same, but more with you. He agrees with me in giving Jocelyn and H. Herbert to the Govt. and also as to my view of Hayes' position and wishes.[9]

8.   These references are to Henry Whitmore (Bridgnorth), and Edward G. D. Pennant (Carnarvonshire). Pennant missed the December division, but Whitmore supported the Conservatives. William B. Hughes, whose vote Young said Pennant could "command," also supported the Government on that occasion. Bonham, then, seems to have been more accurate in judging these men than Young.

9.   The reference was to James Johnstone (Clackmannon and Kinross). The

He transfers from Peelites to doubtful Goulburn, Pennant, Hughes, Wilson Patten and Mure, in which I think he's wrong except as to Goulburn, and probably Hughes, who is too shabby to place any reliance on. Henry Corry is a Derbyite. Hanmer, Mostyn & Milnes—Whigs. But what are G. Harcourt, Sir J. Owen & Laffan? I cannot tell. Bonham says 'somewhat doubtful Anti-Derbyites! What this means I cannot tell.[10]

But after all the Govt. have no command of a majority, and the Death of the Duke of Wellington will take away another of their props. . . . I do not quote, but your meaning when you say 'we should not give any vote against them until etc.'—Does this mean we are to vote with them? or only to stand aloof?

4. Lord John Manners to Benjamin Disraeli, 10 March 1857. *Disraeli Papers* (Hughenden Manor), Manners XIII.

It is assumed that there is a general wish on both sides that the old Tory or Conservative Party should be reorganized. It is necessary to that end to discover the obstacles which stand in the way of such a reorganization. They would probably be found to consist of two sorts. 1st Obstacles of Principles, 2nd Personal Obstacles.

With respect to the first class it is suggested that—The causes of original disunion are now removed, and removed in favour of the Policy of the Minority. They may be roughly summed up as Corn Laws, Sugar Duties, Navigation Acts, followed by Clergy Reserves, Succession Tax. There is no intention on the part of the Majority to reopen any of these questions. . . . Now for the present, what are the . . . causes of disunion under the head of Principles? They are to be found, it seems to me, chiefly in the field of Finance. Custom House duties find favour in the eyes of the Majority, Direct Taxation and Excise, it is feared, in those of the Minority. Mr. Gladstone would probably repeal more Custom House Duties . . . unless he can effect great reductions in the expenditures it would seem that he must increase either the Excise, or the Income Tax.

---

constituencies of the others have been noted previously. Young was right and Bonham wrong in his analyses of Stuart, Dering, Willoughby and Beckett, and Bonham was wrong also about Fitzgerald. Bonham, however, was right in his judgments of Johnstone and Whitmore, and both he and Young were right in judging Jocelyn. Both were wrong about Herbert.

10. The references are to Henry Goulburn, William Mure, and Robert Laffan (St. Ives). Goulburn and Mure voted with the Peelites against the Government in December, so Bonham was wrong about them, but he was right about Patten and Pennant, who missed the division, and Hughes, who voted to sustain the Derby Government. Among the "doubtful Anti-Derbyites," only Harcourt voted against the Conservatives. But Sir John Owen later found his way to the Liberals.

But the Majority is reluctant to cut down Estimates, except as they are proved to be exceptions; and if it is attempted to force them to this course, will you not at once be opposed by the heart and pith of our Party? On the other hand ought not Mr. Gladstone, looking to the enormous concessions made to this policy since 1846 to rest content with them. . . . If he asks more from the Majority than a ratification of the Past he is unreasonable. . . . The Country Party cannot be brought to join in a Crusade against the Custom House, and liberal Military Establishments. . . . Obstacles of Principles continued. Foreign policy? I know of none. Colonial Policy? I know of none. Home Policy? Maynooth and the management of Ireland generally may present difficulties, but not of great moment. Reform? Mr. Sidney Herbert's opposition to Mr. L. King's motion may be taken as a pledge that there is no great difference . . . between the two sections on this head. . . . [11] Education? Here again all . . . are pretty well agreed. I am not aware of any other subject of importance on which a difference in principle is likely to prove fatal to the proposed reorganization.

2d. Personal Obstacles. There are two sorts. 1st, General dislike and mistrust of Mr. Gladstone's political career . . . , but these feelings . . . may be expected to disappear with their causes. 2nd, Clashing of competing claims. These must be left to the Leaders of the two sections to conciliate as best they can; and they have a right to expect and demand that no selfish considerations of that nature should be allowed to prejudice what this Memorandum starts with assuming to be the general wish.

5. Lord Stanley to Lord Malmesbury, June 16, 1850. Malmesbury, *Memoirs*, 262.[12]

Of the ten Peelites whom you give to the Government, he [Lord Aberdeen] expects Ellesmere and Wharncliffe to vote with us, De Grey

---

11. But during the 1857 election campaign Graham took the position that any cooperation with Derby had been "negatived conclusively by my vote and speech on the reform of the county representation, which is the touchstone of adherence to the Derby party." (*PGRA*, 2:304). Graham to Mounsey, 6 March 1857. During the election Herbert also modified his position on reform, and it thus loomed as a considerable obstacle to reunification, even though Derby was able to offer such a measure in 1859.

12. Most of the Peelites mentioned in the letter are familiar enough; a few might require some explanation. The Earl of Ellesmere (1800–1857) was Lord Francis Egerton in 1846; the 2d Baron Ashburton (1799–1864) succeeded his father, who voted against repeal, in 1848; the 2d Baron Cowley (1804–84), whose predecessor missed the 1846 division, succeeded to his title in 1847; the 6th Duke of Atholl (1814–64) voted for repeal in 1846 as 2d Baron Glenlyon; the Bishop of Winchester, Charles R. Sumner, evidently changed his views, as he was a Protectionist in 1846; the 1st Viscount Gough (1779–1869), and the 1st Viscount Hardinge (1785–1856) had been in India in 1846.

to stay away, Ashburton, Bristol, and Cowley to be with them, and Atholl, Churchill, Denbigh, and the Bishop of Winchester he knows nothing about. Of the twelve doubtful Peelites, he expects we shall have Bathurst, Clare, and Howe; Seaton and Shaftesbury are against us; Gough, Hardinge, Wellington, and Ripon will stay away; he knows nothing of Hertford, Northumberland, and Winchester.

Bibliography

PUBLIC DOCUMENTS

Annual Register, or a View of the History, Politics and Literature for the Year, 1845–57.

Great Britain: *Admiralty Papers.* Public Record Office.

Great Britain: *Colonial Office Papers.* Public Record Office.

Great Britain, Parliament, *Hansard's Parliamentary Debates,* 3d ser., Vols. 83–136.

Great Britain, Parliament, *Parliamentary Papers,* "Report of the Select Committee on the Army Before Sebastopol, 1855."

Great Britain, Parliament, *Sessional Papers* (House of Commons) London: Public Record Office.

Great Britain, *Statutes at Large,* Danby Pickering Edition.

Parliamentary Pocket Companion, London, 1845–57.

NEWSPAPERS

Illustrated London News
Liverpool Mercury
Manchester Guardian
Morning Chronicle (London)
Standard (London)
The Times (London)

PAMPHLETS

Coalition Governments Past and Present, A Letter to the Right Honourable the Earl of Aberdeen. London: John Mortimer, 1853.

Election Address to the Tamworth Voters. Robert Peel. 1847.

Coin and Currency in an Address to the Landowners. James R. G. Graham. London: James Ridgway, 1828.

MANUSCRIPT SOURCES

Aberdeen Papers. British Museum.

Brougham Papers. University of London.

Cardwell Papers. Public Record Office.

Colchester Papers. Public Record Office.

Disraeli Papers. Hughenden Manor.

Ellenborough Papers. Public Record Office.

Gladstone Papers. British Museum.

Graham Papers. Netherby.

Granville Papers. Public Record Office.

Goulburn Papers. Surrey Public Record Office.

Iddesley Papers. British Museum.

Martin Papers. British Museum.

Napier Papers. British Museum.

Newcastle Papers. Nottingham University.

Peel Papers. British Museum.

Portland Papers. Nottingham University.

Ripon Papers. British Museum.

Russell Papers. Public Record Office.

Wellington Papers. Apsley House.

ARTICLES IN JOURNALS

Altholz, Josef L. "The Political Behavior of English Catholics, 1850–1867." *Journal of British Studies* 4 (November, 1964).

Baring, F. H. "Lord John Russell's Attempt to Form a Government in 1845." *English Historical Review* 23 (April, 1908).

Conacher, J. B. "Peel and the Peelites, 1846–1850." *English Historical Review* 73 (July, 1958).

Dreyer, F. A. "The Whigs and the Political Crisis of 1845." *English Historical Review* 80 (July, 1965).

Gash, Norman. "Ashley and the Conservative Party in 1842." *English Historical Review* 53 (October, 1938).

———. "F. R. Bonham: Conservative 'Political Secretary,' 1832–1847." *English Historical Review* 63 (October, 1948).

Glickman, Harvey. "The Toryness of British Conservatism." *Journal of British Studies* 1 (November, 1961).

Golby, John, "A Great Electioneer and His Motives: The Fourth Duke of Newcastle." *Historical Journal* 8, no. 2 (1965).

Jones, Wilbur D., and J. Chal Vinson. "British Preparedness and the Oregon Settlement." *Pacific Historical Review* 22 (November, 1953).

Kemp, Betty. "Reflections on the Repeal of the Corn Laws." *Victorian Studies* 5 (March, 1962).

Lawson-Tancred, Mary. "The Anti-League and the Corn Law Crisis of 1846. *Historical Journal* 3, no. 2, (1960).

Roberts, David. "Tory Paternalism and Social Reform in Early Victorian England." *American Historical Review* 63 (January, 1958).

Spring, David. "Earl Fitzwilliam and the Corn Laws." *American Historical Review* 59 (January, 1954).

Thompson, F. M. L. "Whigs and Liberals in the West Riding, 1830–1860." *English Historical Review* 74 (April, 1959).

Ward, J. T. "West Riding Landowners and the Corn Laws." *English Historical Review* 81 (April, 1966).

SECONDARY WORKS

Appleman, Philip, ed. *1859: Entering an Age of Crisis.* Bloomington: Indiana University Press, 1959.

Argyll, Dowager Duchess of, ed. *George Douglas Eighth Duke of Argyll, 1823–1900: Autobiography and Memoirs.* 2 vols. London: John Murray, 1906.

Arnstein, Walter L. *Britain Yesterday and Today.* Boston: D. C. Heath & Co., 1966.

Ashley, Evelyn. *The Life and Correspondence of Henry John Temple Viscount Palmerston.* 2 vols. London: Richard Bentley & Son, 1879).

Bassett, A. T., ed. *Gladstone to his Wife.* London: Methuen and Co., 1936.

Balfour, Lady Frances. *The Life of George, Fourth Earl of Aberdeen.* 2 vols. London: Hodder and Stoughton, 1922.

Bell, Herbert C. F. *Lord Palmerston.* 2 vols. Hamden: Archon Books, 1966.

Benson, A. C., and Viscount Esher, eds. *The Letters of Queen Victoria, A Selection from Her Majesty's Correspondence Between the Years 1837 and 1861.* 3 vols. New York: Longmans, Green and Co., 1907.

Briggs, Asa. *The Age of Improvement.* New York: David McKay Co., Inc., 1959.

Broughton, Lord. *Recollections of a Long Life.* 6 vols. London: John Murray, 1911.

Cole, G. D. H., and Raymond Postgate. *The British People, 1746–1946.* London: Methuen & Co., 1961.

Conacher, J. B. *The Aberdeen Coalition, 1852–1855.* Cambridge: University Press, 1968.

Croker, John W. *The Correspondence and Diaries of the Late Right Honourable John Wilson Croker.* Edited by Louis J. Jennings. 2 vols. New York: Charles Scribner's Sons, 1884.

Davidson, R. T., and W. Benham. *Life of Archibald Tait Archbishop of Canterbury.* London: Macmillan and Co., 1891.

Disraeli, Benjamin. *Lord George Bentinck.* New York: E. P. Dutton, 1905.

Douglas, Sir George, ed. *The Panmure Papers.* London: Hodder and Stoughton, 1908.

Erickson, Arvel B. *The Public Career of Sir James Graham.* Oxford: Basil Blackwell, 1952.

———. *Edward T. Cardwell: Peelite.* Philadelphia: American Philosophical Society, 1959.

Feiling, Keith. *A History of England.* New York: McGraw-Hill Book Co., 1948.

Gardiner, A. G. *The Life of William Harcourt.* 2 vols. New York: George Doran, 1923.

Gathorn-Hardy, A. E. ed., *Gathorne-Hardy, First Earl of Cranbrook A Memoir.* 2 vols. London: Longmans, Green, and Co., 1910.

Gayer, A. D. et al. *The Growth and Fluctuation of the British Economy, 1790–1850.* Oxford: The Clarendon Press, 1953.

Gibbs, Peter. *Crimean Blunder.* New York: Holt, Rinehart & Winston, 1960.

Gooch, G. P., ed. *The Later Correspondence of Lord John Russell, 1840–1878.* 2 vols. London: Longmans, Green, and Co., 1925.

Gordon, Sir Arthur. *The Earl of Aberdeen.* London: Sampson, Low, Marston & Co., 1893.

Guedalla, Philip, ed. *Gladstone and Palmerston, being the Correspondence of Lord Palmerston with Mr. Gladstone, 1851–1865.* London: Victor Gollancz, 1928.

Hindle, Wilfred. *The Morning Post, 1772–1937.* London: George Routledge and Sons, 1937.

Hodder, Edwin. *The Life and Work of the Seventh Earl of Shaftesbury, K. G.* 3 vols. New York: Cassell and Co., 1887.

Jelavich, Barbara. *A Century of Russian Foreign Policy.* New York: J. B. Lippincott, 1964.

Jones, Wilbur Devereux. *Lord Derby and Victorian Conservatism.* Oxford: Basil Blackwell, 1956.

———. *Lord Aberdeen and the Americas.* Athens: University of Georgia Press, 1958.

————. *'Prosperity' Robinson, The Life of Viscount Goderich, 1782–1859.* London: Macmillan, 1967.

Kingsley, Donald J. *Representative Bureaucracy.* Yellow Springs: Antioch Press, 1944.

McDowell, Robert B. *British Conservatism, 1832–1914.* London: Faber and Faber, 1959.

Maclagan, Michael. *Clemency Canning, Charles John, First Earl Canning Governor-General and Viceroy of India 1856–1862.* London: Macmillan & Co., 1962.

Magnus, Philip. *Gladstone.* London: John Murray, 1954.

Malmesbury, Earl of. *Memoirs of an Ex-Minister.* London: Longmans, Green & Co., 1884.

Marriott, J. A. R. *England Since Waterloo.* London: Methuen & Co., Ltd., 1913.

Martin, Kingsley. *The Triumph of Lord Palmerston, A Study of Public Opinion in England Before the Crimean War.* New York: Dial Press, 1924.

Martin, Sir Theodore. *A Life of Lord Lyndhurst.* London: John Murray, 1883.

Martineau, John. *The Life of Henry Pelham, 5th Duke of Newcastle.* London: John Murray, 1908.

Monypenny, W. F., and G. E. Buckle. *The Life of Benjamin Disraeli, Earl of Beaconsfield.* 2 vols. New York: The Macmillan Co., 1916.

Morley, John. *The Life of William Ewart Gladstone.* 2 vols. New York: The Macmillan Co., 1903.

Nechkina, M. V., ed. *Russia in the Nineteenth Century.* Ann Arbor: J. W. Edwards, 1953.

Office of The Times. *The History of The Times.* New York: E. P. Dutton & Co., 1905.

Parker, Charles S. *Sir Robert Peel from his Private Papers.* 3 vols. Second edition. London: John Murray, 1899.

————. *The Life and Letters of Sir James Graham.* 2 vols. London: John Murray, 1907.

Reid, T. Wemys. *The Life, Letters, and Friendships of Richard Monckton Milnes, First Lord Houghton.* 2 vols. London: Cassell and Co., 1891.

Smellie, K. B. *A Hundred Years of English Government.* London: Gerald Duckworth & Co., 1937.

Southgate, Donald. *The Passing of the Whigs, 1832–1886.* New York: St. Martin's Press, 1962.

Stanmore, Lord. *Sidney Herbert, Lord Herbert of Lea: A Memoir.* 2 vols. London: John Murray, 1906.

Strachey, L., and R. Fulford. *The Greville Memoirs.* 7 vols. London: Macmillan and Co., 1938.

Temperley, Harold. *England and the Near East: The Crimea.* London: Longmans, Green, and Co., 1936.

Trevelyan, George M. *British History in the Nineteenth Century, 1782–1918.* London: Longmans, Green, and Co., 1937.

Walpole, Spencer. *A History of England from the Conclusion of the Great War in 1815.* 6 vols. London: Longmans, Green, and Co., 1890.

———. *The Life of Lord John Russell.* 2 vols. London: Longmans, Green, and Co., 1889.

Wellesley, F. A., ed. *Secrets of the Second Empire, Private Letters from the Paris Embassy, from the Papers of Henry Richard Charles Wellesley, First Earl Cowley, Ambassador at Paris, 1852–1867.* New York: Harper Bros., 1929.

Wood, Anthony. *Nineteenth Century Britain, 1815–1914.* London: Longmans, Green, and Co., 1960.

Woodward, E. L. *The Age of Reform, 1815–1870.* Oxford: Clarendon Press, 1962.

Yonge, Charles D. *The History of the British Navy from the Earliest Times to the Present Time.* 3 vols. Second edition. London: R. Bentley, 1866.

Young, George M. *Victorian England: Portrait of an Age.* London: Oxford University Press, 1960.

Index